ART
ARTIST
ARTICLES

Roger Peters

EXHIBITION CATALOGUE
(2026)

Thirty three works mentioned or visible
in Press Clippings and Publications
from 1972 to 2024

PROSPERO PLACE

PERCY THOMSON GALLERY

STRATFORD DISTRICT LIBRARY

ART
ARTIST
ARTICLES

(1972-2024)

Exhibition Catalogue

Copyright © 2026 Roger Peters

All rights reserved.

ISBN 978-0-473-76805-8 (pbk)

Page setup by Maree Horner

QUATERNARY IMPRINT

Published for the Quaternary Institute

www.quaternaryinstitute.com

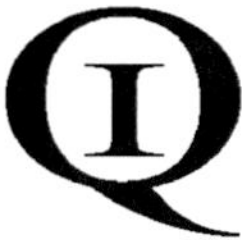

PREFACE

NOTEBOOK 6 Thurs 1st Aug '85

I can leave you alone· I can come to you with an apparent ease· I can look about and absorb the night of my vision· I can touch you and be uplifted· That is me — that is me — nothing without you·

The heartache of Ruapehu leaves me in tears· I long for the solitude of its thunderous majesty· My heart bears witness to its unequivocable might· I am in a sea of images that knows its destiny· I am a stone that knew a rock· You are the delight that captures my eternal motions· You and I live in the same chasm called space·

I have an offering for you· It takes its form from the leaves and white water that know you so well· The animal dreams of man assault its basaltic imagination· Already the crystals of your love pierce its understanding·

I love your friends· Mallarme and Lorca know the subtle strength of our relationship· The Chilean Neruda grasps my soul with the image of his tongue· The poetry of their flesh and stones crushes my feelings like a herbal arrogance· Duchamp and Brancusi have a part to play in the pure skin of inspiration· But it is the Andes and the Pyrenees that tacks my skin close to the board·

Drained of venality I am confronted by the inescapable lure of a wing beat, a halo of vowels and consonants, of moonlight and oranges and look to the expression of a dream·

The NOTEBOOK Quotations throughout the Catalogue are from 27 NOTEBOOKS kept between 1981 and 2017

Other titles by Roger Peters

William Shakespeare's Sonnet Philosophy
(Four volume, slipcase set - 2005)
Volume 1
How Shakespeare structures
his nature-based philosophy into the *Sonnets*
before he publishes them in 1609
(***Volume 1,*** second edition - 2019)
Volume 2
A line by line analysis
of the 154 individual sonnets using
the *Sonnet* philosophy
as the basis for their meaning
(***Volume 2,*** second edition - 2018)
Volume 3
An analysis of individual plays and poems
to show that the *Sonnet* philosophy
is the basis for their meaning
(***Volume 3,*** second edition - 2020)
Volume 4
How the works of
Wittgenstein, Duchamp, and Mallarmé
led to an appreciation
of Shakespeare's philosophy
(***Volume 4,*** second edition - 2019)

Shakespeare's Global Philosophy (2017)
exploring Shakespeare's nature-based
philosophy in the sonnets, plays and Globe

Shakespeare & Mature Love (2017)
how to get from nature to love in Shakespeare

Shakespeare's Philosophy Illustrated (2018)
Quaternary teaching aids

Quaternary Essays (2020)
applying Shakespeare's nature-based Sonnet
philosophy to life and art

Songs of the Earth (1972 to 2021) (2021)
Exhibition Catalogue

Play Commentaries to Williams Shakespeare's 1623 Folio (2022)
using Shakespeare's nature-based philosophy from
his 1609 Sonnets to understand the plays

QUATERNARY IMPRINT
Published for the Quaternary Institute

CONTENTS

THE PERCY THOMSON GALLERY

ART	ARTICLES	DATE	VENUE	PAGE
BEING IN A SPACE	*NZ Herald/Auckland Star*	1972	Air New Zealand Award	2
SONGS OF THE EARTH	*Auckland Star*	1975	Auckland City Art Gallery	6
FOUR MEN ON CLOUD ONYX	*The Daily News*	1990	Govett Brewster Art Gallery	8
KATIE BUST	*The Daily News*	1990	Govett Brewster Art Gallery	10
SONGS OF THE EARTH II	*The Daily News*	1991	Govett Brewster Art Gallery	12
TERESA BUST	*Stratford Press*	1991	Artist's Studio	14
KAREN BUST	*The Daily News*	1992	Gallery 79 Hawera	16
THE WRESTLERS' BALL	*Wanganui Chronicle/ Wellington Post*	1994	Sarjeant Gallery	18
ROCKS	*NZ Herald*	1998	Artspace Auckland	22
BLUE LADDER	*NZ Herald*	1998	Artspace Auckland	24
Dick Habershon	*Reference*	2001	Stratford	26
QUATERNARY INSTITUTE	*Stratford Press*	2002	Quaternary Institute	28
THE SECRETS OF THE SONNETS	*The Daily News*	2005	Quaternary Institute	30
David Loye	*Email*	2006	California	32
MAREE RECLINING	*Opunake & Coastal News*	2017	Artist's Studio	34
SONNET WALL	*Opunake & Coastal News*	2017	Quaternary Institute	36
SNOW	*Towards a History of the Contemporary*	2018	Wellington	38
TALIA BUST	*Biograview*	2021	Artist's Studio	40
LEAVES	*Opunake & Coastal News*	2021	Pihama, South Taranaki	42
BLOCKS	*Opunake & Coastal News*	2021	Pihama, South Taranaki	44
SONGS OF THE EARTH (1972 -2021)	*Art New Zealand*	2021	Pihama, South Taranaki	46
TUBES	*Art New Zealand*	2021	Pihama, South Taranaki	48
STEPS	*Art New Zealand*	2021	Pihama, South Taranaki	50
MIRROR	*Art New Zealand*	2021	Pihama, South Taranaki	52
SHAKESPEARE INTERVIEWS	*Bryan Vickery Media*	2022	Quaternary Institute	54
PLAY COMMENTARIES TO WILLIAM SHAKESPEARE'S 1623 FOLIO	*Whanganui Chronicle*	2024	Quaternary Institute	56

THE STRATFORD DISTRICT LIBRARY

ART	ARTICLES	DATE	VENUE	PAGE
THE DOLLSHOUSE	*Stratford Press*	1984	Stratford Gallery	62
1609 SONNET COMMENTARIES	*Stratford Press*	1996	Quaternary Institute	64
WILLIAM SHAKESPEARE BUST	*Stratford Press/Daily News*	1997	Artist's Studio	66
SONNET COMPETITION & TROPHY	*Stratford Press*	1998	Artist's Studio	68
THE SECRETS OF THE SONNETS	*The Daily News*	2001	Quaternary Institute	70
LUCY BUST	*Biograview*	2021	Artist's Studio	76
QUATERNARY DISPLAY CARTS	*The Daily News*	2024	Quaternary Institute	80

ACKNOWLEDGEMENTS

The Quaternary Institute gratefully acknowledges the following publications
for the use of the Press Clippings and other material
that form the basis of this exhibition

THE AUCKLAND STAR
Catalogue pages 4 & 6

NZ HERALD
Catalogue pages 2, 5, 22 & 24

THE DAILY NEWS
Catalogue pages 8, 10, 12, 16, 30, 60, 70, 72, 73, 80, 82, 83 & 84

THE STRATFORD PRESS
Catalogue pages 14, 28, 62, 64 & 68

DOMINION POST
Catalogue pages 20

THE WHANGANUI CRONICLE
Catalogue pages 18, 56 & 58

OPUNAKE & COASTAL NEWS
Catalogue pages 34, 42 & 44

TOWARDS A HISTORY OF THE CONTEMPORARY
Catalogue page 38

BIOGRAVIEW
Catalogue page 40, 74, 75, 76 & 78

ART NEW ZEALAND
Catalogue pages 46, 50 & 52

ART
ARTIST
ARTICLES

(1972-2024)

PERCY
THOMSON
GALLERY

Catherine Rhodes

Director

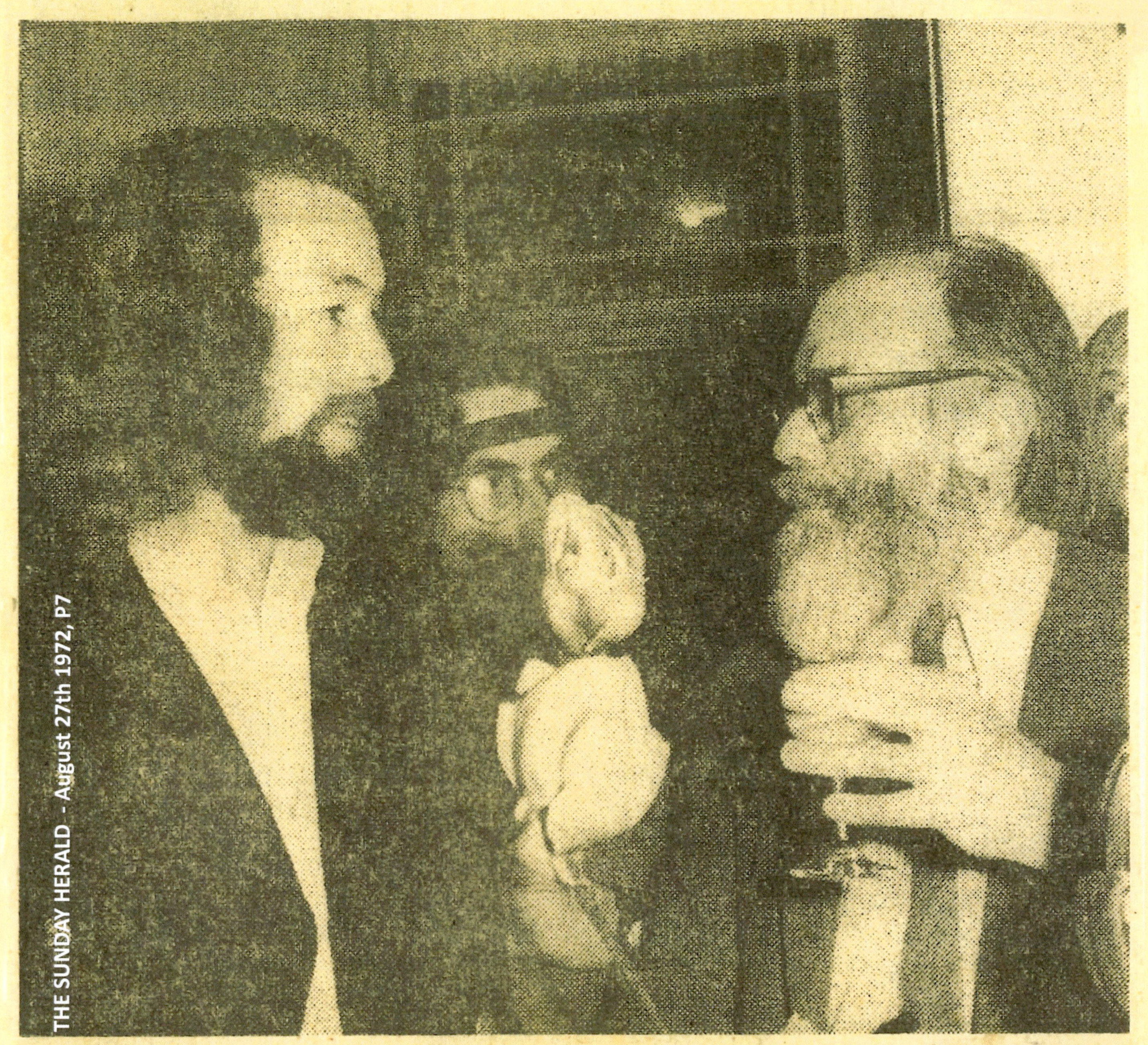

The dean of the Faculty of Fine Arts, Professor Paul Beadle, with Roger Peter, winner of the Air New Zealand prize, at the opening of the Auckland University Festival of Fine Arts.

NOTEBOOK 7 Tues 10th Dec '85

In summer the sun sets into the edge of my back room· I can look out across the trees and grass to the long lines of its light picking out the patches of yellow where shadows have yet to fall· Across the pond and willows its bright evening glow echoes the residue of warmth I feel within my heart at the end of the day·

Even at the calculation's end, that streak of warmth is enough to save a soul· The regulated pattern of meals and work find their ease in the hour that proceeds the shining depths of night· These are the moments a Backroom comes into its own· The fowlhouse, the woodshed, the goats' paddock and fruit trees are the greens and greys to my gazing mind·

The light blue sky has the intensity that belies the heat of the day and fills the room with reading light and casts in silhouette the dreams I have of tomorrow· This room is not a room of yesterday· Rather it is full of images of untried desires hinging on memories barely substantial· The spark of love encouraged by the evening air seeks to enliven the creativity this little room promises·

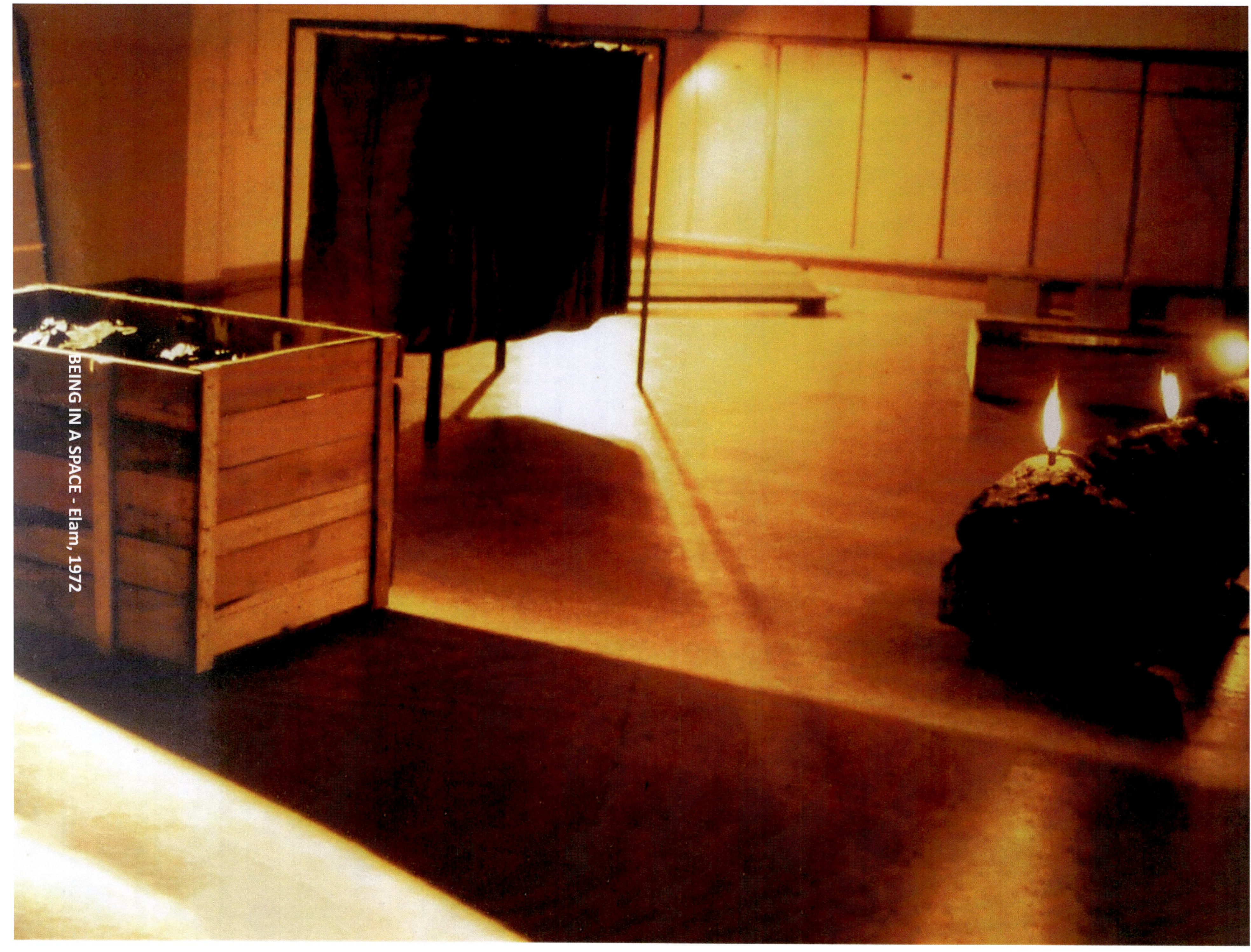
BEING IN A SPACE - Elam, 1972

Scrappy, confusing— but quality's there

Weekender's **ART** news & reviews By HAMISH KEITH

To describe the 14th Universities Arts Festival exhibition as an exhibition is stretching the word too far. It is a shambles, a disorganized hochpotch that for display and presentation deserves to score a miserable nought out of 10.

Flung at the walls and floors of the large white mansion on the corner of Wakefield and Symonds Streets, the show does less than justice to the quality of the work in it.

Among the hundred or so pieces collected for the show are a great many that are full of energy and rich with ideas. It is a great pity that the potential which seems to exist in them has not merited even the kind of attention usually given to an end-of-term display of work by primary-school children.

The exhibition coincides with the Air New Zealand Fine Arts Award, which this year has been given to an intriguing collection of warm sensations gathered together in one space by **Roger Peters**.

Peters has put together a kind of factory boiler-room environment full of visible heat, suggested energy, power and the comfortable smell of clean sacks and warm oil.

Leaning against one wall is a ladder, the rungs made from red-hot heater elements. Against another is a box of coal lumps. Ranged along a third are three lit gas jets spouting from the tops of scoria lumps. Fastened to a fourth wall are three thin chains descending from a rod into three containers of whitish, plastic glop.

In the centre of the room is a rack of sacks, and on the floor is a shallow bath of heated oil and a wire grid supported by a flat square of black plastic. As a reminder of the potential expenditure of human energy, there is a heavy wooden pallet with thick rope handles at either end.

PETERS has given his bits and pieces the general label "Being in a Space," which is a fair-enough assessment of the experience he provokes.

The pleasant thing about this room is that familiarity with it increases the visitor's relationship with what is going on; it may be entered reluctantly, but after a while the room becomes the kind of space that it is unpleasant to leave.

Certainly the ladder rungs will burn the incautious. So will the gas jets. The warm oil is a trap, and any attempt to lift the pallet could produce a slipped disc or a crushed toe.

Peters has, however, produced a feeling of heat and energy under control, and the latent danger of his assemblages only emphasizes who is in command. In this case it is a sensation given to anyone who stands within the room.

Next door to "Being in a Space," **Bruce Barber** has constructed a very different kind of environment. Three plastic strips on the floor, each with a tension strip behind or in front of it and one with test tubes stuck to it at regular intervals; a desk lamp; some diagrams on the wall; and a continuous tape recording of science jargon, breathlessly and incompetently read — these are his raw material.

With all this Barber seems to aim a good, solid kick at ivory-tower technology. It's a good environment for falling asleep in out of sheer boredom — the same kind of ambience as many remote university lecture halls.

ON THE SECOND floor, Kimberly Gray offers a piece of participation in a situation involving four shaving mirrors and a swivel chair. You can swivel on the chair and then pin a piece of paper to the floor indicating where you think it should have been placed.

The rest of the show is difficult to see, but some things make their presence felt. **J. Hurrel** has three fine, richly encrusted paintings, the best being "Backyard Business," where all kinds of things and beasties emerge from luscious swirls of enamel-like paint.

S. Lawrie offers a horrendous line-up of meat sandwiches, three being ham and the one in the middle, complete with a dead fly, being labelled "man," rather like some vegetarian nightmare.

Two of the three entries by **Lyndon Welbourne**, "Diamond Star Hubcap Halo" and "Homage to the Valkyrie Fountain," are strong, mature images that cry out for better treatment than they have been given in this confusion.

AS MIGHT be expected from a student show, there are a lot of obvious influences, but it is a promising development that more of the borrowings are from other New Zealand painters and sculptors than from glossy art magazines.

Like the display, the catalogue is scrappy and confusing. It is hard enough to locate individual works in it, but any attempt to find out something about the origins of any given exhibitor is completely fruitless.

Presumably the collection has been gathered up from all over the country. It would have made sense to give some idea of what area each contributor came from, if for no better reason than to explain why some of the more promising have not been heard of here before.

New Zealand is not so well endowed with talent in the visual arts that new work of this quality can afford to be hidden under the proverbial bushel.

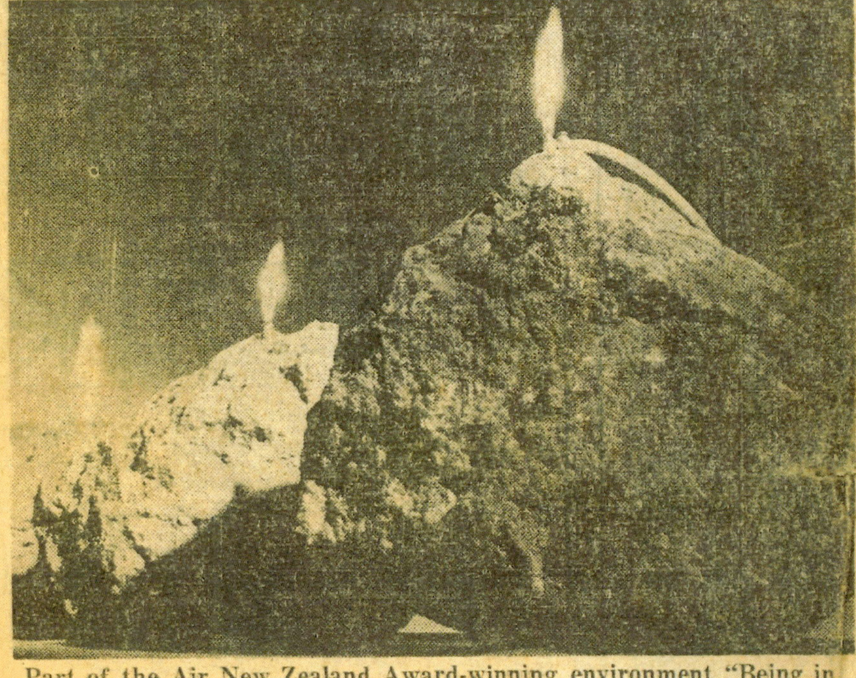

Part of the Air New Zealand Award-winning environment "Being in a Space," by Roger Peters, at the Universities Arts Festival exhibition.

NOTEBOOK 1 Fri 18th Sept '81

Reading of Wittgenstein again makes me jerk into a state of clarity and realights the foundations for a great No of my attitudes which I find I have now sublimated and not so much taken for granted rather accept in contradiction to the values held by many of those I associate with – more to that later.

NOTEBOOK 1 Mon 28th Sept '81

There seems no doubt to me of the correctness of W's idea that philosophy qua philosophy is a dead end – that changes if they are to recur and be enduring must rise from grass roots otherwise you get the shadow of change without substance and the blind formality and conservatism and short-sighted beliefs that follow. To come – symbolism (natural)

NOTEBOOK 8 Mon 3rd Nov '86

Mallarme, Duchamp, Wittgenstein suddenly your constellations have resolved themselves into perceptible Galaxys. Hope has, for me, assumed the dimensions of the Universe. Your lights are now but part of the reflection of life. I have flipped through the invisible grasp of your magnetic fields. Now each of you seems to highlight a particular facet of my Human Being. Like a rocket you have combined to launch my fragile craft into the reaches of space.

The novelty of this realisation has me wondering as to its consequence and reminiscing over its development. None of you has held tightly to the vanity of your achievements. You have each been conspicuous in your disavowal of the seminal aspects of your efforts. What then constitutes this rupture I proclaim from a period of intense devoteeship on my part.

For the last 15 years or more your names have been the lead lights in the abbey of my deliberations. How now can I say that I can see through the doors, cast open, to the sunlight of my life. In seeing you in coloured glass I have no desire to disparage you. Not at all! But I do see you, at last. No longer do I feel the need to look at life through the refractivity of your mediums.

Though I baulk at changing your designations from Pater to 'Frere' it is in a sense of Brotherhood that I would feel most comfortable with you now. If only because I have persisted with you over the years and ever hoped to gain from the sense of integrity and values you shewed that I might say now that you have allowed me a freedom, that though new born, is nonetheless real. That faith in you is renewed in love. Your battles are over – mine are just begun.

NZ HERALD - Tuesday August 22nd 1972, P2

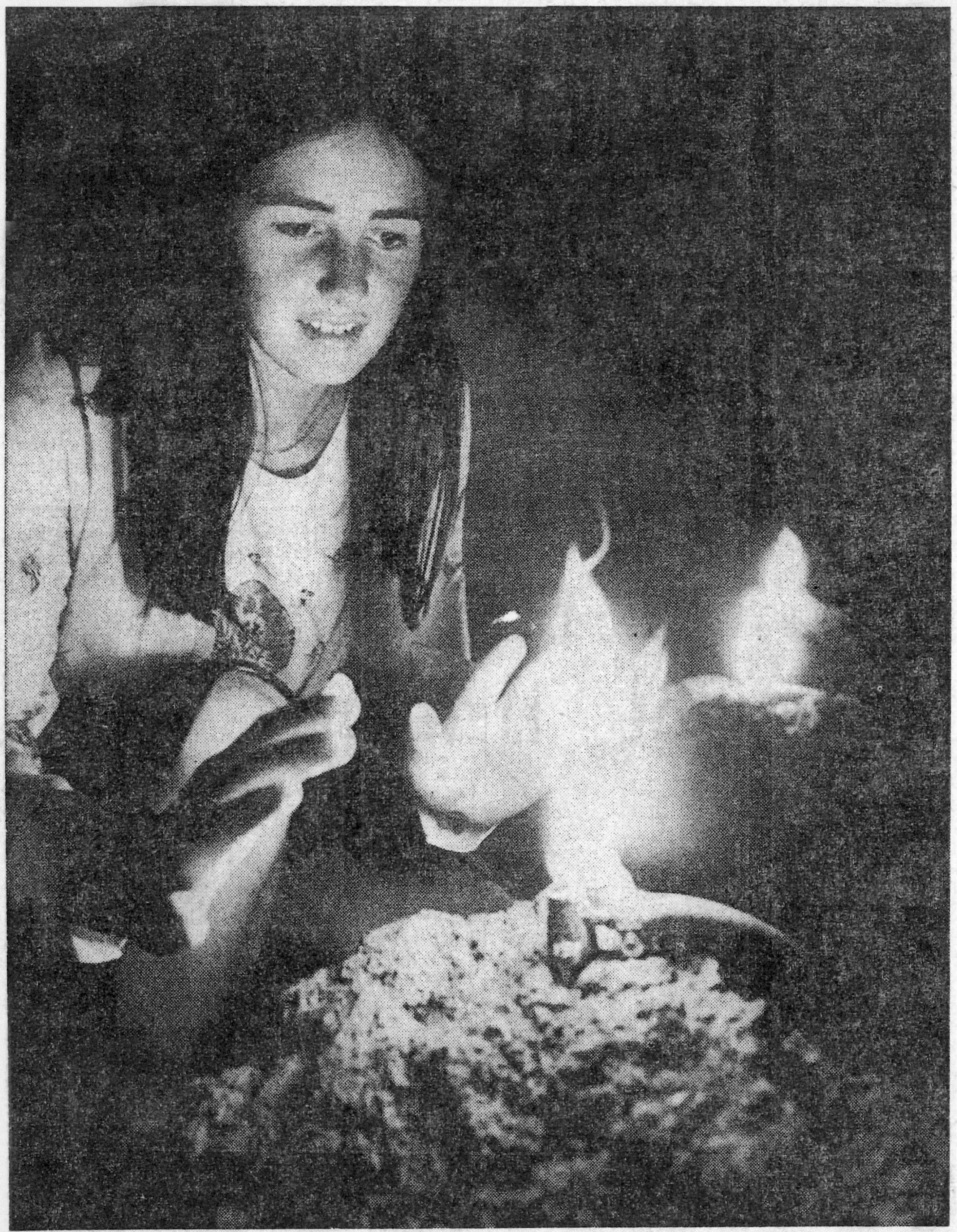

Miss Kathleen Gallagher (19), on holiday from Christchurch, warms her hands by the flame from one of the exhibits by New Zealand artist Roger Peters at the Auckland Art Gallery. The works in this exhibition portray the elements.

Grey Lynn bypass

A new by pass into Williamson Ave, Grey Lynn, opened yesterday.

Traffic can now avoid the

Diver "rising"

INVERCARGILL, Today (PA). — The diver recovering from the bends on the Penrod 74 oil rig in Foveaux Strait is under a controlled

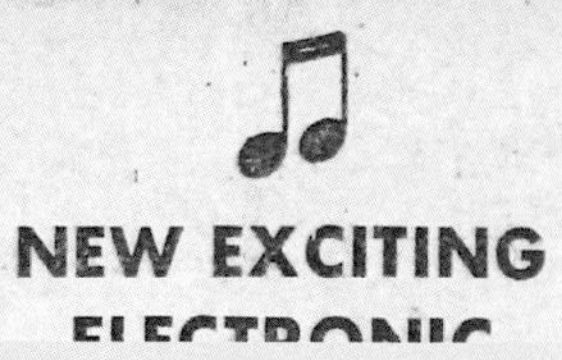

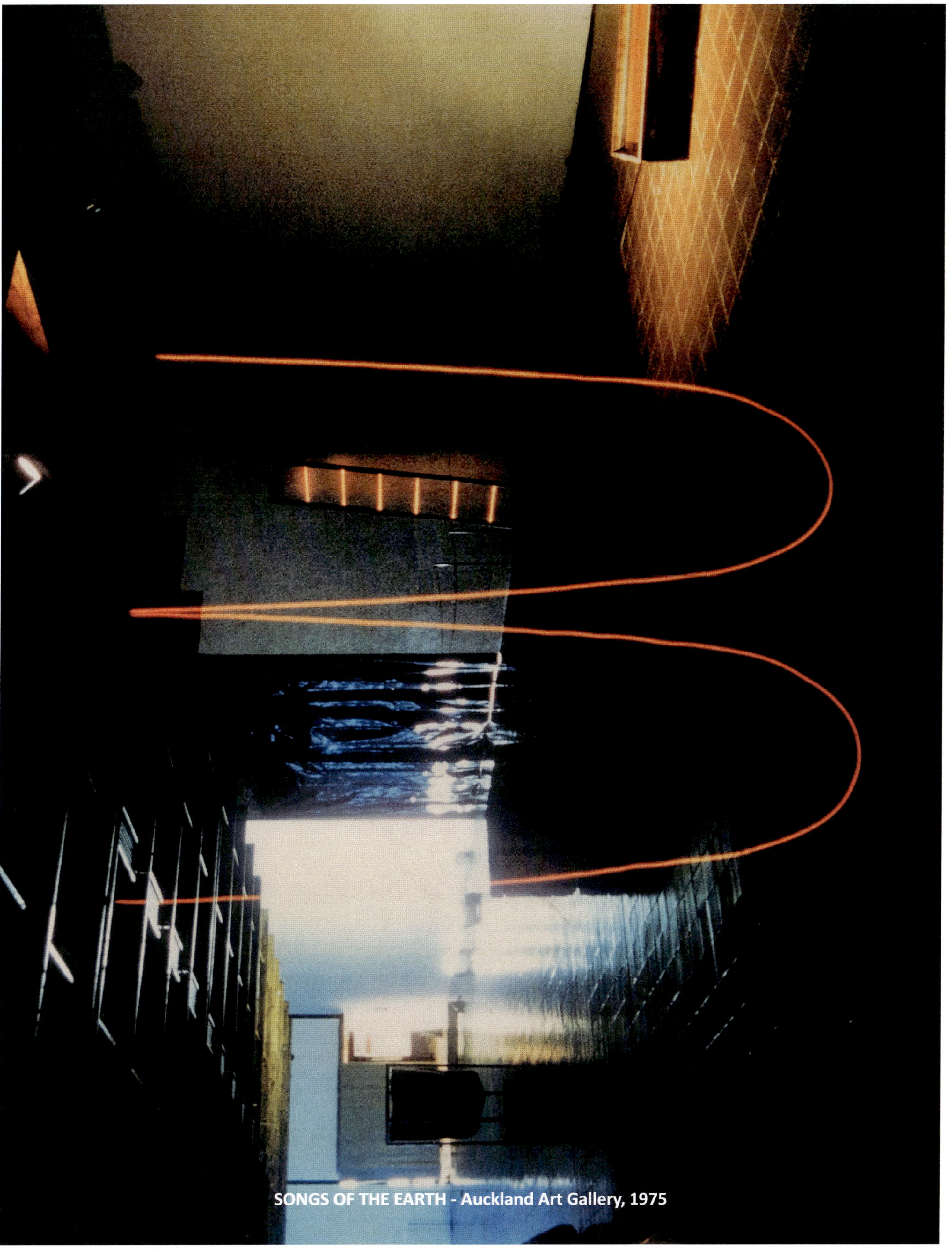

SONGS OF THE EARTH - Auckland Art Gallery, 1975

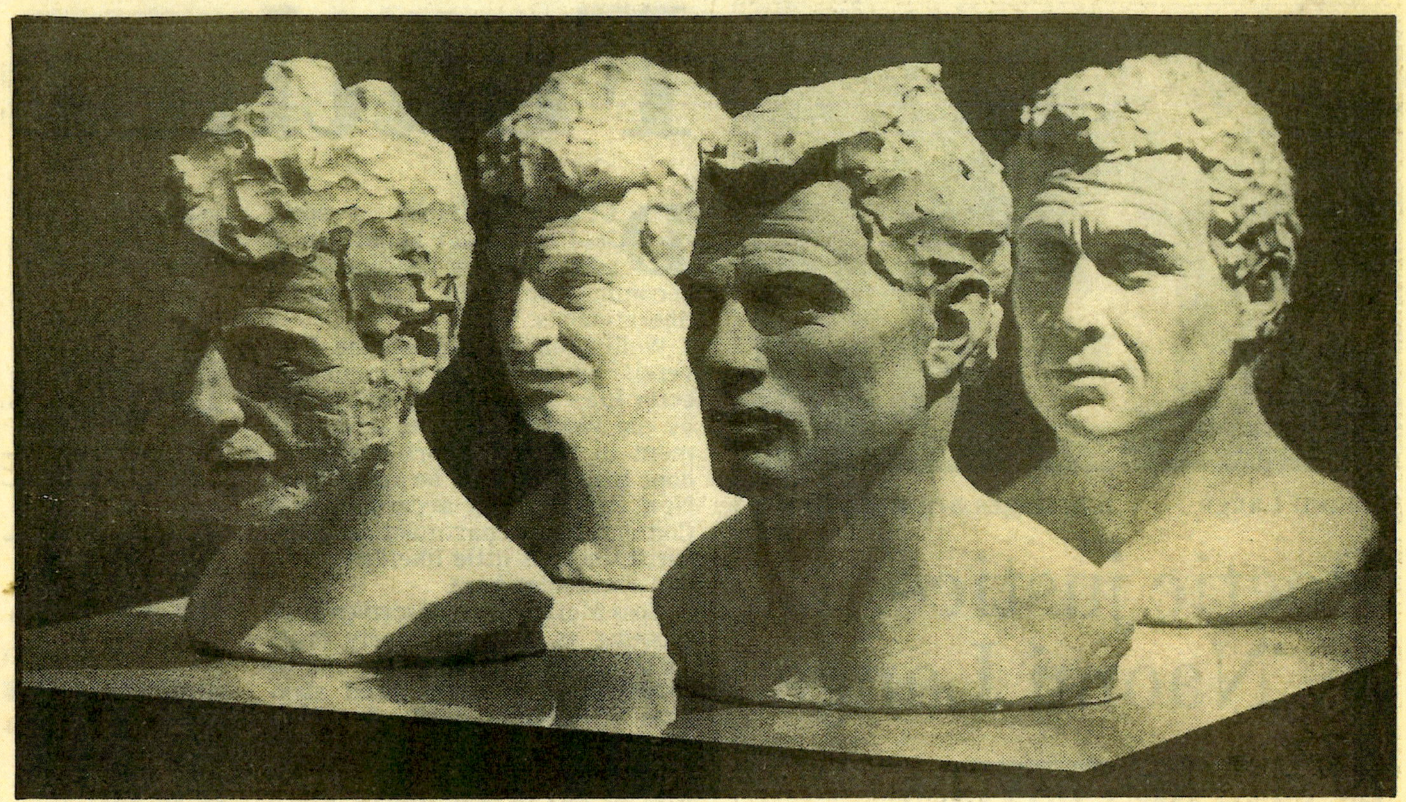

My pick, but not the judges . . . "Four Men on Cloud Onyx" by Roger Peters reveals an awareness of form.

Photo: Dwayne Senior

Losers were great, so winners must be good

GALLERY REPORT with PAM WALKER

WRONG again! As usual, I speculated about the two major award winners while mooching around the Govett-Brewster Art Gallery in New Plymouth during a visit to the annual 'Taranaki Review' exhibition.

Roger Peters' fine plaster of paris portrait heads "Four Men on Cloud Onyx", and the bronze pair "Sisters" revealed awareness of form, lively modelling (note the calligraphic flourishes of the young girls' hair) and a sensitivity to texture evident in the intriguing contrasts between matt and glossy surfaces.

My other favourite was Mike Spencer's stubby little stoneware teapot; full of character.

Next morning, Alan Carter's oil painting "Top Dressing 1" and Dave Hegglun's andesite carving "A Fair Slice of the Cake for Nga Ruahine" proved to be the winners. Ah well, no doubt they deserved it.

Carter's painting is vigorous, and Hegglun's work has certainly improved since the fairly recent days when he incorporated pot plants into his paintings, a

You can help decide the two awards for the most popular works in this year's review by voting for them when you visit the exhibition, which continues until October 7.

● The Taranaki Review — the look, the format and the selection process — is the subject of a discussion evening to be held at the Govett-Brewster Art Gallery at 7.30pm on Tuesday. The discussion will be chaired by Kinsley Sampson, with an introduction by gallery director John McCormack, and opening contributions from Egmont Community Arts Council chairperson Margaret Scott, and Okato artist Dale Copeland. The discussion will be open to general debate and organisers hope anyone with something to say about the Review will attend and generate some lively and constructive discussion.

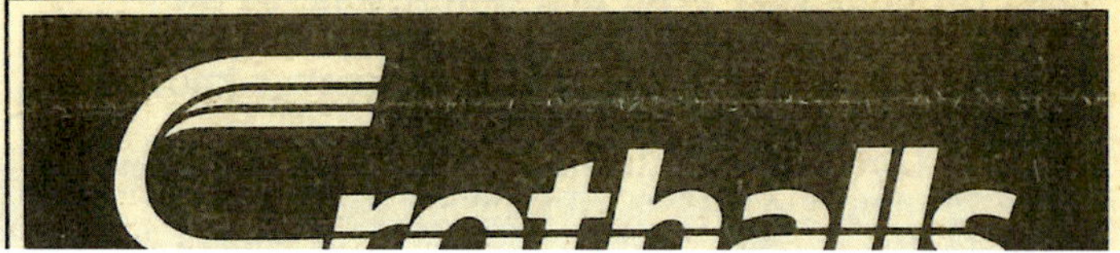

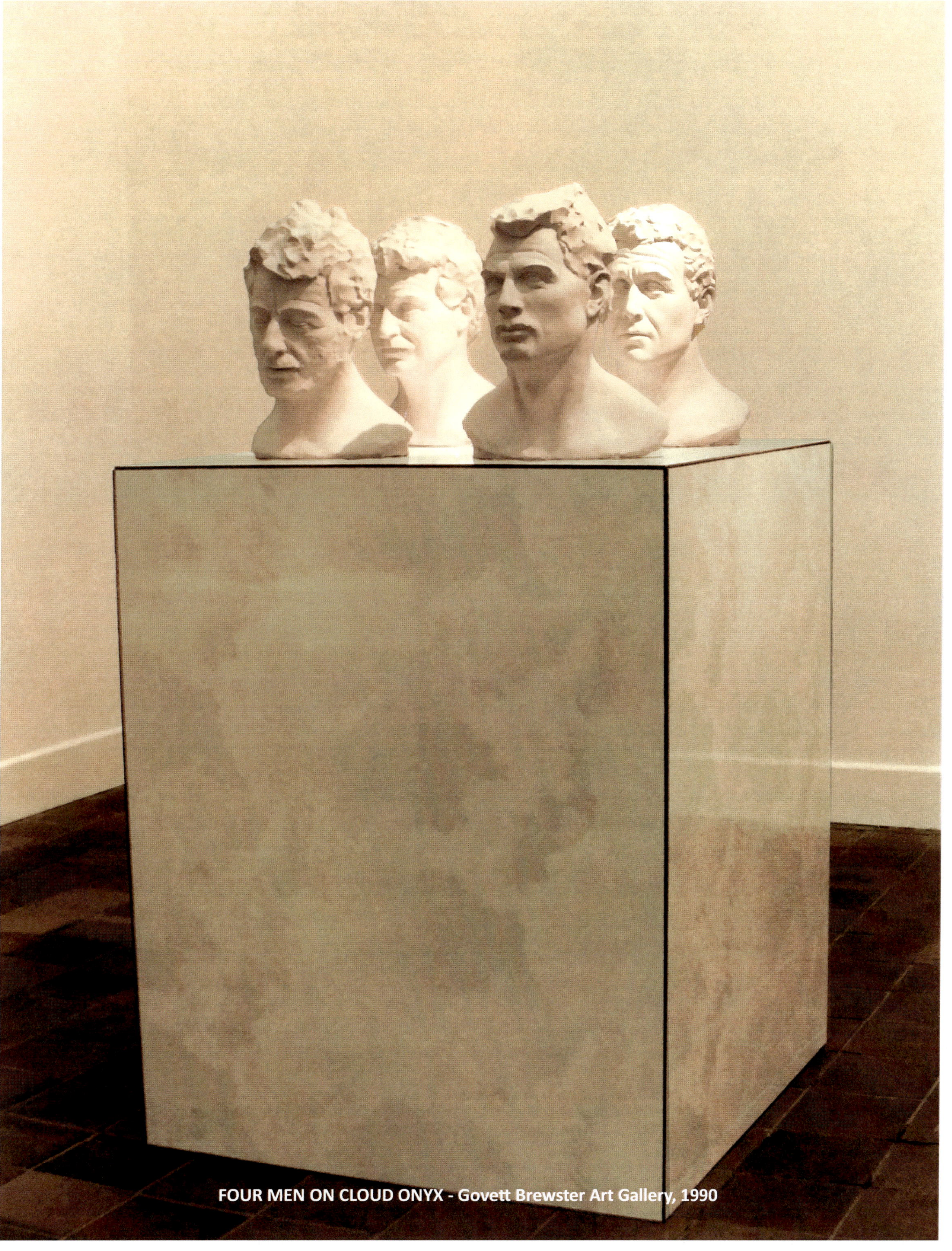

FOUR MEN ON CLOUD ONYX - Govett Brewster Art Gallery, 1990

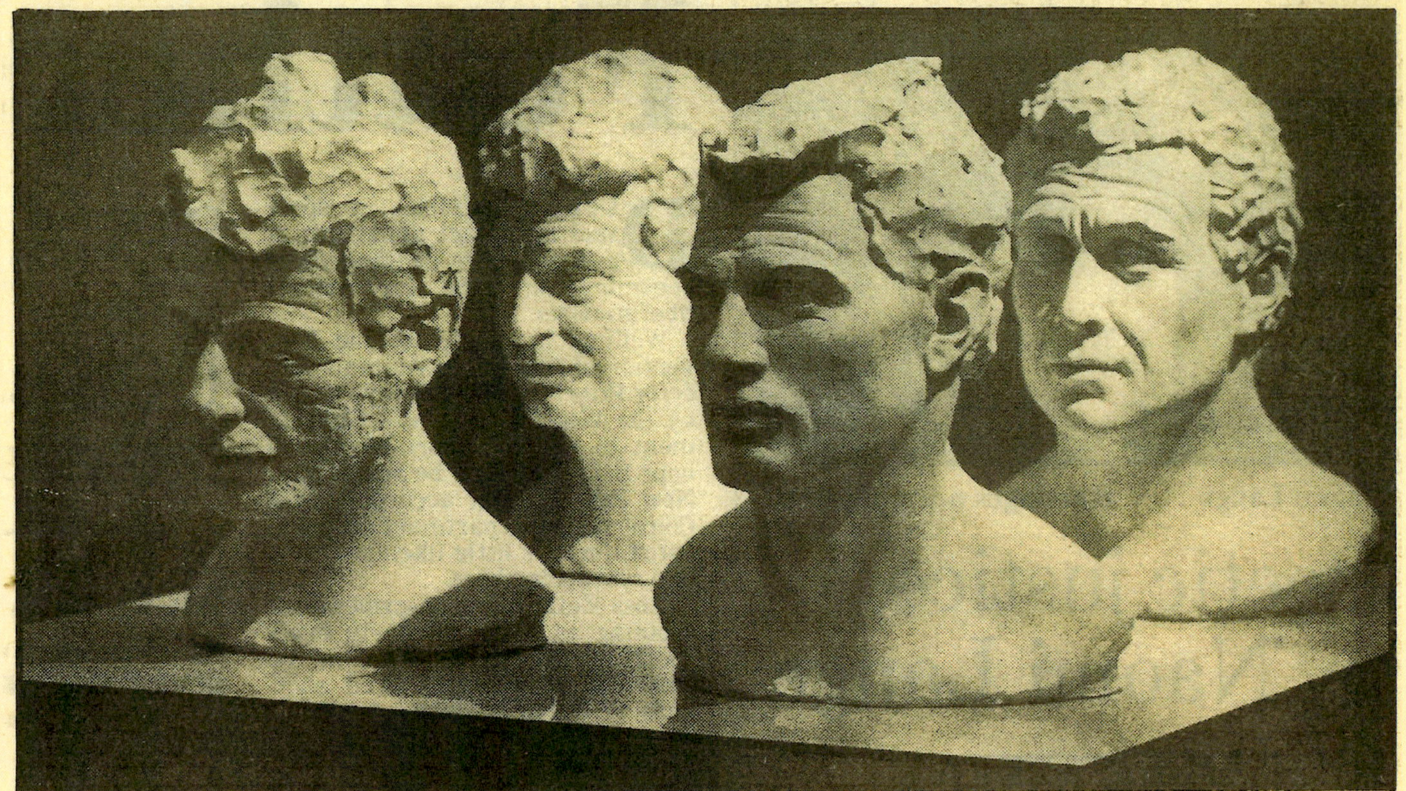

My pick, but not the judges . . . **"Four Men on Cloud Onyx"** by Roger Peters reveals an awareness of form.

Photo: Dwayne Senior

Losers were great, so winners must be good

WRONG again! As usual, I speculated about the two major award winners while mooching around the Govett-Brewster Art Gallery in New Plymouth during a visit to the annual 'Taranaki Review' exhibition.

Roger Peters' fine plaster of paris portrait heads "Four Men on Cloud Onyx", and the bronze pair "Sisters" revealed awareness of form, lively modelling (note the calligraphic flourishes of the young girls' hair) and a sensitivity to texture evident in the intriguing contrasts between matt and glossy surfaces.

GALLERY REPORT with PAM WALKER

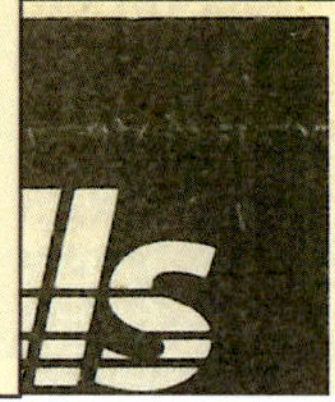

THE DAILY NEWS - September 15th 1990, P15

10

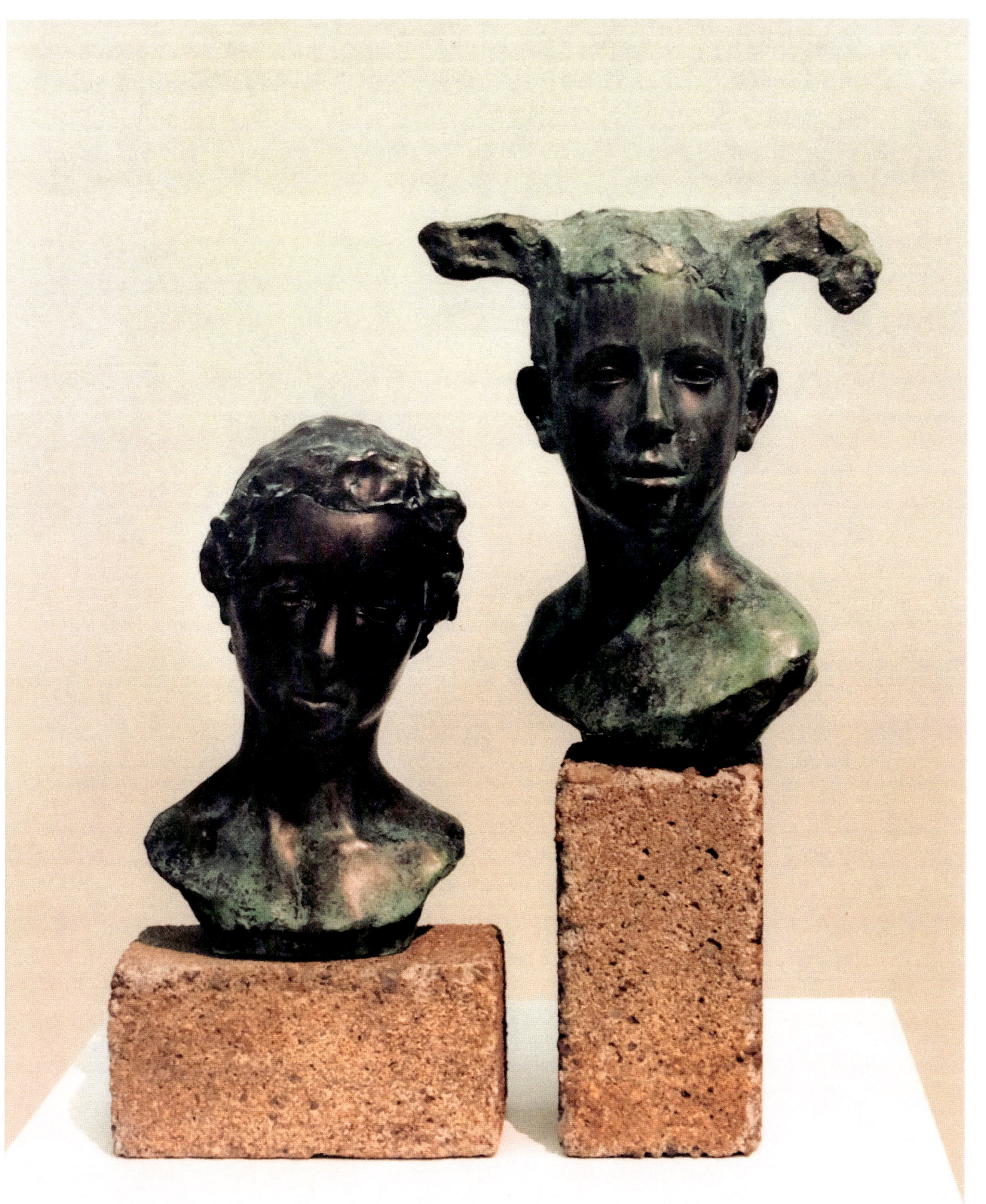

'SISTERS' TALIA & KATIE - BRONZE, Govett Brewster Art Gallery, 1990

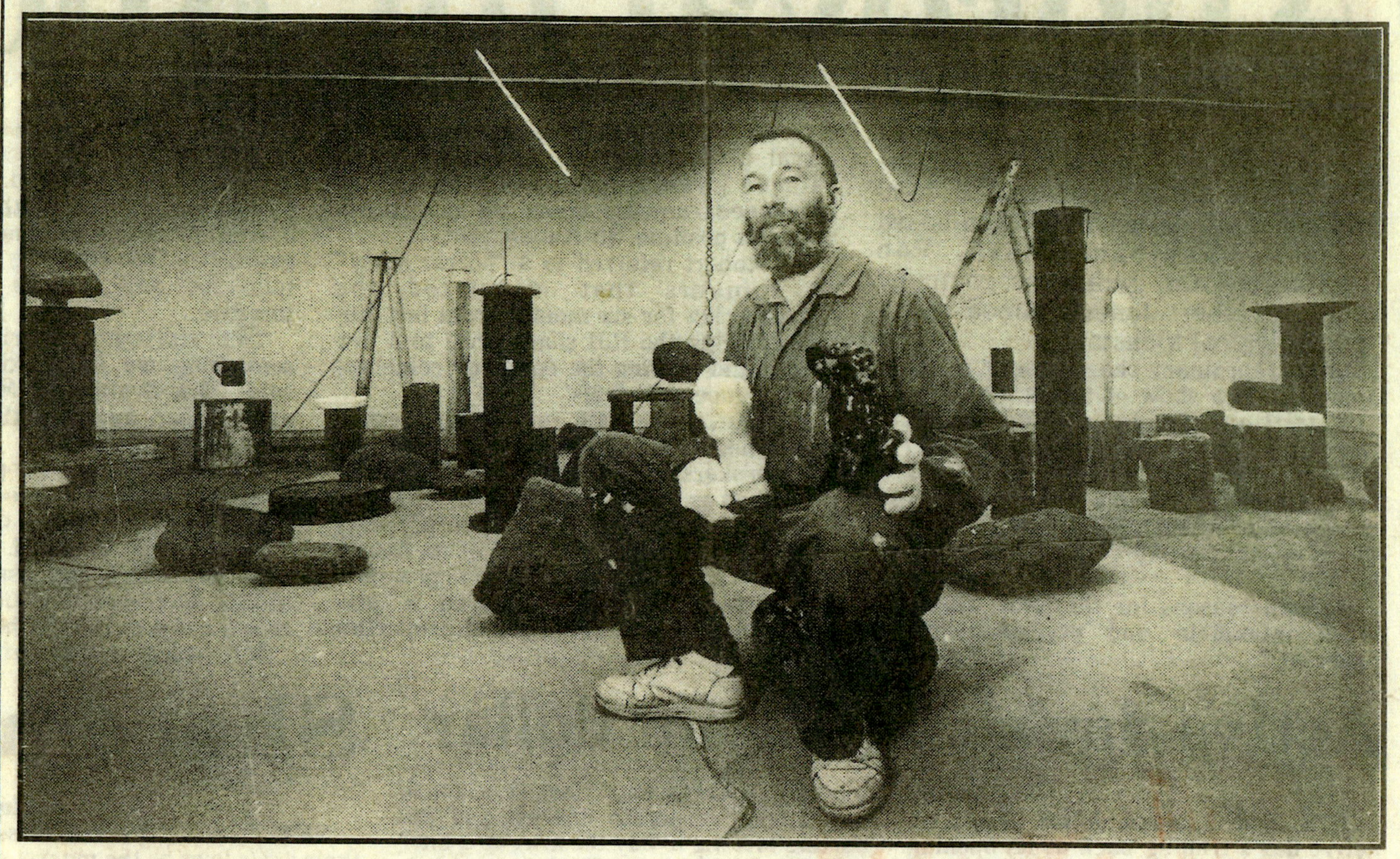

Roger Peters takes time out from setting up his work 'Songs of the Earth II'. Photo: DWAYNE SENIOR

Kaponga artist sets up installation

A SCULPTURAL installation by a Kaponga artist who describes himself as a bit of a magpie opens at the Govett-Brewster Art Gallery in New Plymouth on Saturday.

Roger Peters said the theme of the installation, entitled "Songs of the Earth II", had strong links with an earlier exhibition he held in the City Art Gallery in Auckland.

The installation would take up three levels at the gallery and encorporated a variety of materials and elements including rocks, wood, metal and the use of neon lighting.

"Mine is a found object type of work. I tend to be a bit of a magpie. I've never had it together in this sort of arrangement so I'm looking at the gallery space to make the work function properly."

Over the last five years Mr Peters said he had been concentrating on figurative work and he had introduced the concept in the installation. "I like the idea of saying something about the way we are and using matter in a more meaningful poetic way. If it is working it should give rise to a number of interpretations. And it provides a way in for people because at least they can relate to figures."

And each piece which went to make up the installation had a special significance, he said.

"Even with rocks — I'd walk along the river but there's only some rocks I'd pick up. There has to be a definite element of empathy with the materials I'm using."

THE DAILY NEWS - May 1991

NOTEBOOK 7 Sun 27th Apr '86

I know I have a clod of earth about my visionary compass which will not pass until the etching of time is complete upon my blade· The scratching on the doors by a thousand hoofs and claws and flames impart a dimension of clustered granite meteorites into the darkness of our hearts·

Baying, Baying, Baying the sweetness of a love song rides the moving earth· The trembling stone leaves no vacuum for our deepest feelings· Our hands and lips are sealed in an expression without reserve· I can see a delightful sequence of flowering transits across the face of the sun — with droplets buoyed up — refracting the beauty of our collision in the depths of space· I learn from your mastery of the howling rage·

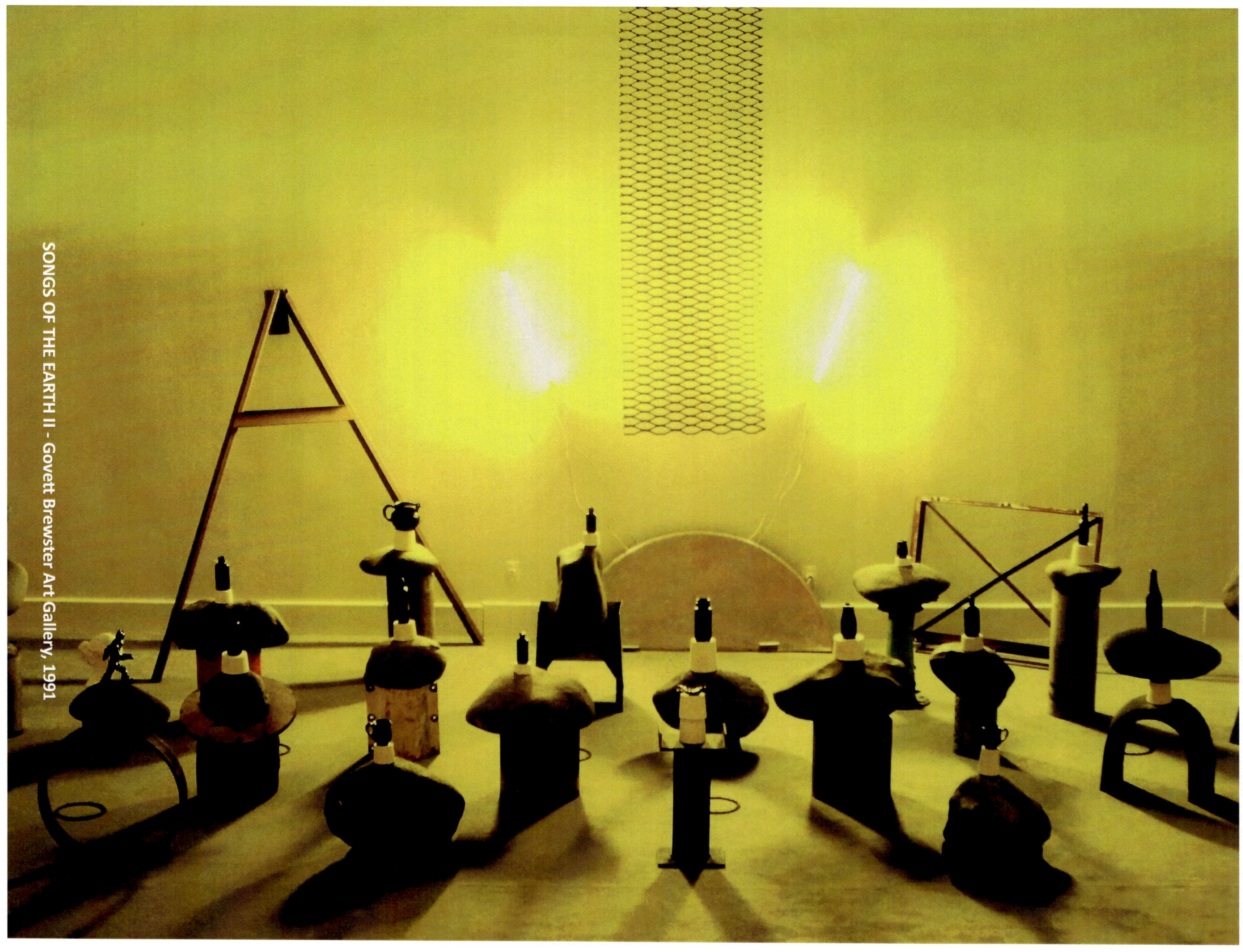
SONGS OF THE EARTH II - Govett Brewster Art Gallery, 1991

Figurative work by Kaponga artist

Roger Peters of Kaponga is an artist one is sure to hear more about in the future.

A worker in the three dimensions, Peters is a modeller and sculptor who covers the whole range from abstract installations to classical figurative work.

His current work is modelling figures, an art he has taught himself and worked on for the last three years.

He creates sensitive and empathetic models of the human form, mainly head and shoulders, which are lifesize or smaller.

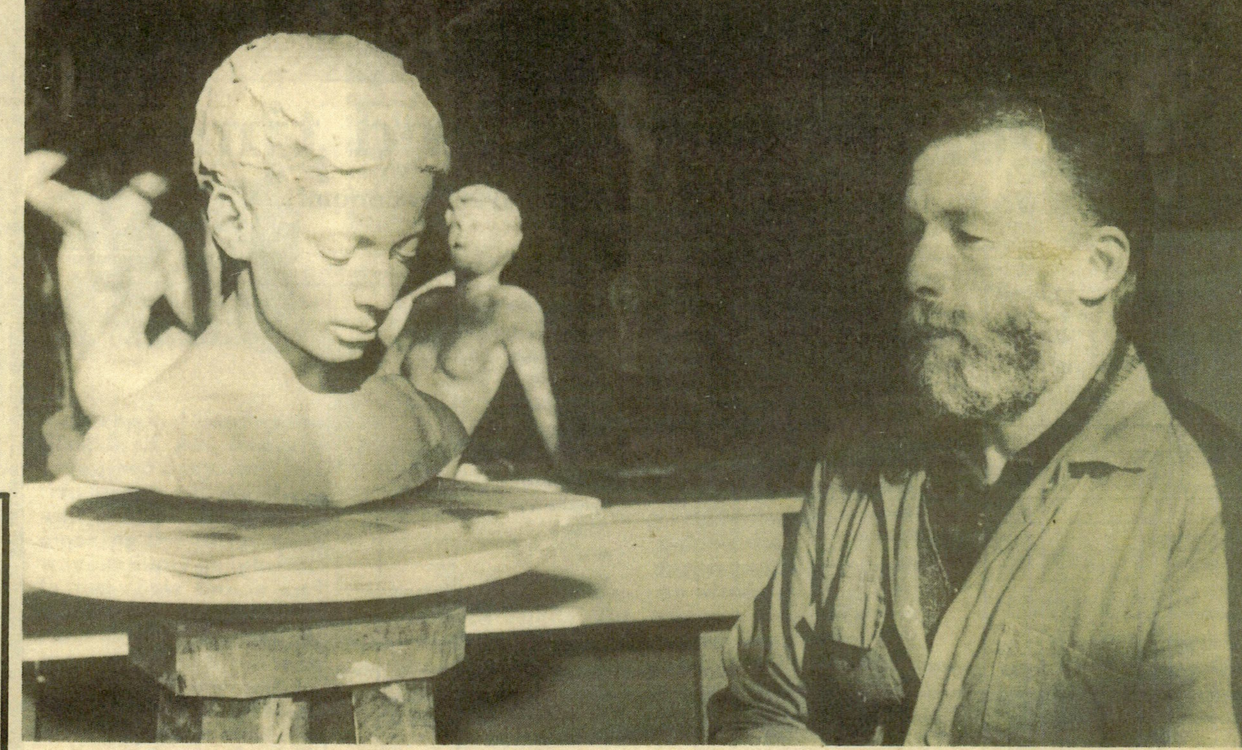

Roger Peters with a head modelled from his daughter Teresa in his Kaponga workshop.

He works with clay, plaster of Paris, bronze and concrete and his figures have been either classical or modelled from friends or local people.

Peters was born in Wanganui, studied at the Auckland School of Architecture for three years and the Elam School of Fine Arts for four years, graduating in 1974.

He majored in sculpture, receiving the second year prize in that area and winning the Air New Zealand National Tertiary Award in 1972.

He exhibited in the Auckland City Art Gallery in 1975 and his work during that time involved forms such as ladders, boxes, rings and loops using heat and light sources.

He began looking at working with the human form, an ambition which was partially realised in the quasi-figurative aluminium cut-outs made between 1979 and 1980, halted by a move to South Taranaki in 1981.

Songs of Desire was exhibited at the Govett-Brewster Art Gallery in 1981.

"My return to sculpture lead to a marquette of a large cut-out which was exhibited at the 1986 Arts Festival in Hawera. However I had a strong feeling of dissatisfaction with the possibilities of cut-outs," he said.

"In 1987 I began teaching myself the basic technical and formal skills involved in figure modelling and casting in bronze, concrete and plaster."

The early fruits of this work were exhibited in the Taranaki Reviews of 1989 and 1990 at the Govett-Brewster, earning a place in the finals each year.

In May this year he diverted from his figurative work to produce an installation exhibited in the Govett-Brewster Art Gallery.

This work harked back to some of his works from the earlier days and entitled 'Songs of the Earth II', comprised of groupings of rocks, wax formed objects, models and other mediums.

He created four groupings suggesting different themes and expanded the content by using the human form.

He is now returning to creating figures and his workshop at the Eltham Road farmhouse he shares with his partner and three children abounds with completed and current beautifully crafted heads and torsos, from copies of classical busts to models of family and friends.

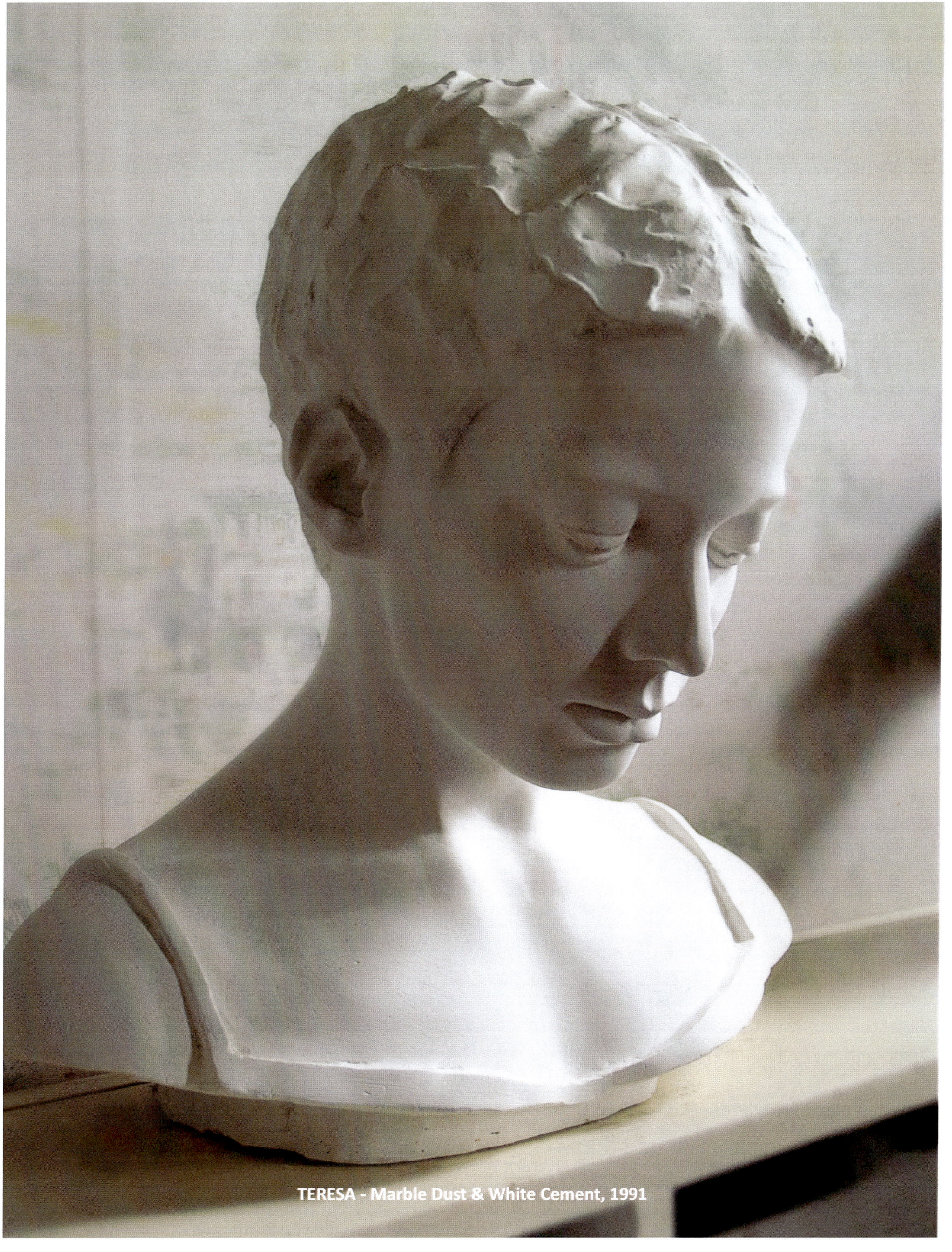

TERESA - Marble Dust & White Cement, 1991

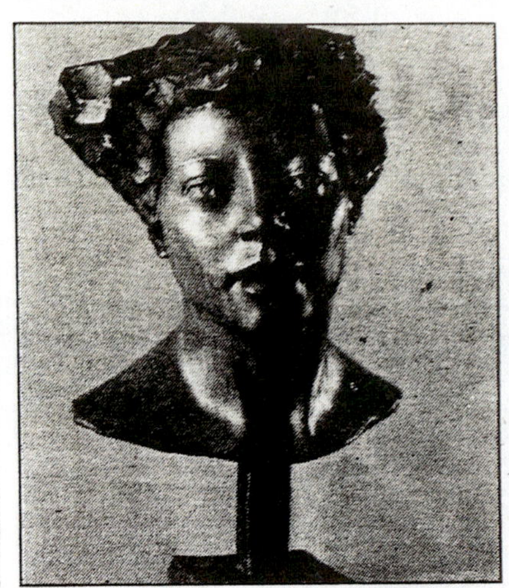

KAREN: A bronze bust by Roger Peters at Gallery 79, Hawera.

Artist delights in stretch of the human form

By PAM WALKER

ROGER PETERS' Projects and Bronzes finshes tomorrow at Gallery 79 in Hawera.

Improvising on the formal means he's patiently taught himself and mastered, Peters has modelled about 40 quarter-sized male nudes expressing not only the activity of the flesh but of the spirit, the anima, so that these little figures are charged with a quivering intensity.

Six groups variously disport themselves in, around, over, on and beneath boxes, planks, branches, wires, strings and stumps. Modelling is rudimentary, detail ignored to focus on gesture.

The energy and humour of these swarms of little figures express Peters' delight in plasticity, in the stretch an swing, contraction and flexion of the human body.

Although the scale, angularity, weight and resistance of the materials used as settings for each group symbolise the relationship between humanity and the physical world of natural and man-made structures, this relationship is comfortable rather than hostile.

Spun around a vortex of wires, dwarfed but not intimidated by tall branches and planks, bracing themselves against or tumbling up and down sheer walls, the little men are deft and assured.

Any notion you may have that the rawness of the figures isn't intentional will be dispelled by two highly finished bronzes, one a study after Michelangelo's noble head, Down, and the other a portrait bust.

THE DAILY NEWS - Wednesday November 25 1992, P19

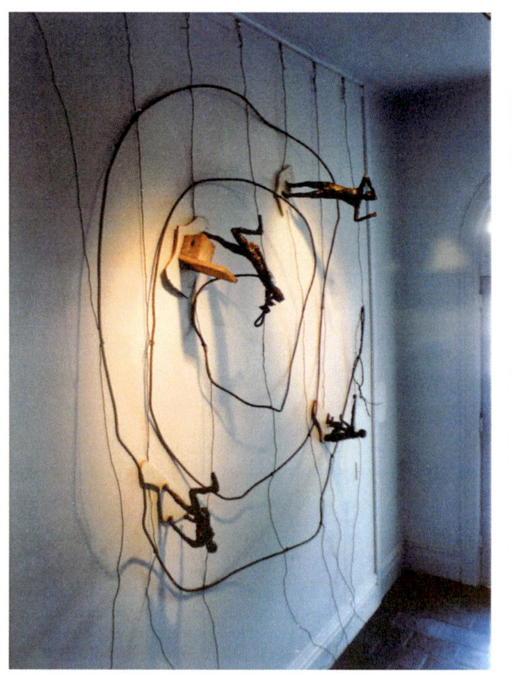

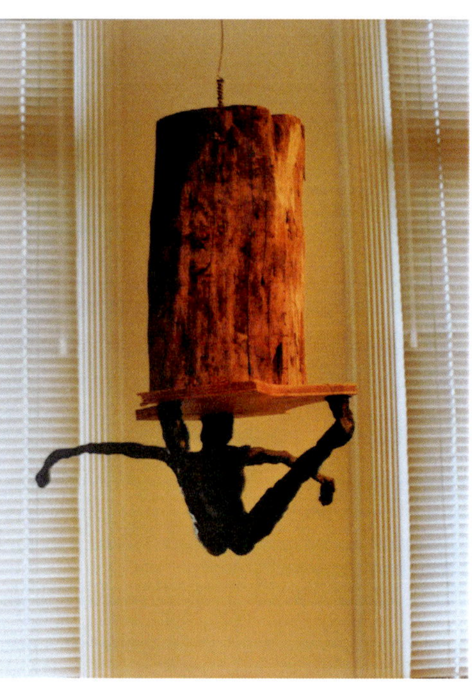

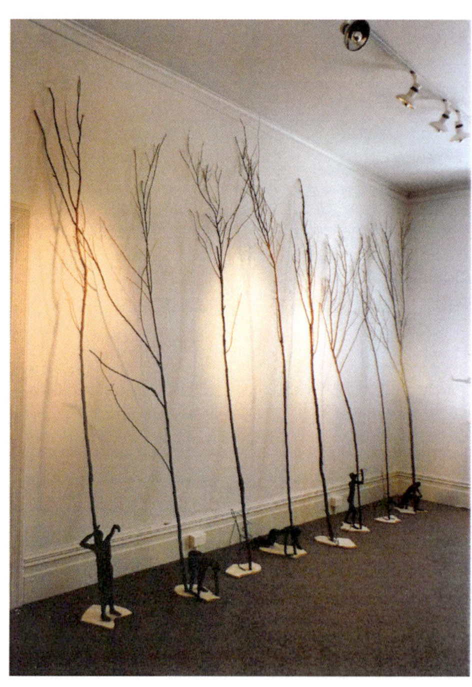

16

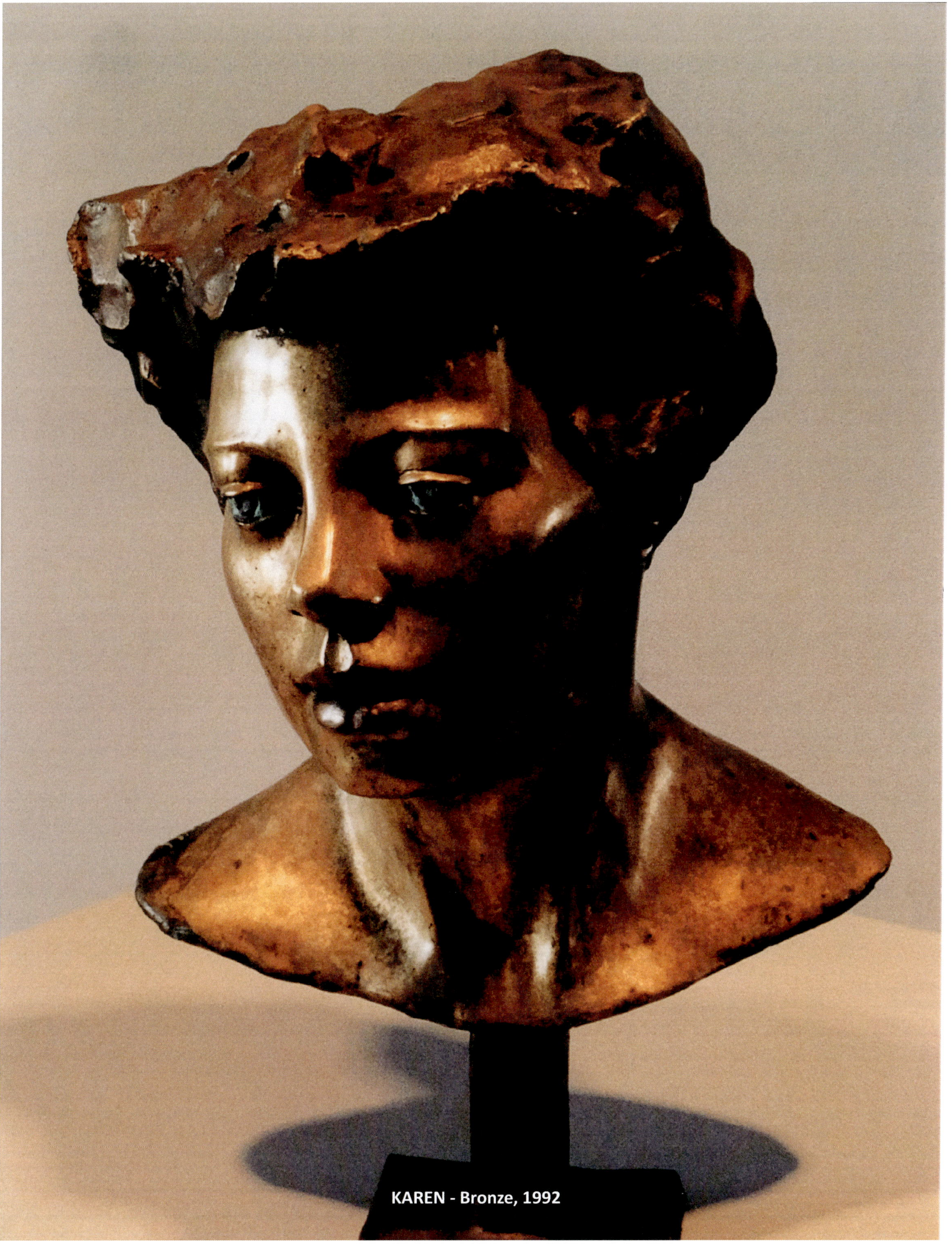

KAREN - Bronze, 1992

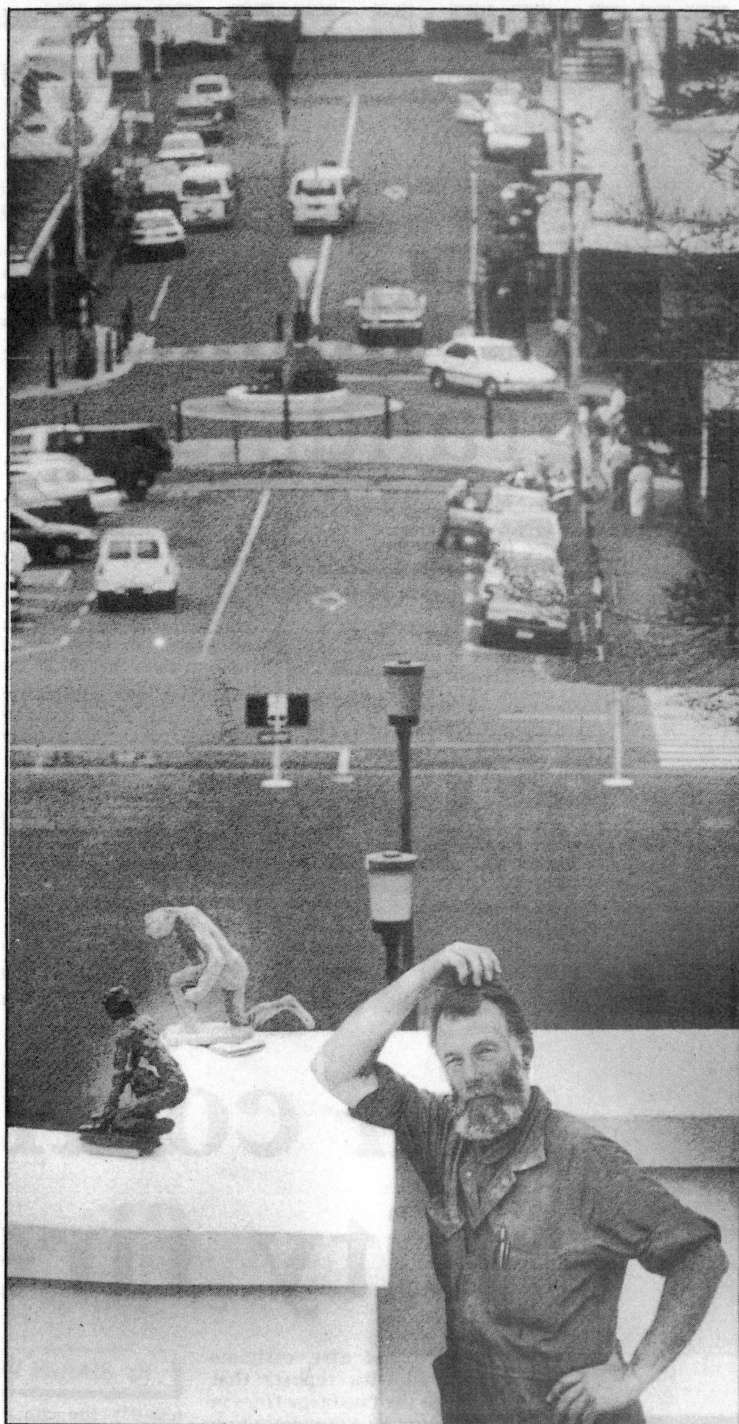

Wrestlers have returned to Wanganui's Sarjeant Gallery, as can be seen by these two sculptural figures on the gallery's parapet pictured with the sculptor, Roger Peters, of Kaponga.

As well as being on the outside of the gallery, sculptures of wrestlers in a variety of positions feature in the gallery's dome area.

Made of plasticine coated with resin, they are part of the dome installation, which is on display until March 27.

Entitled "The Wrestlers' Ball", albeit not intentionally, it is a reminder of the copy of the third century Greek marble sculpture "The Wrestlers" which was the focus of the dome area until removed in 1980.

Mr Rogers has a strong interest in architecture and said he knew the gallery well from his childhood visits to Wanganui to see grandparents Tony and Antica Borich and also his father's family.

The gallery was unique in New Zealand and had a "body quality" about it, he said.

In the sense of the marble wrestlers being Grecian they were a significant metaphor for the building itself Mr Peters said.

"In my work I wanted to explore the dome as a creation of the human mind, as an exquisite repository for particular human needs, desires and aspirations.

"The dome in Wanganui, in New Zealand may seem an anachronism in terms of the land and in terms of indigenous art.

"Yet the dome, in its own terms is a space of tremendous power."

In installing "The Wrestlers' Ball" Mr Peters climbed by rope up into the centre of the dome, and is possibly the first person to have done this.

A sacred cow?

Sir.— Is the Sarjeant Gallery some sort of sacred cow we must treat with holy reverence? I applaud gallery staff for being different.

The building is indeed a valuable asset historically and otherwise but its main function is to house and exhibit art. Art, as an expression of creative spirit, should stimulate feelings, thoughts and debate. The latter has certainly been achieved.

History is a living thing. It is part of us.

I don't see "The Wrestlers' Ball" as a desecration but an enhancement of our cultural identity.

K. ANDERSON
Ahu Ahu Valley

Gallery applauded

Sir.— We were astonished and upset reading the quotes of Judge Treadwell about the exhibition of the Sarjeant Gallery.

Being two tourists travelling around New Zealand we visited Wanganui for three days last week. We were informed about the gallery and its modern and interesting exhibitions.

We went to see it and were impressed by the sculpture "The Wrestlers Ball". For us it seemed to be a fantastic dialogue between modern art and an historic building.

So Judge Treadwell speaks not for us and other tourists we met.

We think Wanganui can be proud of the work of the gallery trust board and its decision for those sculptures.

The city of Wanganui we'll keep in our minds.

MICHAEL SCHLICKWEI
Munster (Germany)

ABOVE: THE WANGANUI CHRONICLE
April 8th 1994

LEFT: THE WANGANUI CHRONICLE
January 25th 1994

RIGHT: THE WRESTLERS' BALL
Pamphlet (front cover)

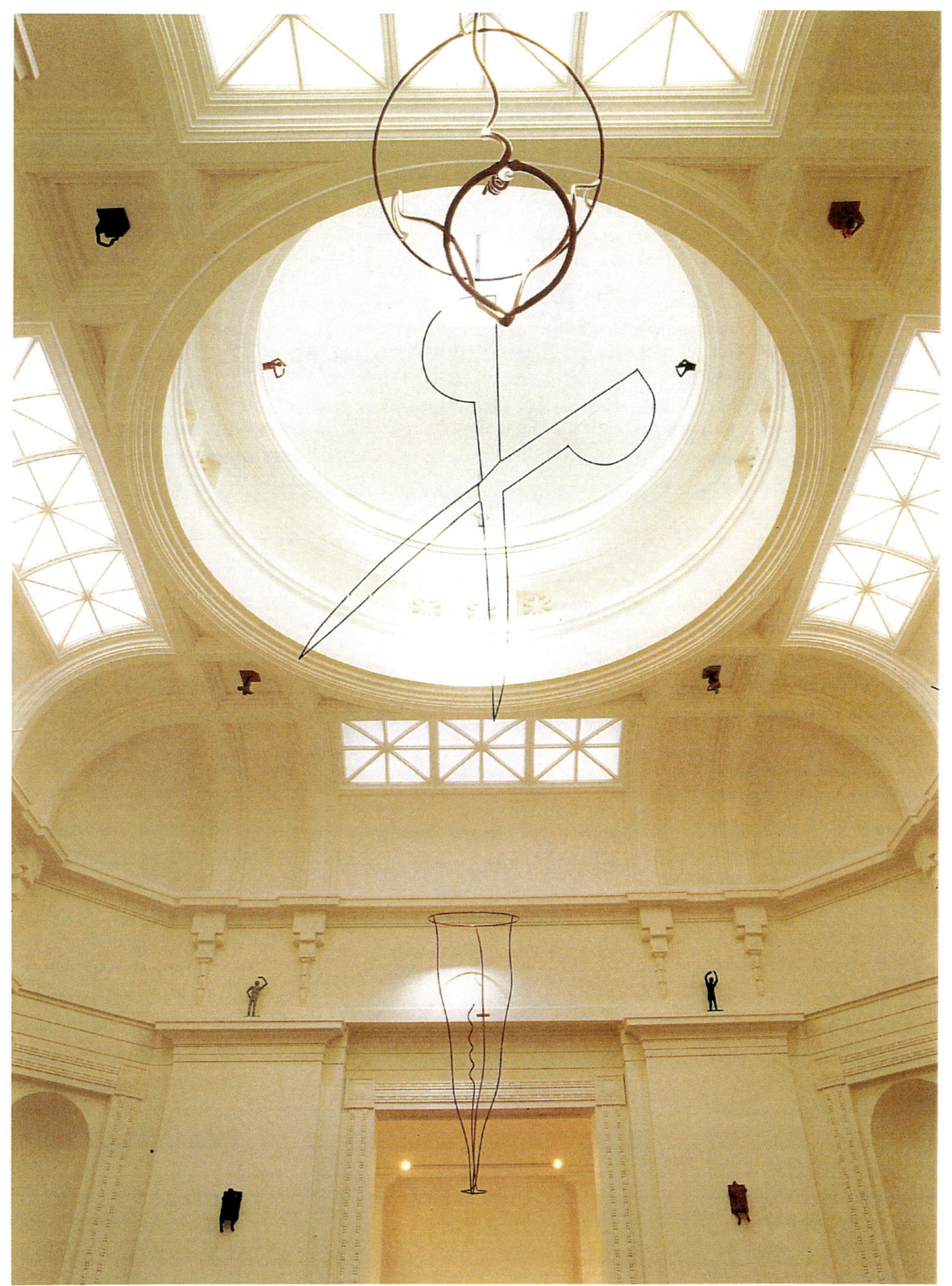

THE **WRESTLERS'** *BALL*

QUEEN'S PARK, WANGANUI, NEW ZEALAND.   P.O. BOX 998, PHONE 06 345-8529, FAX 06 345-5516

PROGRAMME 25   ISSN 0112-7934   MARCH 1994

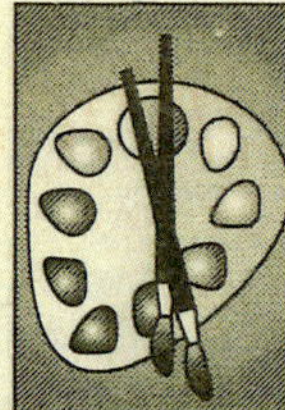

Escape from Sarjeant

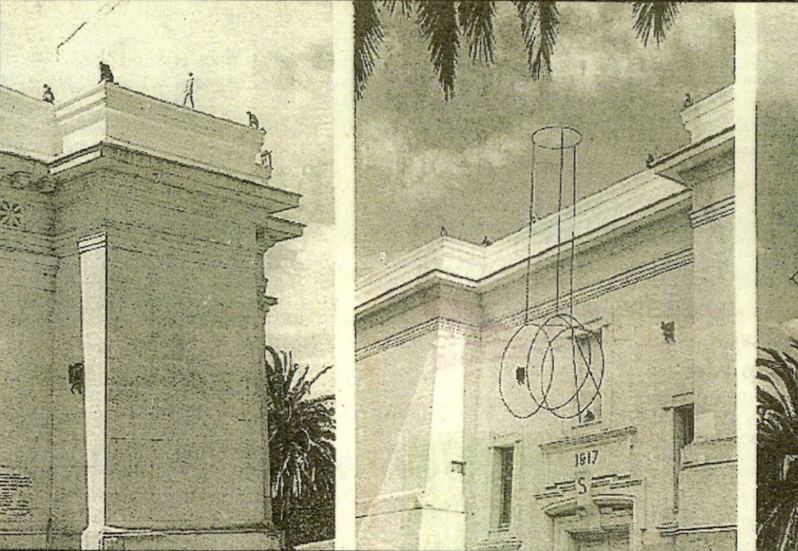

ART ON THE OUTSIDE: sculptor Roger Peters' installation at the Sarjeant Gallery

NOW that we've survived another (mainly performing) arts bash and await the appointment of the next International Festival of the Arts' director, it is timely to remind ourselves that in the visual arts at least we are able to feed our addiction, even if on a slow drip, without significant disruption.

Apart from the programmes offered by the region's public galleries and art museums, Wellington also has a diverse range of commercial galleries which offer a broad diet of visual experiences at no cost to a festival-depleted wallet.

Because these galleries ch[ange] shows every two to three wee[ks the en]thusiastic viewer has to plan ah[ead].

A walkabout at lunchtime or [Sat]urday morning, armed with the [latest] exhibition guide and combined [with fre]quent cafe stops, should be a [rewarding] experience.

WANGANUI'S Sarjeant Gallery h[as attract]ed some flak from the local cha[pter of the] Historic Places Trust with its la[test instal]lation project by sculptor Roger [Peters.]

Not content with filling the a[rchitectural] niches and plinths inside the fi[ne building] that is the Sarjeant, Peters' fi[gures and] abstract shapes wander over t[he outside] of the building.

Horror of horrors, how dare [the artist] and gallery engage in a con[temporary] dialogue with a historically liste[d building!] Much better to leave the struc[ture alone] to die and become a financial li[ability, gut] it and, finally, preserve the faca[de so that] it can be appliqued to some nev[v structure] as a morbid memorial plaque. O[r is it?]

The poor old State Coal bu[ilding,] reduced to a decorative existe[nce by a] new theatrical venture on W[ellington's]

[lic] histories which provide [some] of the dialogue the late [Cooper insisted on pro]...

[re]alise it, the closing date of [it is] upon us and the works will [be in] their crates as they depart [and eventually their own]ing to the City Gallery — [free] — and catch the [together] with the other of...

[the amazing energy dis]... [the] festival in the Tu[...] and concert and the ex[...] a Toi Maori programmes [against] the overrated and [dozen] dance photos of Lois [at She]d 11, make sure you [see the] Reaching Out show at [a space in] Porirua.

[most] important contempo... [and] Pacific Island artists' [show, s]een there till April 24.

[...s] fortnightly art column al[ternates with] Patricia Cooke's theatre [column.]

WANGANUI'S Sarjeant Gallery has attracted some flak from the local chapter of the Historic Places Trust with its latest installation project by sculptor Roger Peters.

Not content with filling the architectural niches and plinths inside the fine building that is the Sarjeant, Peters' figures and abstract shapes wander over the outside of the building.

Horror of horrors, how dare the artist and gallery engage in a contemporary dialogue with a historically listed building! Much better to leave the structure alone to die and become a financial liability, gut it and, finally, preserve the facade so that it can be appliqued to some new structure as a morbid memorial plaque. Or is it?

THE DOMINION - Saturday April 2nd 1994, P25

NOTEBOOK 10 Thurs 21st Jan 88

Is the world becoming clearer to me or am I merely submitting to it· Up until recently I have been seemingly happy to be obscure, to be misunderstood and even to be barely legible as if there was some secret strength in disguising the depths of my ignorance· – Now with no really perceptible change in my state of knowledge but maybe with a significant change in attitude clarity seems in order – and at that it seems no great fuss – no fuss in the sense that what I imagined was there before was such a chimera it comes to nothing and what I now wish to say seems so obvious that saying it simply and clearly is the best way of expressing its feelings and even its possible complexities·

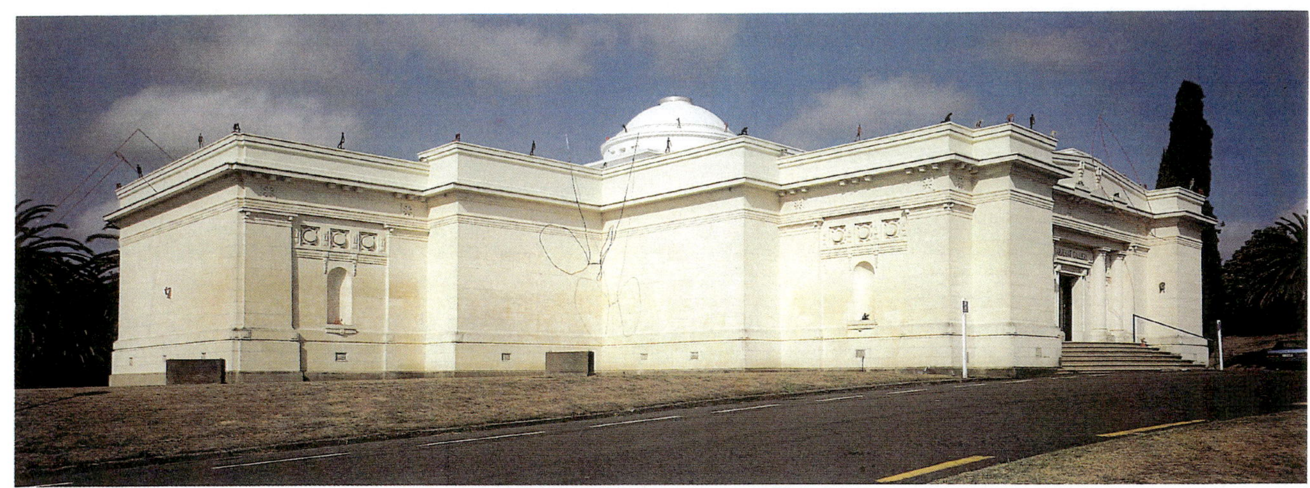

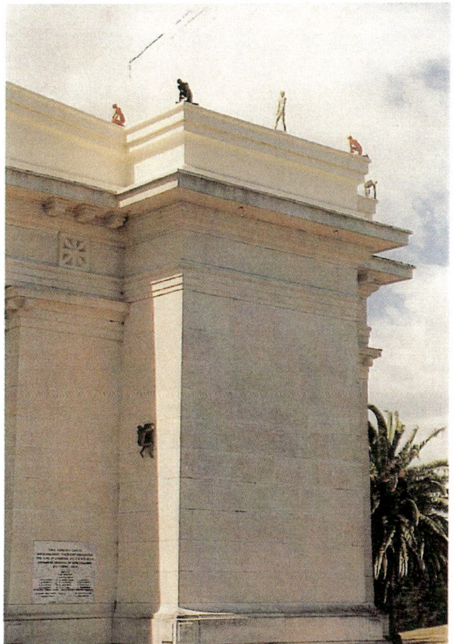

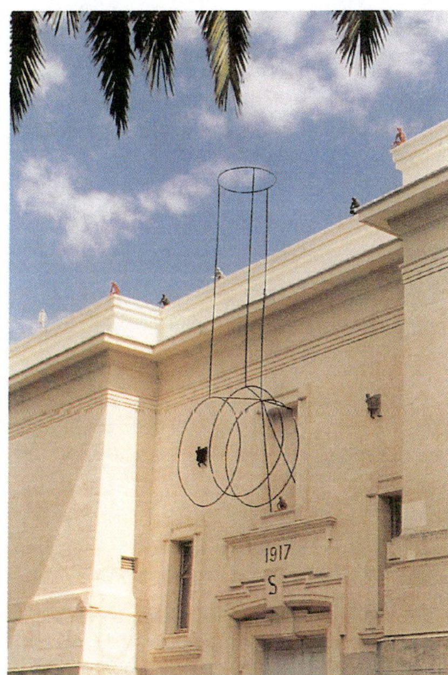

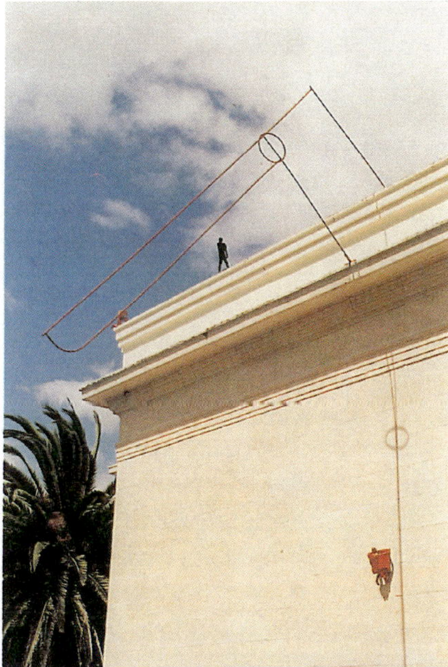

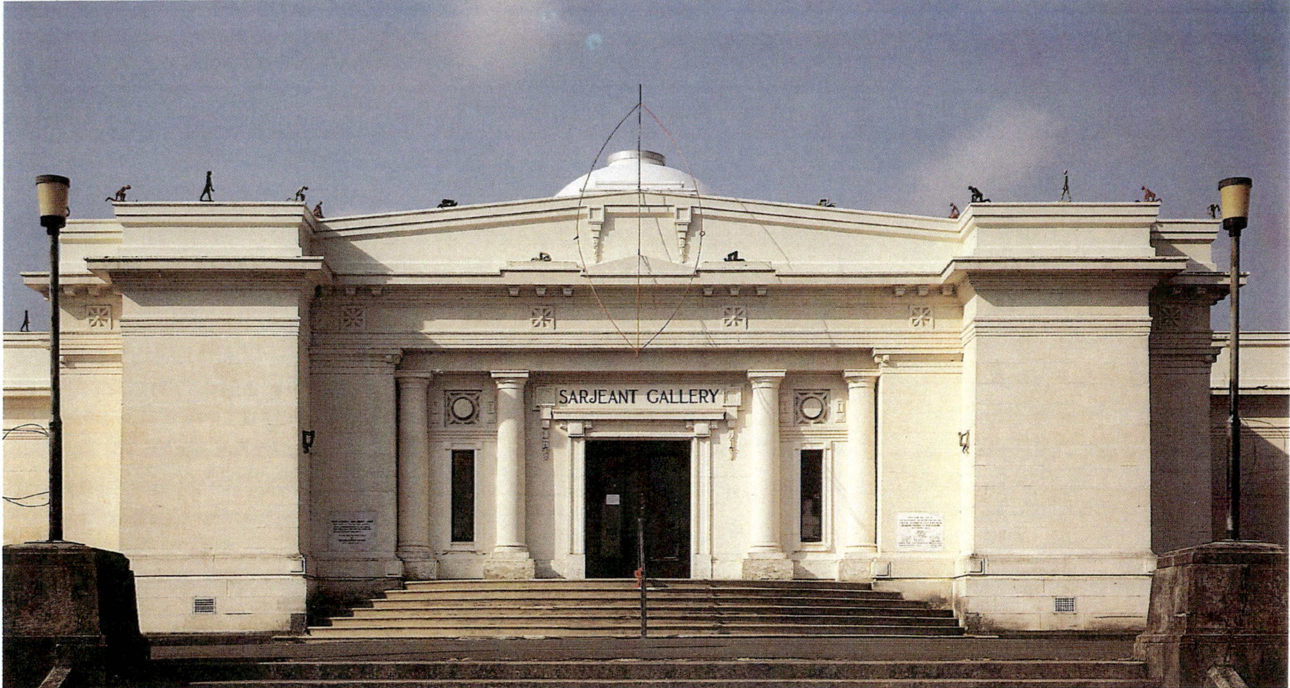

Roger Peters   The Wrestlers' Ball   Dome Installation No. 19

THE WRESTLERS' BALL - Pamphlet (back cover)

Flaming reminder of our radical '70s art

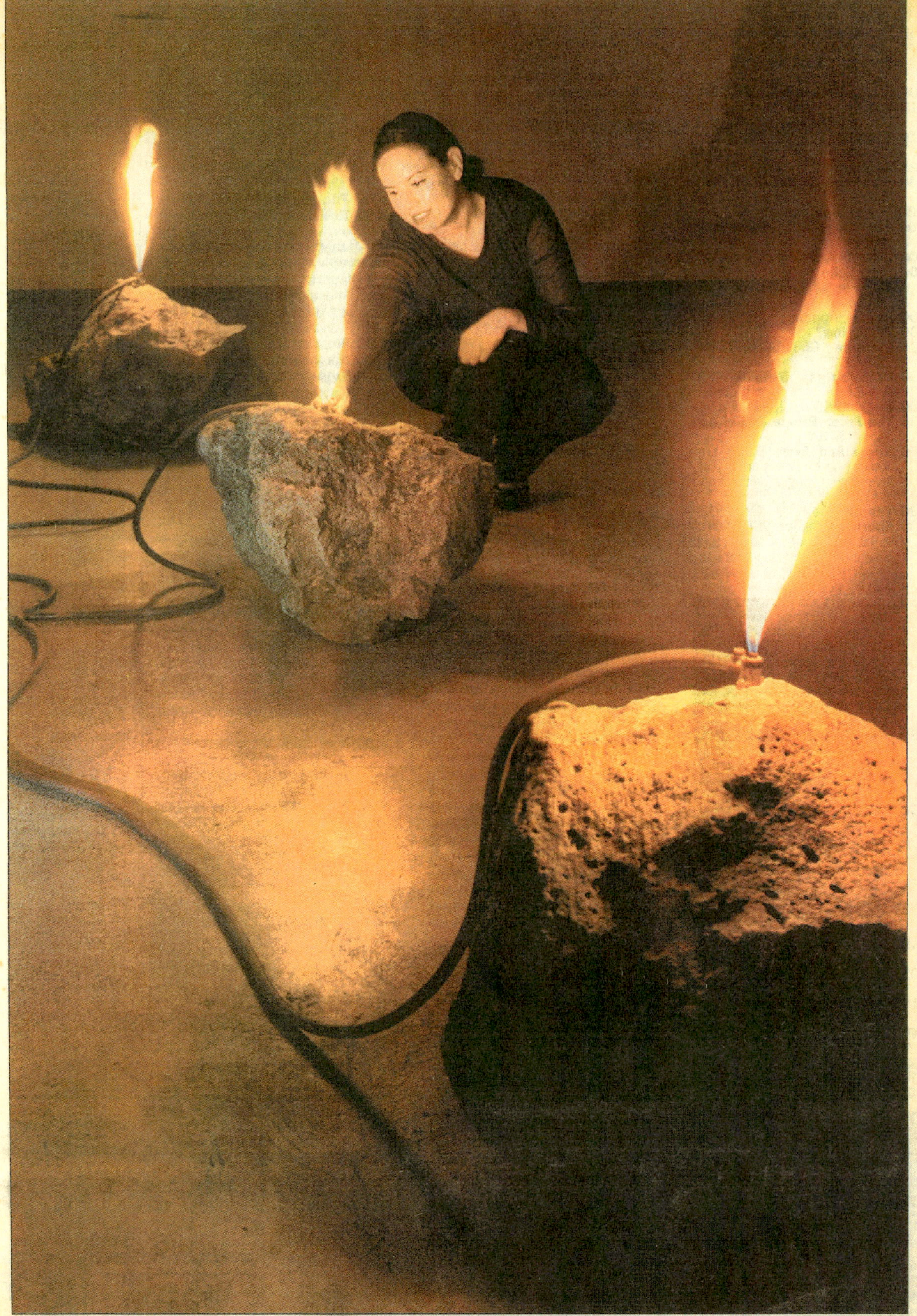

Auckland Artspace Gallery administrator Kelly Carmichael lights the final flame of the artwork *The Rocks*, by New Zealander Roger Peters. The work, which features rocks collected from Mt Eden, is one of several pieces from the 1970s on show at the gallery. Kelly Carmichael says the '70s were largely ignored as a period of radical art in New Zealand. "The aim here is to recover a lost chapter in contemporary New Zealand art." The Artspace has had to turn off its fire alarms because *The Rocks'* flames would set them off constantly. The exhibition finishes tomorrow and will be replaced by another show featuring more works from the '70s.

NZ HERALD - October 16th 1998

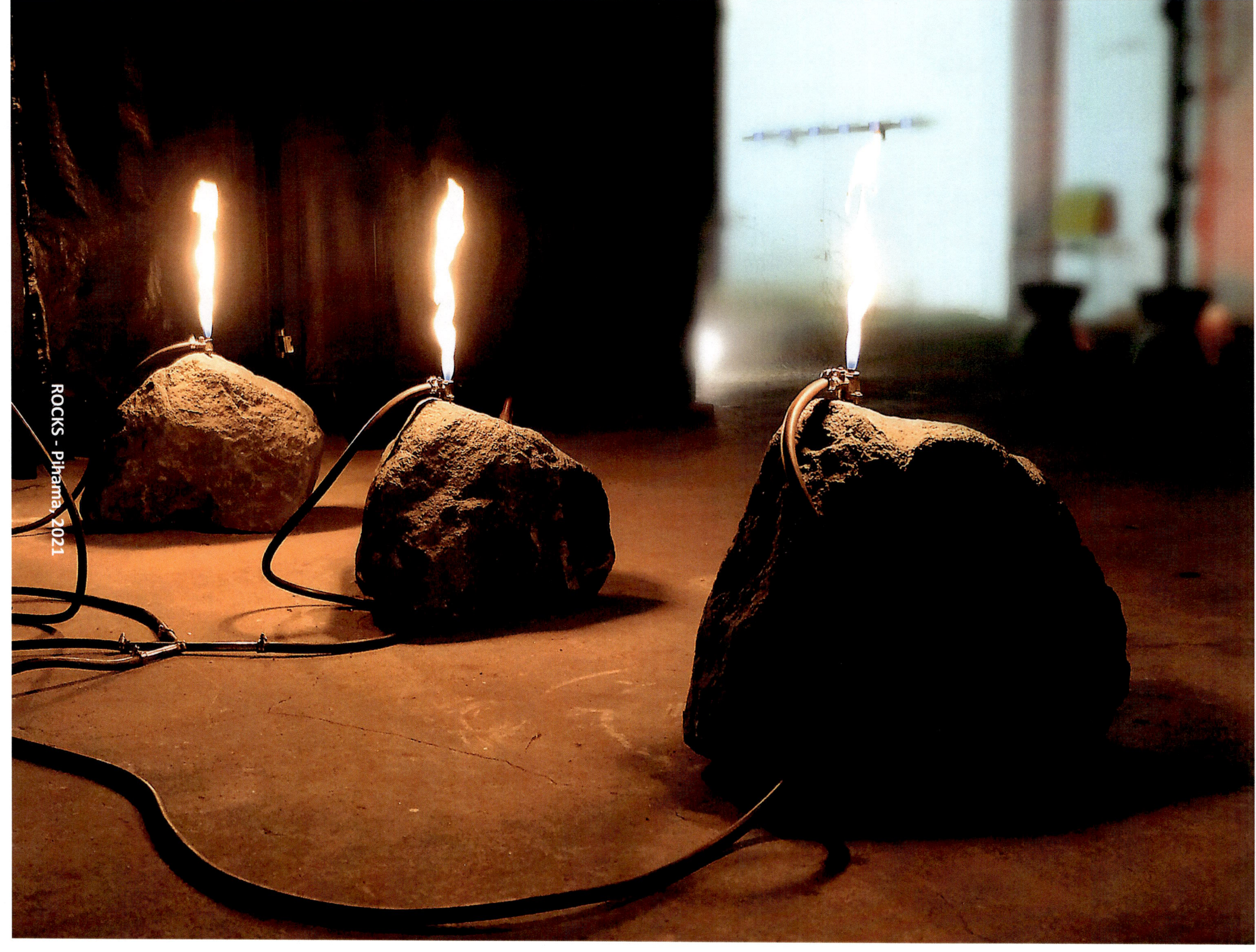

ROCKS - Pihama, 2021

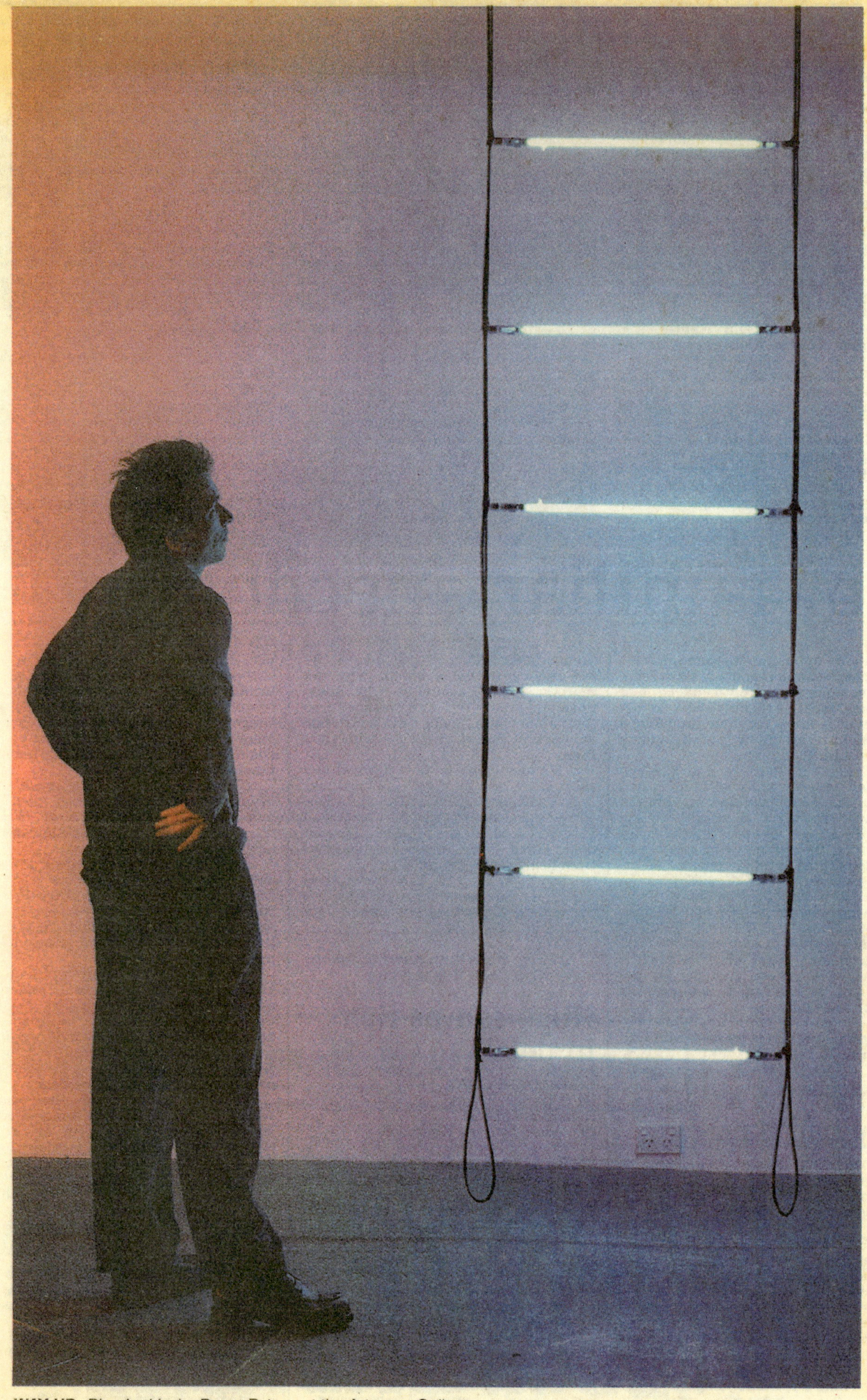

WAY UP: *Blue Ladder* by Roger Peters, at the Artspace Gallery.

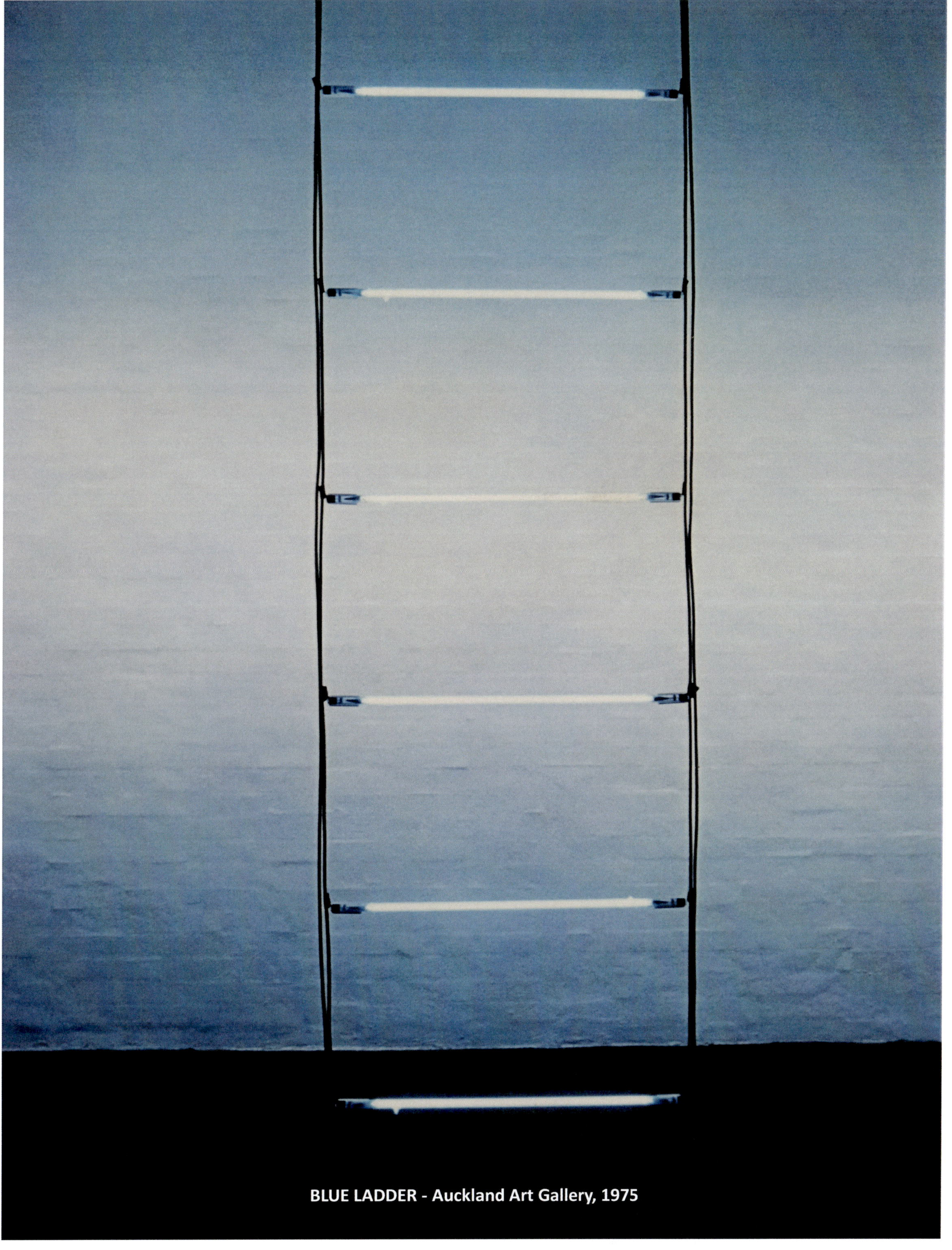

BLUE LADDER - Auckland Art Gallery, 1975

43 Brecon Road
STRATFORD

8 March 2001

<u>To Whom It May Concern</u>

This statement attests that the undersigned has known Mr Roger Peters since 1995.

In this time the writer has become aware-intensely - of the quality and depth of Mr Peters' studies of Shakespeare's poetry.

He was first aware of the Peters' interest in Shakespeare in the course of a series of poetry discussions and tutorial groups.

It was soon obvious that this interest had resulted in an ever-deeper probing and delving into the origins, ideas, structure and significance of the sonnets.

In October, 1996, Mr Peters began an ongoing column in the "Stratford Press" devoted to a study and explanation of individual sonnets.

There followed a major treatise which analyses the sonnets in extraordinary depth. The scholarly input is in the proper sense of the word-awesome.

The writer thought that in the course of his university studies and many years of teaching he had some understanding of Shakespeare's writings. Alongside the Peters' insights this understanding is trite, superficial and inadequate.

The work that Mr Peters has produced is not merely a work of discovery: it is a masterpiece of analysis which breaks new ground and compels by its logic a new view of the sonnets.

R.G. HABERSHON, M.A.; B.Ed.; A.C.C.M.; Dip.Teach.

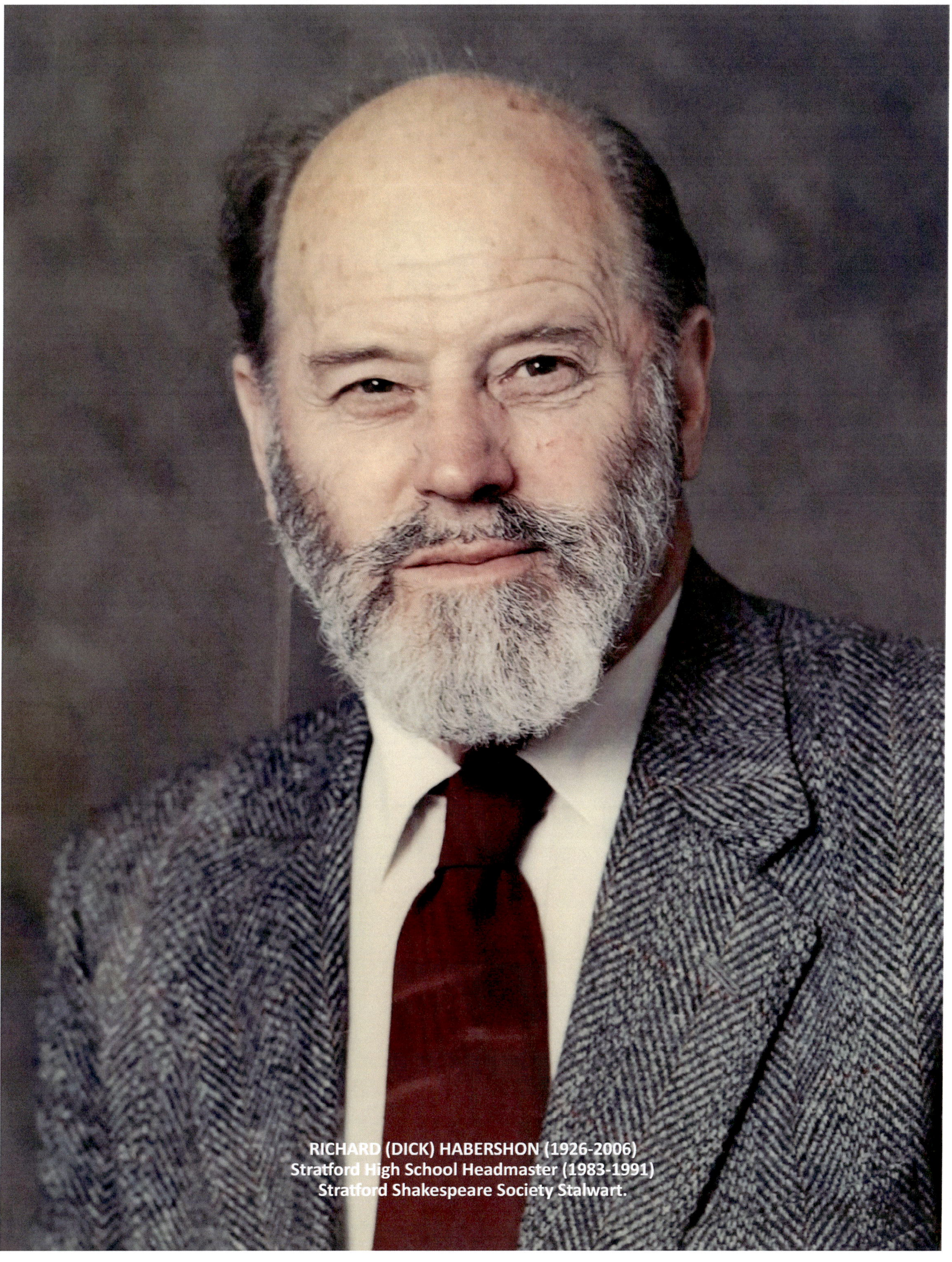

RICHARD (DICK) HABERSHON (1926-2006)
Stratford High School Headmaster (1983-1991)
Stratford Shakespeare Society Stalwart.

'Quarternary' phase in the study of Shakespeare

Stratford' with its Shakespearean name and links, has long held a superficial attachment to all things relating to the bard, but over the past few years research at a much deeper level has been continuing right on our doorstep.

Today marks the last Sonnet Column to be published in the Stratford Press - a column which has over the past five-and-three-quarter years attempted to explain the deeper philosophy behind the writings of Shakespeare, as seen in his sonnets.

Column author Roger Peters of Kaponga, said that now that commentaries on the full set of 154 sonnets had been published, he would continue his work by producing four volumes on Shakespeare, the first two of which were already complete.

"Volume 1 is a critique of Shakespeare's philosophy, Volume 2 contains the sonnet commentaries, Volume 3 is an analysis of all Shakespeare's works and Volume 4 deals with the people whose work I studied to come to the understanding I now have of Shakespeare," he said. He is also developing a website.

Mr Peters said that he had 'run up against tertiary minds and thinking' when trying to disseminate his ideas about Shakespeare's works.

"I have written ideas that didn't exist so far in the world of literary comment," he said. "My work belongs in the category past tertiary level (quaternary). I think there is another way of viewing this (Shakespeare's works) consistent with the tertiary view but which can also take in the bigger picture."

Early influences

A change in course from studying architecture, as a rather mediocre student in Auckland, to fine arts which saw him win an award for his work, set Mr Peters on the road of discovery.

"I began to ask myself, 'What is it that makes an artwork function at a mythic (spiritual) level?" he said. "I was trying to understand the principles behind that."

A chance involvement in a sonnet reading weekend in Wanganui in 1994, led Mr Peters to see that there was a philosophical understanding in these works which paralleled what he had discovered in his own artwork. That got him thinking and for several months his mind was 'buzzing' with themes and number systems he was discovering in the sonnets.

"I was really grabbed by what I had discovered," he said.

A number of artists and scholars had influence on the development of his thinking before and during this time, including the French artist Marcel Duchamp, Austrian/

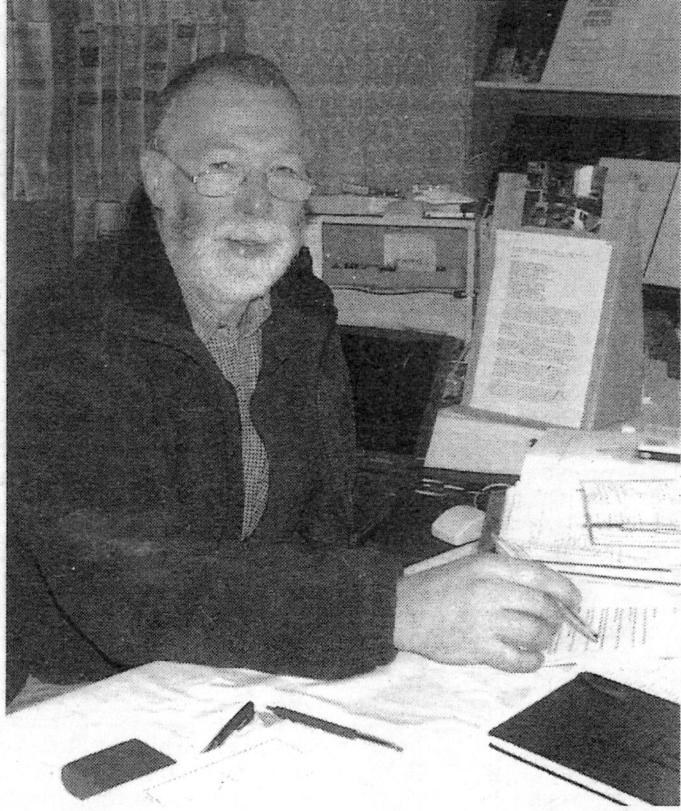

A new era: Roger Peters in his 'den' surrounded by Shakespearean 'paraphernalia', including a bust, charts of the bard's work, and books.

English philosopher Ludwig Wittgenstein, and scientist Charles Darwin.

Local support

"I started the sonnet column in the Press as a challenge initially but it became a habit," he said. "I found sponsorship for each column from local businesses. Over 100 businesses have contributed in this way and only a very few have been unwilling or unable to support the column. It was a great way to get to know the town.

"Now when I head into Stratford I have to remind myself that I don't have to go round businesses today!"

Although the column did not evoke response in the Press, Mr Peters did receive comments.

"Some people told me that they had difficulty understanding what I had written but most people who spoke to me said they were regular readers," he said. "A few of them have become friends and some have wished to know more about the sonnet philosophy."

Mr Peters said that he was grateful to the Stratford Press for publishing his column, to those who prepared it for printing, to all those who had sponsored it over the years, and to those who had commented either way about it.

THE STRATFORD PRESS - July 10th 2002, P6

Unemployment stats looking good

At the end of the March quarter this year 389 Stratford people were registered with WINZ as actively seeking employment.

Regional PR manager for WINZ, Gail Bennett, said, "These figures differed slightly from a household labour force survey done by the Department of Labour over the same period, because WINZ figures are taken only from people registered with them or those receiving a benefit of some kind".

WINZ figures showed that employment had been found for 112 people over the preceding three months.

While the average rate of unemployment throughout the country stood at 5.6% Taranaki's unemployment rate has continued to fall and was now an estimated 4.9% which was a drop of 1% from the previous quarter.

The figures also show Taranaki to be holding third equal place along with Auckland and Hawkes Bay as regions with the lowest rates of unemployment.

Ross Brown Rugby

West won the annual Ross Brown primary schools rugby tournament played recently at Kaponga.

They beat Central 52-0, North by 10-0 and South by 5-0.

Boys selected for the Taranaki primary schools squad from the Stratford Press distribution area are:

Kawana Cassidy (Stratford Primary), Hamish Nicholls (St Joseph's, Stratford), Jordan Walters (Ngaere School), James Dunlop (Matapu)

HOME PAGE www.quaternaryinstitute.com

The Quaternary Institute

THE INSTITUTE FOR THE QUATERNARY EVOLUTION IN SHAKESPEAREAN THOUGHT

MOTTO: Know you not that I must be about my mother's business

- **QUATERNARY INSTITUTE: INTRODUCTION** (View Site Map)
- **CONDITIONS OF ENGAGEMENT**
- **QUATERNARY PROGRAM of ADVANCEMENT**
- **WILLIAM SHAKESPEARE'S SONNET PHILOSOPHY: VOLUME 1**
- **WSSP: VOLUME 1: GLOSSARY of PIVOTAL CONCEPTS**
- **WSSP: VOLUME 2: 154 SONNET COMMENTARIES & EMENDATIONS**
- **WSSP: VOLUME 3: 4 POEM & 5 PLAY COMMENTARIES**
- **WSSP: VOLUME 4: OUT of DARWIN, WITTGENSTEIN, & DUCHAMP**
- **QUATERNARY ONLINE JOURNALS & INVESTIGATIONS** JAQUES & INQUEST & QUIETUS & ACQUITTAS
- **Books & e-publications QUATERNARY IMPRINT**
- **QI Newsletter, Videos & Art QUATERNARY INTERMEDIA**

PRESS RELEASE April 2023

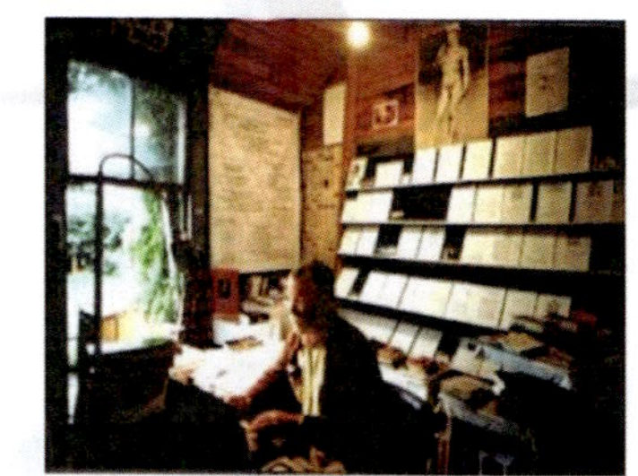
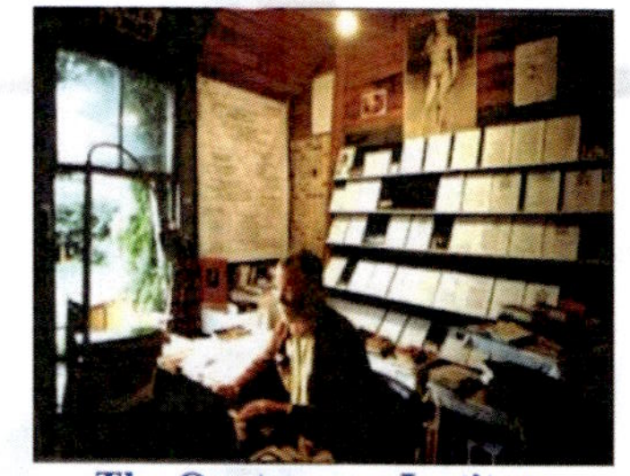

The Quaternary Institute

Foundation Director : Roger Peters **CONTACT**

Updated 4 February 2026

SATELLITE PAGES

THE QUATERNARY INSTITUTE
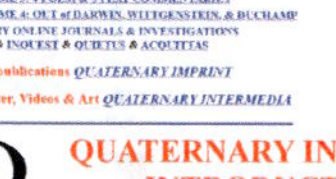

QUATERNARY INSTITUTE INTRODUCTION

THE QUATERNARY INSTITUTE
CONDITIONS OF ENGAGEMENT

THE QUATERNARY INSTITUTE
QUATERNARY PROGRAM

THE SONNET PHILOSOPHY

William Shakespeare's Sonnet Philosophy details the logical structure of the philosophy in Shakespeare's 1609 Sonnets.

Volume 1: Contents and Introduction (45 book pages)

- Contents and Introduction
- Nature and the sexual dynamic
- The increase argument
- Truth and beauty
- The logic of myth
- The cryptic numerology
- Appendices
- Glossary

CONTENTS & INTRODUCTION

SONNET COMMENTARIES

The commentaries show how to apply the Sonnet philosophy to individual sonnets, and to avoid the inadequacies of the traditional paradigm.

- INTRODUCTION
- SONNETS 1-9
- SONNETS 10-24
- SONNETS 25-33
- SONNETS 34-45
- SONNETS 46-57
- SONNETS 58-69
- SONNETS 70-81
- SONNETS 82-93
- SONNETS 94-105
- SONNETS 106-117
- SONNETS 118-129
- SONNETS 130-141
- SONNETS 142-153
- SONNET 154
- EMENDATIONS

INTRODUCTION

SATELLITE PAGES

PLAY COMMENTARIES

Each commentary applies the Sonnet philosophy to the plays and poems of Shakespeare to reveal their inherent meaning.

- Introduction
- Venus and Adonis
- Rape of Lucrece
- Phoenix and Turtle
- A Lover's Complaint
- Love's Labour's Lost
- Measure for Measure
- Macbeth
- Twelfth Night
- Henry VIII

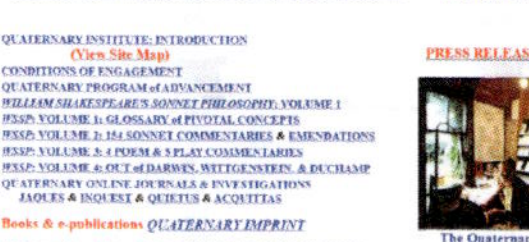
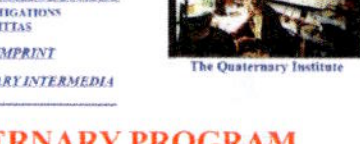

INTRODUCTION

DARWIN, WITTGENSTEIN, MALLARME & DUCHAMP

The mature works of Darwin, Wittgenstein, Mallarme and Duchamp were based in aspects of natural logic. Their work when combined enabled an insight into the comprehensive articulation of natural logic in Shakespeare's Sonnets.

- Preface
- Introduction: Duchamp to Shakespeare
- Chapter 1 Duchamp
- Chapter 2 Wittgenstein
- Chapter 3 Darwin
- Chapter 4 Shakespeare & Back

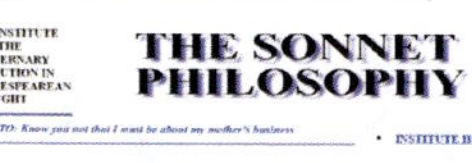

PREFACE

GLOSSARY

The explanation of key terms in the Glossary contextualizes each word within the logic of the Sonnet philosophy.

- INTRODUCTION & A-B
- GLOSSARY C-I
- GLOSSARY J-M
- GLOSSARY N-Sh
- GLOSSARY Si-Z

Return to: VOLUME 1: CONTENTS AND INTRODUCTION

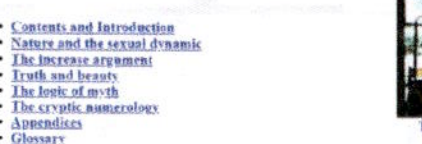

INTRODUCTION & A-B

SATELLITE PAGES

JAQUES

JAQUES (*The Journal for the Advancement of the Quaternary Evolution in Shakespeare*) has been established to foster an appreciation of the philosophy of William Shakespeare that is given logical and evocative expression in his Sonnets.

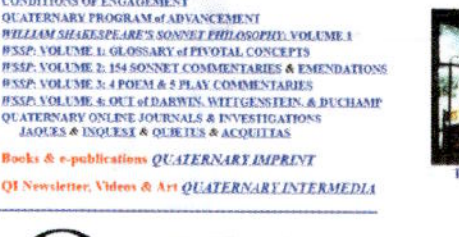
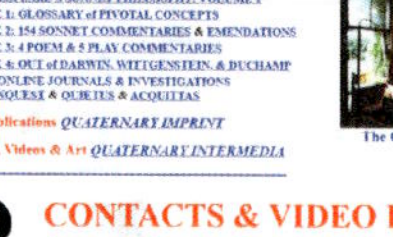

- Jaques Editorial
- How to use the Nature Template (New)
- Common Ground: Duchamp to Shakespeare
- Stephane Mallarme & Symbolic Deaths
- Wittgenstein in Shakespeare - Nature & Rules
- Nietzsche & Wittgenstein - Mirror Wrong
- Criteria for Quaternary

JAQUES EDITORIAL

INQUEST

INQUEST (*The Inquiry into the Quaternary Evolution in Shakespearean Thought*) will critique scientists, philosophers and commentators who have failed to appreciate the philosophy in Shakespeare's Sonnets, poems and plays.

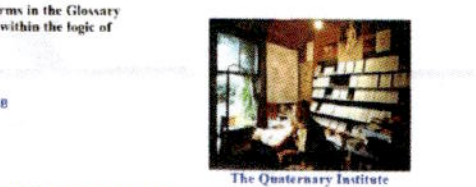

- Inquest Editorial
- Freud & Jung - Psycho Drama
- Joyce & Eliot - Which 30-th
- Booth & Vendler - Obsessive Misinterpretation
- Germaine Greer - Women Issues
- 1+1 = 2 True or False
- From Tertiary to Quaternary Creativity

INQUEST EDITORIAL

QUIETUS

QUIETUS (*The Quaternary Investigation into the Evolution Toward the Quipuscous in Shakespeare*) examines the social and political implications of a consistent philosophy in Shakespeare's Sonnets, poems and plays.

- Quietus Editorial
- Shakespeare and Democracy
- Jefferson & The Declaration of Independence
- Lahoff & Johnson - Flesh in the Mind
- From male to female - where the default lies (New)
- Upending from Tertiary to Quaternary (New)

QUIETUS EDITORIAL

ACQUITTAS

ACQUITTAS (*Assize Court for the Quaternary Investigation of Tertiary Travesties Against Shakespeare*) has been promulgated to prosecute the literary crimes against the works of William Shakespeare in ignorance of the consistent and comprehensive nature-based philosophy given evocative expression in his 1609 Sonnets.

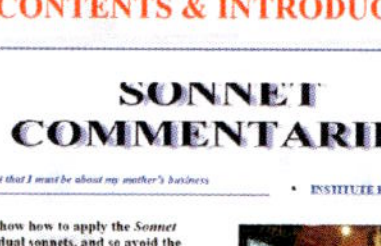

- ACQUITTAS - Comments & Cases
- ACQUITTAS - Prefatory
- ACQUITTAS - Preliminary Remarks
- ACQUITTAS - Parameters and Procedures
- ACQUITTAS - Evidential Cases

ACQUITTAS ASSIZE COURT PROCEEDINGS

Contact

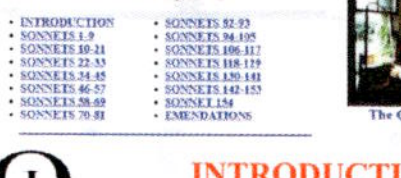
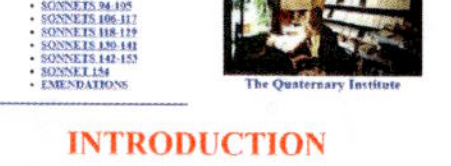
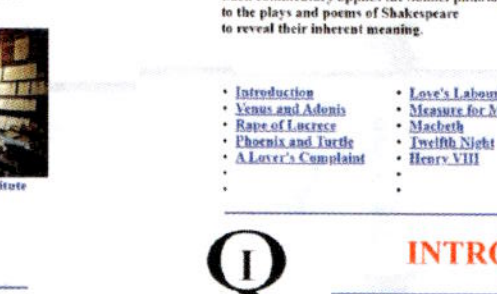

- QUATERNARY INSTITUTE: INTRODUCTION (View Site Map)
- CONDITIONS OF ENGAGEMENT
- QUATERNARY PROGRAM of ADVANCEMENT
- WILLIAM SHAKESPEARE'S SONNET PHILOSOPHY: VOLUME 1
- WSSP: VOLUME 1: GLOSSARY of PIVOTAL CONCEPTS
- WSSP: VOLUME 2: 154 SONNET COMMENTARIES & EMENDATIONS
- WSSP: VOLUME 3: 4 POEM & 5 PLAY COMMENTARIES
- WSSP: VOLUME 4: OUT of DARWIN, WITTGENSTEIN, & DUCHAMP
- QUATERNARY ONLINE JOURNALS & INVESTIGATIONS JAQUES & INQUEST & QUIETUS & ACQUITTAS
- Books & e-publications QUATERNARY IMPRINT
- QI Newsletter, Videos & Art QUATERNARY INTERMEDIA

CONTACTS & VIDEO LINKS

THE QUATERNARY INSTITUTE WEBSITE - launched 2001

Secrets of the sonnets

Roger Peters has completed the major work of his life — a massive interpretation of Shakespeare's sonnets. VIRGINIA WINDER tried to get into the mind of the eccentric scholar

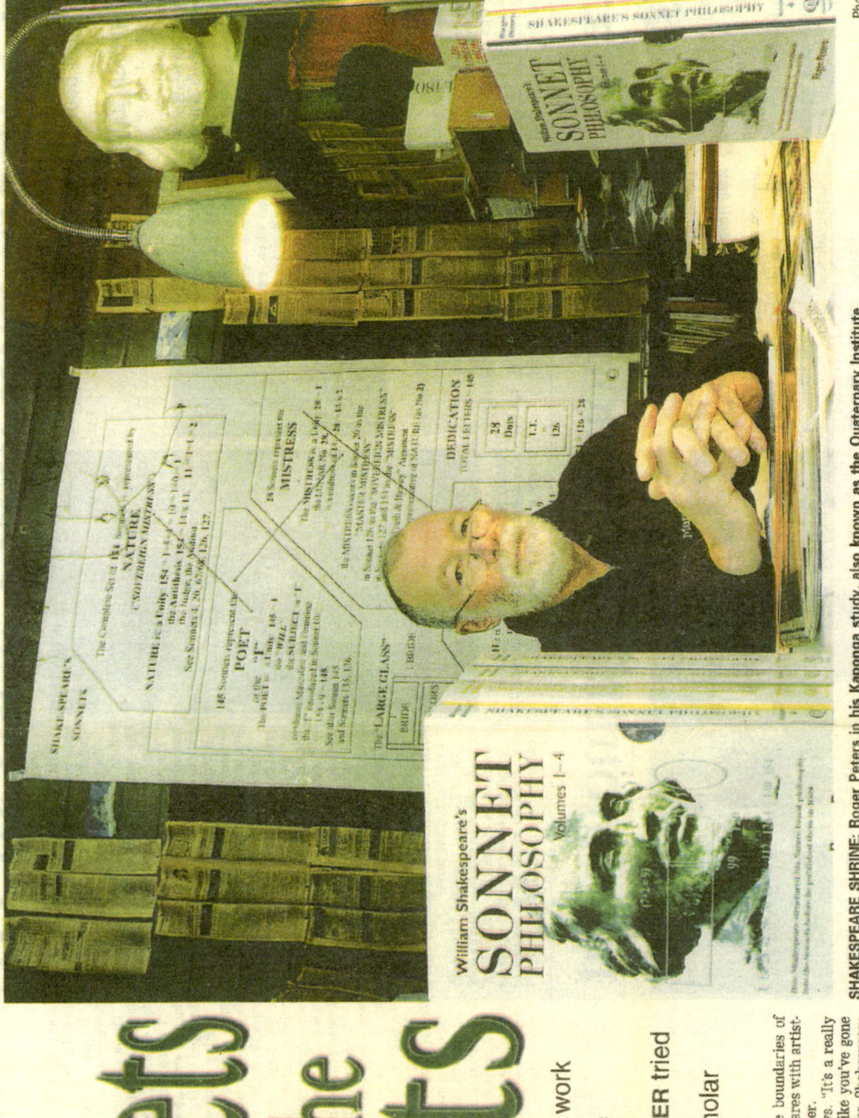

Photo: PIP GUTHRIE

SHAKESPEARE SHRINE: Roger Peters in his Kaponga study, also known as the Quaternary Institute.

GENIUS or madman — that is the question.

It is difficult to decipher the truth — if there is one — about Kaponga-based scholar Roger Peters.

For the past 10 years he has dedicated himself to studying William Shakespeare's 154 sonnets.

Now he has published his four-volume work — 1760 pages — revealing Shakespeare's Sonnet Philosophy. He has been able to do this with help from a $30,000 Taranaki Electricity Trust grant.

"Shakespeare published the philosophy of the sonnets in 1609, a full 20 years after writing his first play, to present the philosophy behind all his plays and longer poems," Peters says.

The story of how Peters got to this place is a long and winding one. But first, let's go to the end, to his place of work and profound thought.

On Eltham Rd near Kaponga is a letterbox marked Peters and Horner, which heralds a house of unusual and amazing thoughts.

Up the long farm track, past a field being grazed by a white donkey called Alf, stands a church-like building. There is a high window emblazoned with a large Q, an I standing to attention inside the one-legged circle. It looks like a religious symbol, a Latin-like letter with some higher meaning.

In this case it stands for the Quaternary Institute or its publishing arm, Quaternary Imprint. The literal definition of quaternary is "having four parts" and in geological terms it refers to the most recent part of the Cenozoic period, which is this era.

In Peters' world it stands for study beyond tertiary level, but the institute doesn't exist beyond the boundaries of the Kaponga home he shares with artist-teacher wife Maree Horner.

"It's my space," he says. "It's a really nice space to be in. It's like you've gone to this new land. It's like Shakespeare did the surveying."

Entering his place is a surreal experience. The door to the Q-marked building is softened by a jasmine vine, the flowers beginning to bloom like just-dusk stars.

Peters looms on the doorstep of his workplace, a quiet presence with trimmed white beard and metal-rimmed glasses low on his nose.

The Q space is part of an old church, he says. It does look like a place of worship, not to God or gods, but to academic thought and, of course, the man himself.

A huge plaster head of William Shakespeare holds a lofty position in the institute, a great brain to be looked up to. There are other heads here too — bright-white sculptures of

> 'I'm not a businessman and I got so stressed I could barely walk'

the 58-year-old's now grown-up daughters. Talia (33), Teresa (27), Katie (24) and Lucy (21) have all left home, leaving behind serene artworks moulded by their dad's hands.

The near-sacredness of the stand-alone building is accentuated by the use of a white table-cloth on the desk-table, white cover on bench seat and huge white charts filled with words and numbers.

These depict his weighty ideas about the numerical codes, the life philosophies hidden in the sonnets.

"Shakespeare structured the basic elements of his philosophy into the set of 154 sonnets, with the whole set representing Nature, the 28 sonnets to the Mistress representing the female and 126 sonnets to the Master Mistress representing male," he says.

"The set of sonnets has a numerological structure consistent with the natural logic of the philosophy."

To decipher Peters' Da Vinci Code-like mind, it is necessary to step back in time. Not to 1564, when Shakespeare was born, but to Auckland's Elam Art School in the 1970s. That is where Peters, an architecture student turned art scholar discovered the works of artist Marcel Duchamp (1887-1968) and philosopher Ludwig Wittgenstein (1889-1951). Peters was so affected by them that he set himself a goal of reading everything he could on subjects like biology, philosophy, psychology, poetry, physics and mythology.

"I was trying to create some sort of context to what I was getting out of Marcel Duchamp and Wittgenstein."

So, after art school, when he and Horner moved to Eltham, Peters dedicated himself to reading Dante and Darwin, and Milton. He would get dozens of books from the local library and plunge into the world's greatest minds.

On the art scene, Peters had had a successful show at the Auckland City Art Gallery, which eventually bought his Hot Wires work. That glowing sculptural piece took him about seven months to make.

"I wasn't a natural artist. I could get there but it wasn't easy for me. I was to discover later that I could mould faces," he says.

Meanwhile, he spent three years working for the Taranaki Electricity Board — his only full-time job — until a staff syndicate of five won $100,000 from a Golden Kiwi ticket. In 1983, his $20,000 share was enough to begin a new venture.

"I left the power board and I thought I could make a business out of making these dolls' houses," he shows a picture of a many-angled construction.

"I'm not a businessman and I got so stressed I could barely walk."

At the time, Peters and his family were living in the Jenkins House on Conway Rd, also known as Ladies Mile. During his slow recovery (it took about five years), he walked many miles on that path.

"I started having this sense of clarity at that time," he says.

He wrote his thoughts and published them in a thin red book. He holds one of the 10 produced and fans through dust-gritty pages, which hold his early ideas on life, body, mind, will and word.

Next came Peters' foray into the field of figures, which led to a show at the Sarjeant Gallery in Wanganui, the town of his birth.

From 1987 to 1994, he studied the works of sculptors Michelangelo, Rodin and Donatello, and taught himself the techniques of headmaking. You can see his bronze head of Shakespeare outside the library in nearby Stratford. For the Sarjeant Gallery outing, he made 130 small figures.

> 'Shakespeare nails down the philosophy we live by'

"That was my own graduation show," he said, referring to his personal years of body-building.

"There are leftover people hanging about the Kaponga place, including a number crawling upside down across the kitchen ceiling. Other rooms are hung with giant donkey paintings by Horner, who has been inspired by Alf.

Peters' reconnection with his birthplace continued when he joined a friend at monthly readings of Shakespeare in Wanganui. In early 1995, the group decided to read the sonnets over two weekends. Hearing all the sonnets read out, Peters had his Shakespeare awakening.

"I was able to sense that what was in there was what I was looking for in Duchamp," he says, talking quickly, but calmly. "Over the next few months, I was just sparking. I was waking up in the middle of the night."

He also began to see the number patterns in Shakespeare's sonnets.

Like a devoted Christian referring to passages of the Bible, Peters talks about particular sonnets and their meanings.

"Shakespeare nails down the philosophy we live by, whether we think we do or not," he says. "He's so amazing, he's ordinary. He's commonsensical. He discovered things that are in this world rather than inventing things beyond this world."

Some Shakespeare experts believe Peters' findings are rubbish, but the discoverer is adamant he is right.

"It's like saying Darwin is bullshit."

While he is quietly pleased to have his box-set published, Peters is careful not to get too elated, believing the downside could be depression. So, like a gold medal-winning athlete who asks, "what now?", the scholar has mapped his future. He has already outlined Volume 5 — a handbook to go with the first four — and is now working on a play commentary and plans to dissect all of them.

His dream though, is this: "What would excite me more than anything would be for somebody to say, 'I know all this, but did you know this ...'" □

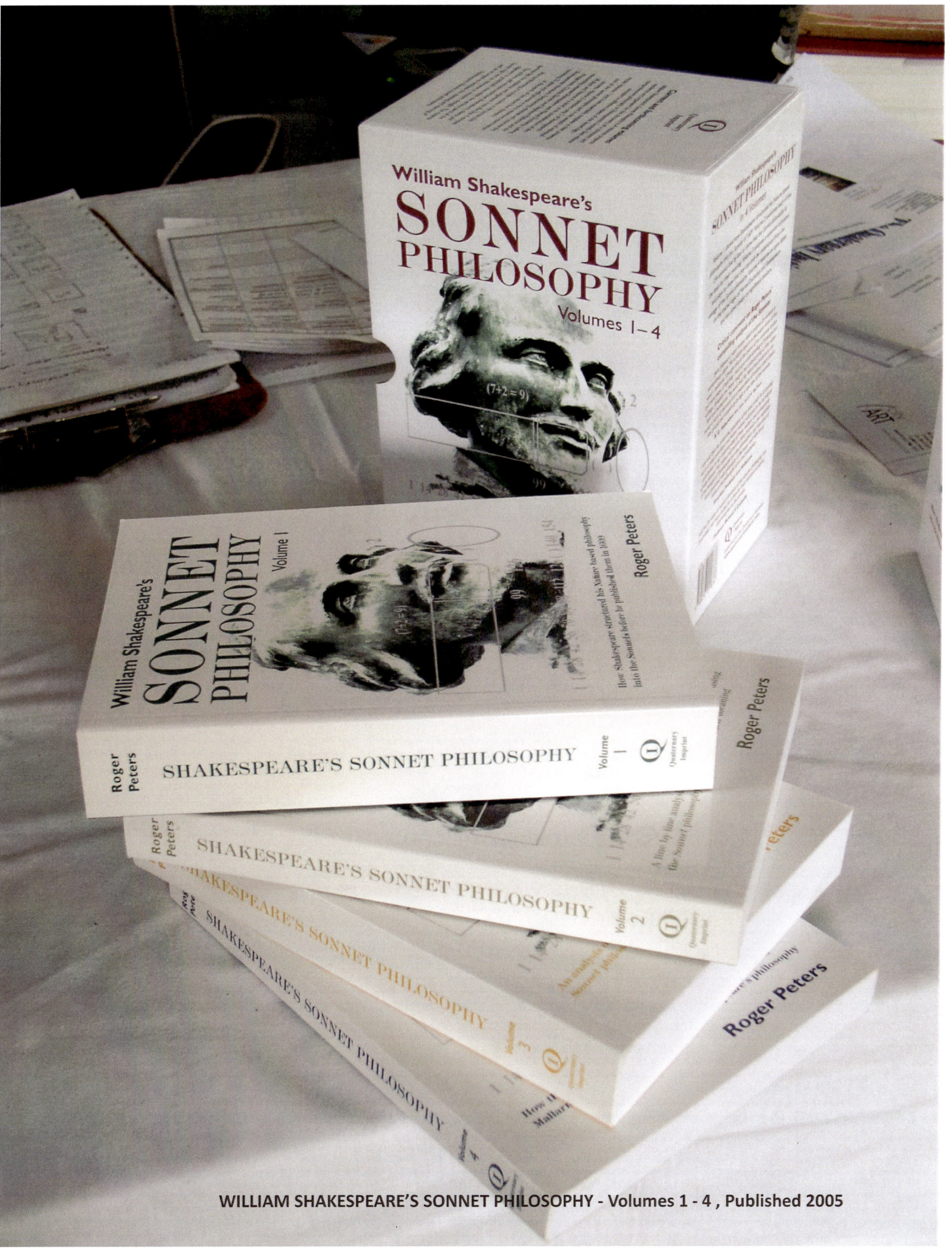

WILLIAM SHAKESPEARE'S SONNET PHILOSOPHY - Volumes 1 - 4 , Published 2005

From:	"David Loye" <loye@thedarwinproject.com>
To:	"Roger Peters" <roger.peters@xtra.co.nz>
Cc:	"riane eisler" <eisler@partnershipway.org>; "Sohail Inayatulluh" <s.inayatullah@qut.edu.au> "Marcus Anthony" <marcusadude@yahoo.com.au>
Sent:	Monday, 21 August 2006 3:42 a.m.
Subject:	Your books

Dear Roger Peters: Your impressive four vol book set on the philosophy
embedded within Shakespeare's sonnets arrived safely. We've been beyond
usual overloaded so only I have had a chance to read into vol four,
which prompts these thoughts:

1. The initial problem on being confronted with the idea of a central
nodule of wisdom being embedded in Shakespeare, corroborated by Darwin,
Duchamp, etc. is, as I'm sure you know, that this is the work of an
obsessive crank. On reading into vol four, however, I'm greatly
impressed with the caliber of your thinking, impressive range of
references, with the increasing conviction you are expressing something
of profound importance. Let me try to articulate it, then I'll deal
with your commentaries on Darwin and Riane's work.

2. Well, actually I find they provide a good springboard. What has long
impressed me about Darwin is that the deeper one gets into the real,
complete Darwin (which unfortunately only my work does so far at all
well), the more one is impressed by his rare grasp of a central vision
of how much of the mystery that confronts us is put together.

4. The image that keeps coming to me is of the old story of the blind
men feeling the elephant. One feels a leg and says it is a tree trunk.
  Another feels the tail and says it is a rope. Another feels an ear
and says this is the leaf of some giant plant.

I think what you are onto is that transcending the training of the
specialties, transcending the bureucraticalization (sp?) of modern
thinking (as Max Weber saw it), transending all the diminishment that is
the reason why my chief allegiance is to the field of evolutionary
systems science, is this rare central wisdom, and rare cohort of people
who perceive it, of the elephant as elephant not something else.

5. Then it make sense that this could be something that Shakespeare
saw, along with Darwin, Duchamp, etc., out of widely different lives and
disciplinary careers. Marx and Engels, too, along with Freud and
Einstein glimpsed it.

All good wishes,

David Loye

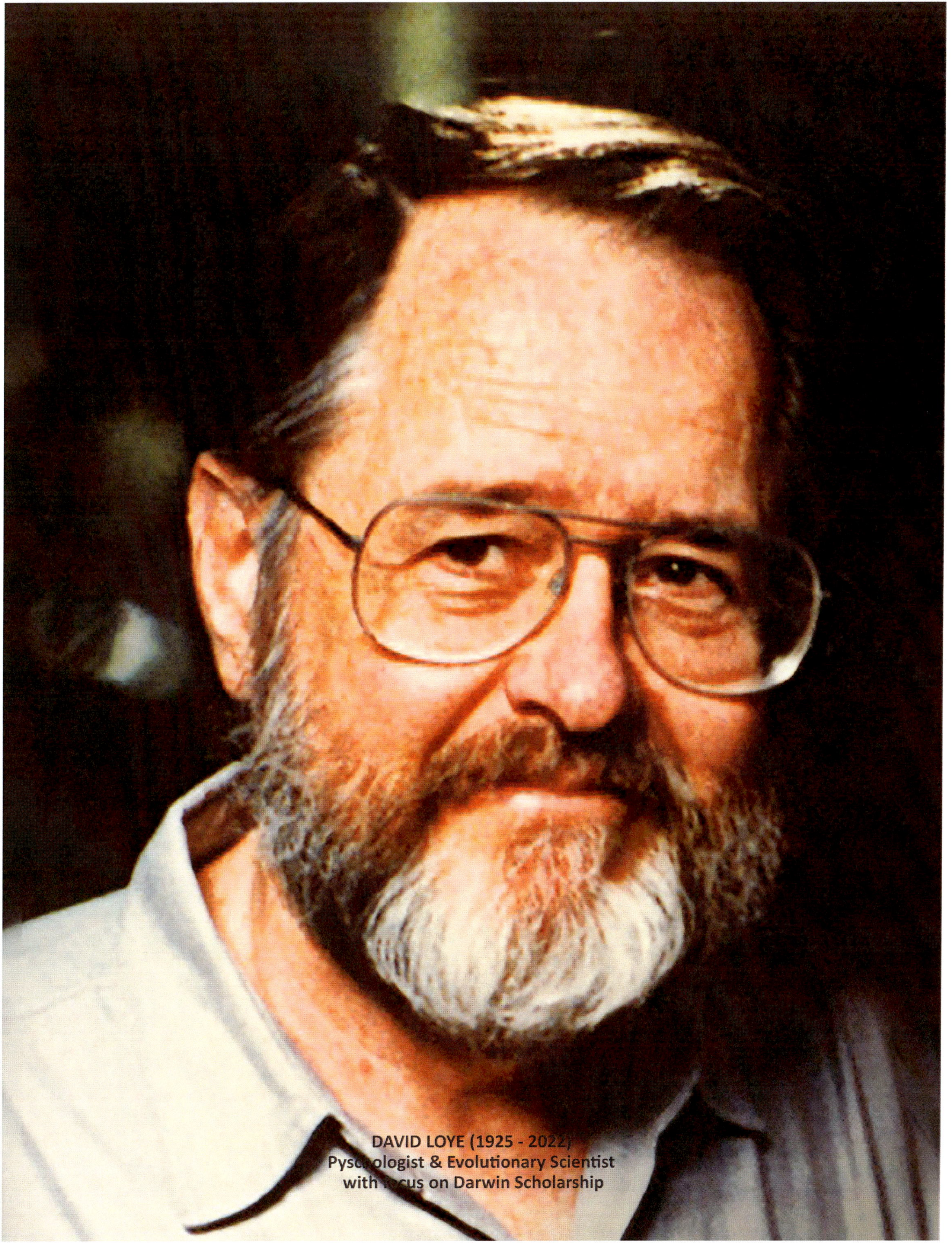

DAVID LOYE (1925 - 2022)
Pyschologist & Evolutionary Scientist
with focus on Darwin Scholarship

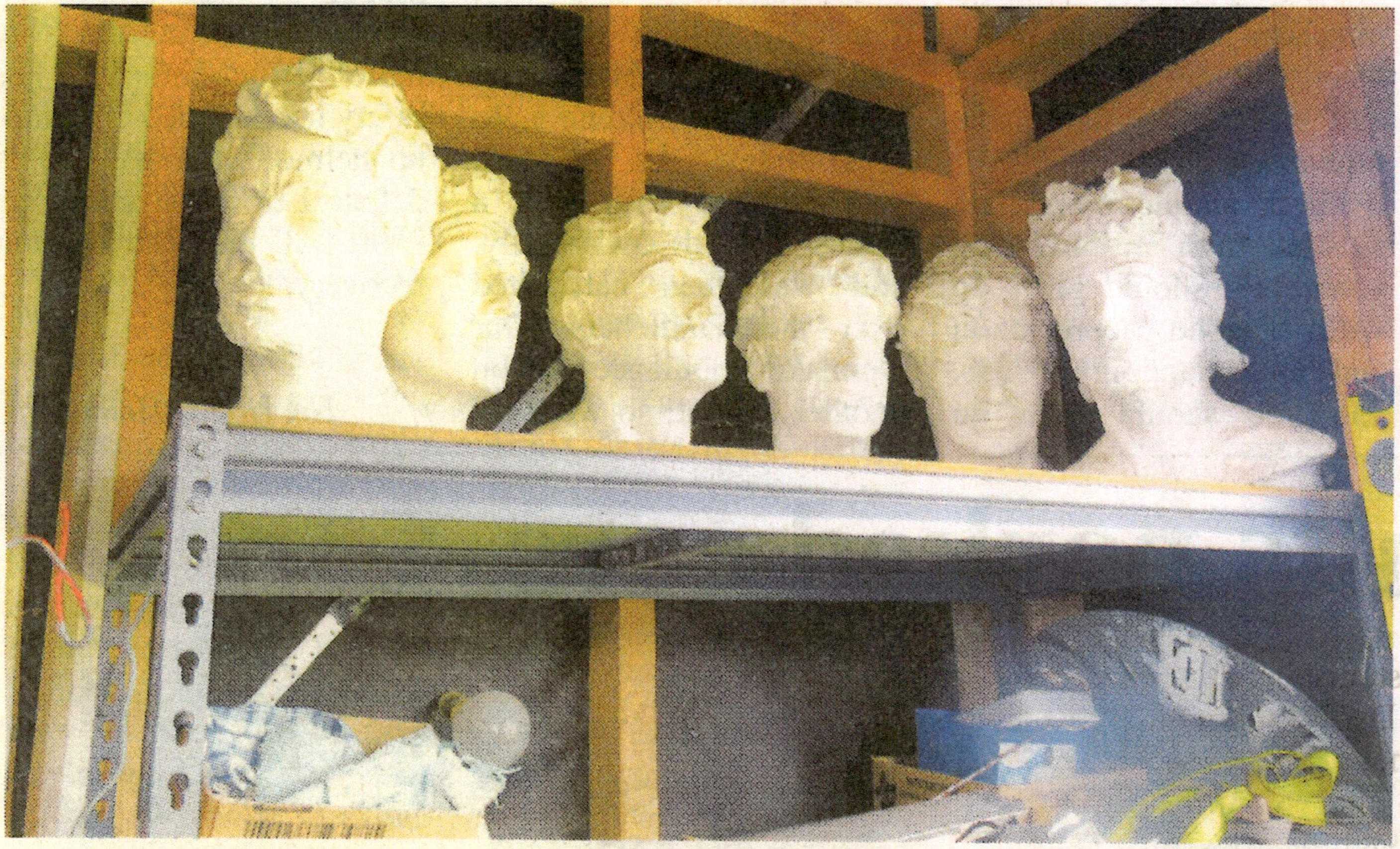

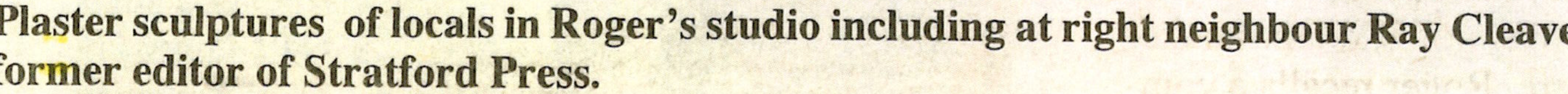

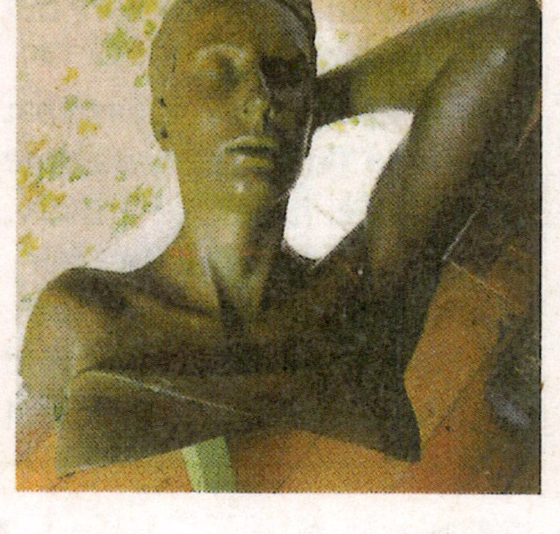

Another of Roger's works, a sculpture of his wife Marie cast in bronze.

Plaster sculptures of locals in Roger's studio including at right neighbour Ray Cleaver, former editor of Stratford Press.

THE OPUNAKE & COASTAL NEWS - Friday August 4th 2017

NOTEBOOK 21   Tues 17th Jan '95

Many crystals have I salted away in the hairiness of my dreams· The night is not the same without the glow of darkness and insistent melody of your tears· The double tree of light sheds stones upon my shackled feet reflecting the sound of rapids where once words were sweet· Glace flowers now foster an artificial buzzing in my fingertips reaching out for the softness of your sighs· The mists of size and quality have descended giving a million reasons for the circles of fear awaiting an indication from the chrysalis of the cortices· I leave you with a reminder of the persistence of dreams·

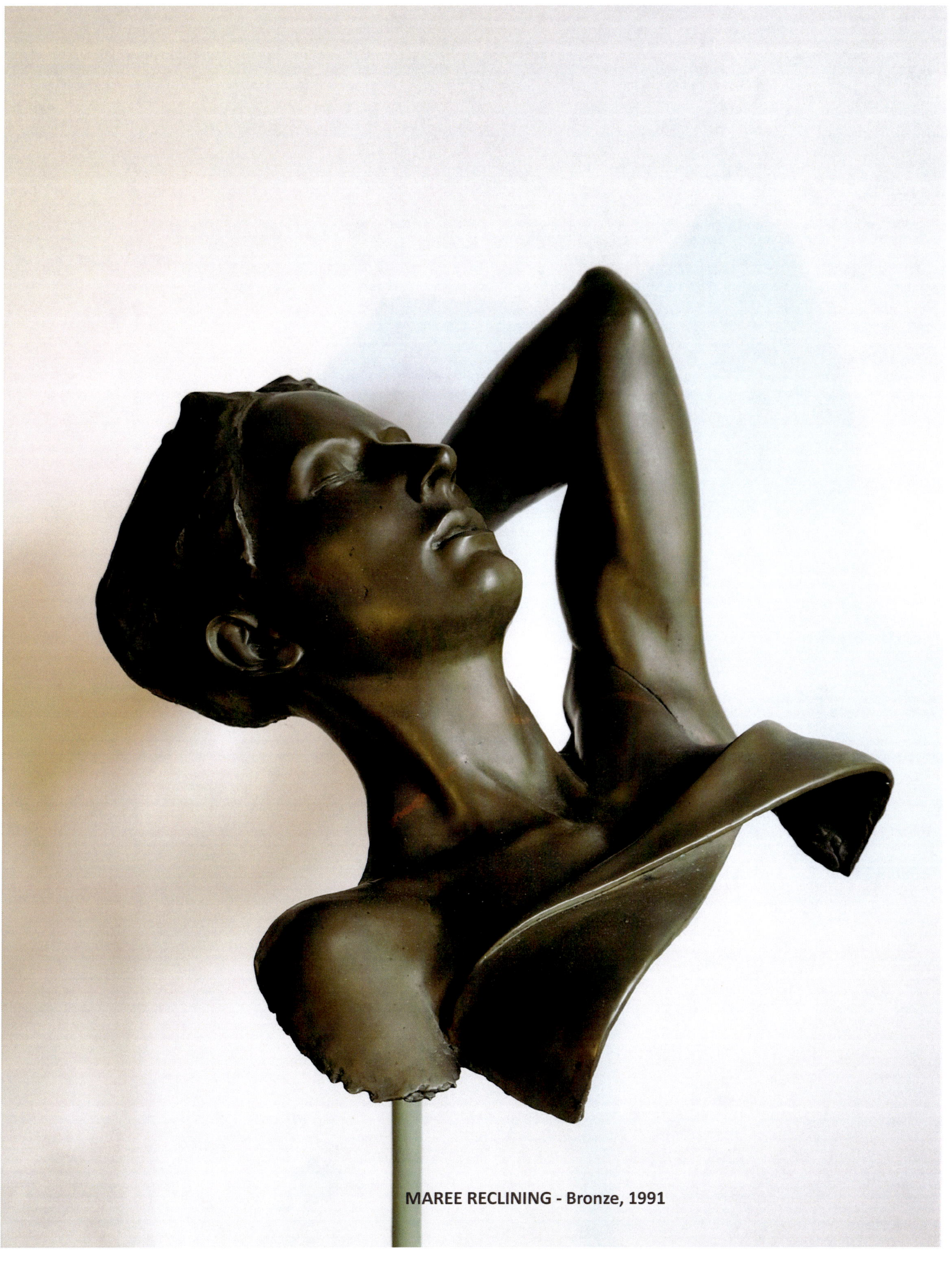

MAREE RECLINING - Bronze, 1991

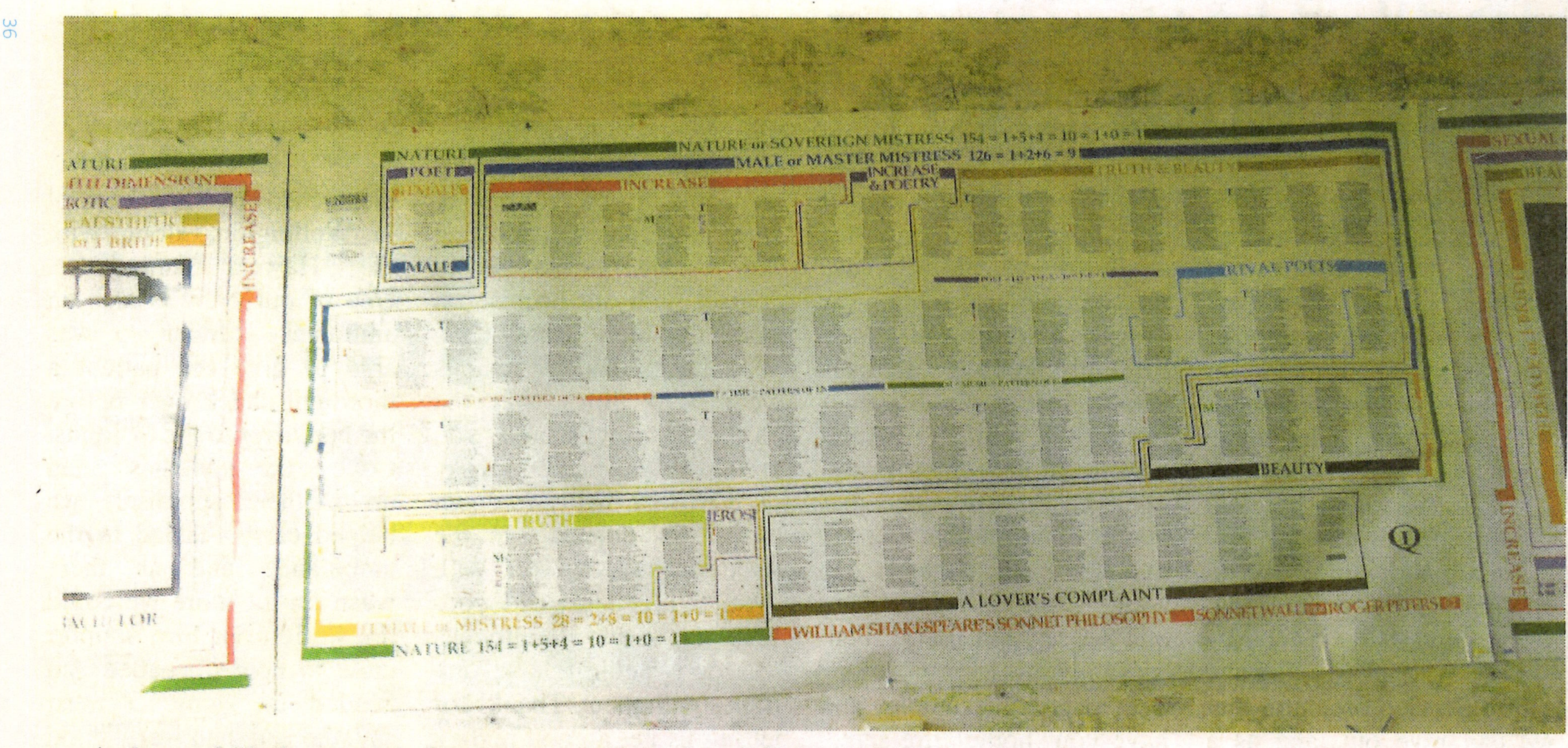

A chart of Shakespeare's Sonnets according to how Roger has categorised them.

THE OPUNAKE & COASTAL NEWS - Friday August 4th 2017

NOTEBOOK 9 Wed 2nd Sept '87

I have had an insight and I will not let it go – it will have to die of itself in my hands!! This insight has grown out of my artistic efforts and my philosophic understanding combined with an empathy with the landscape of my youth and a feel for the unaffected in people· I am going to push this insight – encourage it – so that in the end it will achieve a maturity that discovers recognition· Up to now I have been pushing myself – it is time to begin nudging the world about!!

Another day in this body. The head to think is as a vapour in a rock yet we can't do without it.
I have died in Ruapehu. There is only life after an eruption of thought. That is the mystery. A week
and a day in the Centre of the N. Island. It is not difficult to learn nothing. That is the sense I have
— I have no notion as to what may have seeped in through the skin. Can I depend upon it.

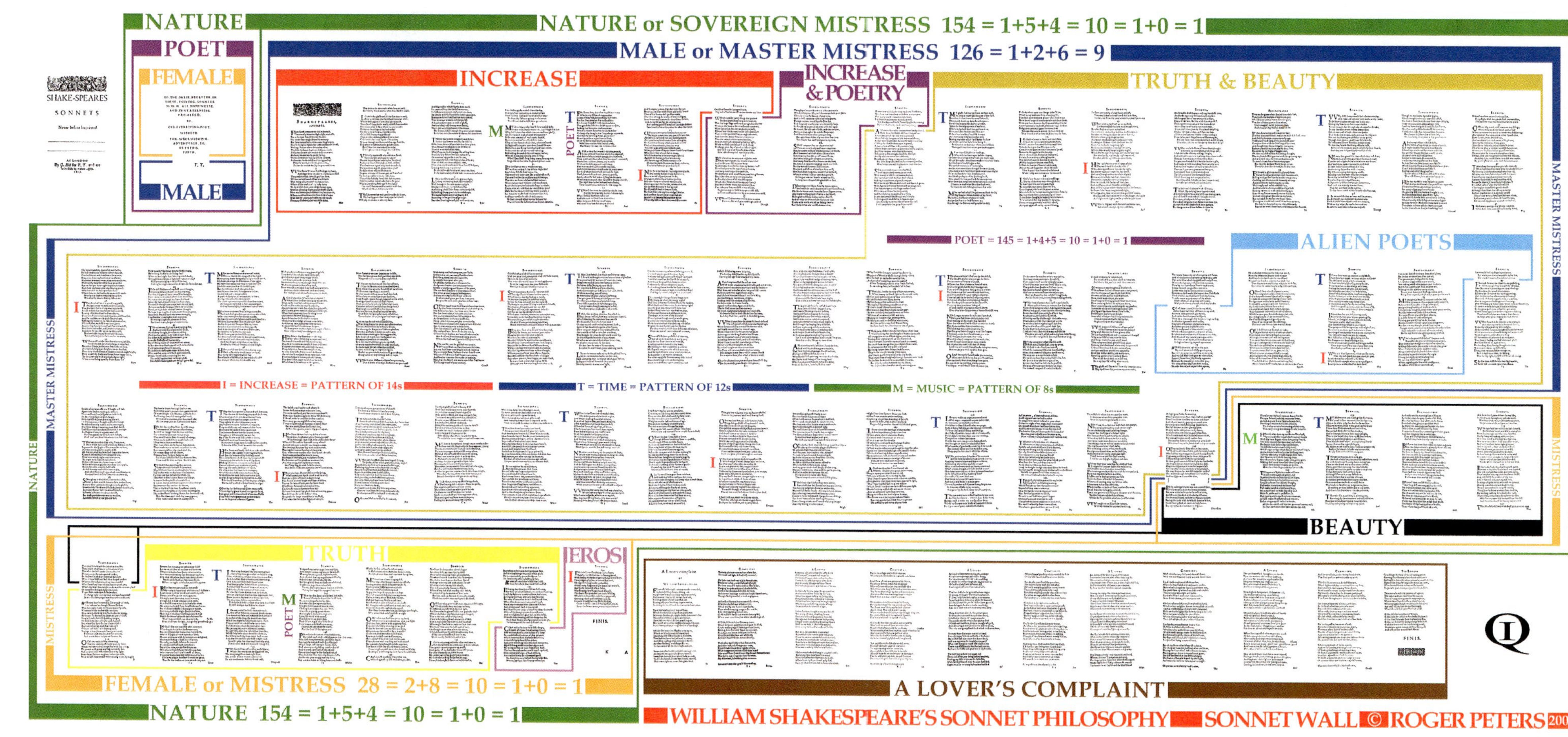

THE SONNET WALL CHART, 2006

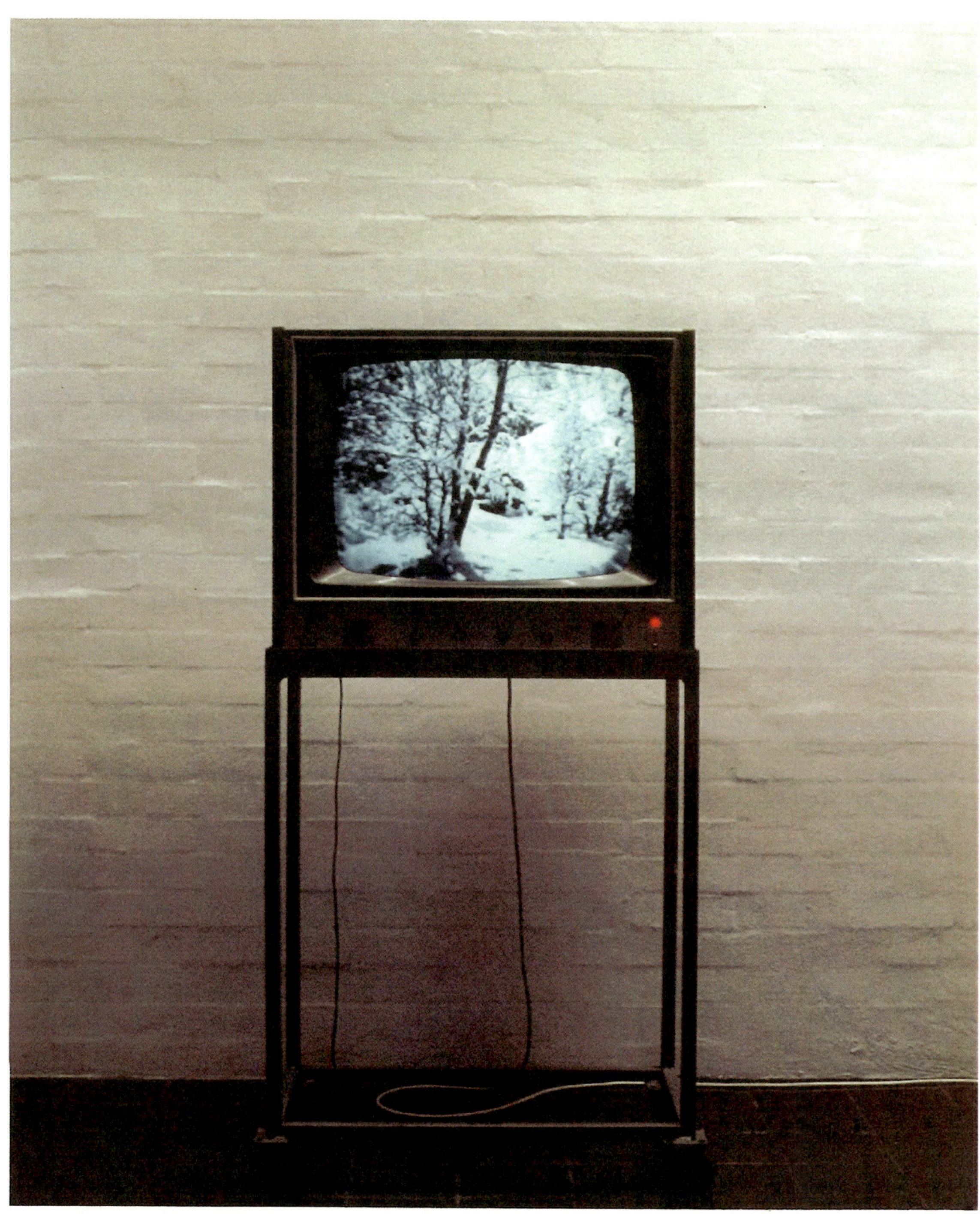

Roger Peters, *Snowfall*, installation with closed-circuit television, 1975, part of *Songs of the Earth*, Project Programme, Auckland City Art Gallery, courtesy of the artist and the E.H. McCormick Research Library, Auckland Art Gallery Toi o Tāmaki (photo: John Daley).

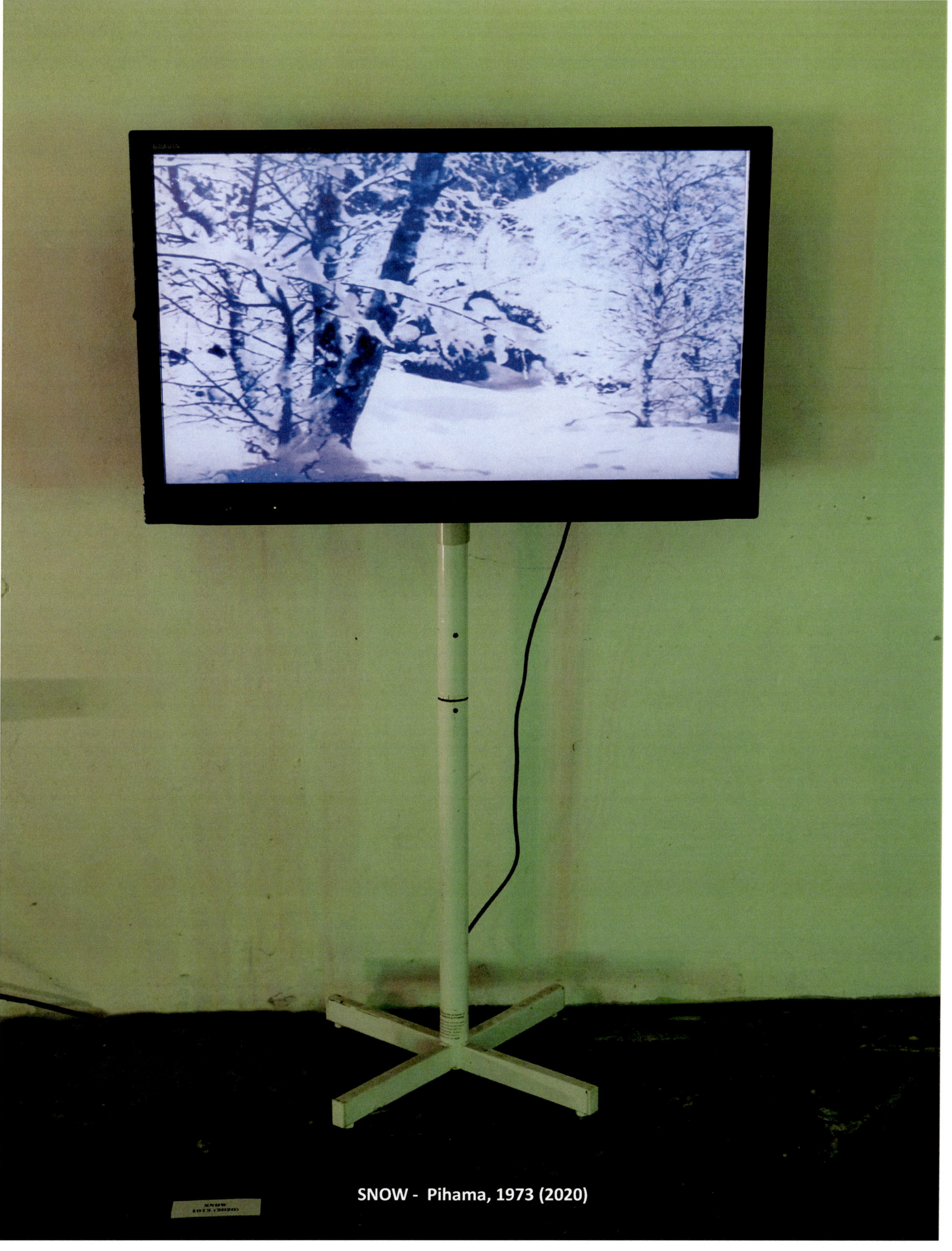

SNOW - Pihama, 1973 (2020)

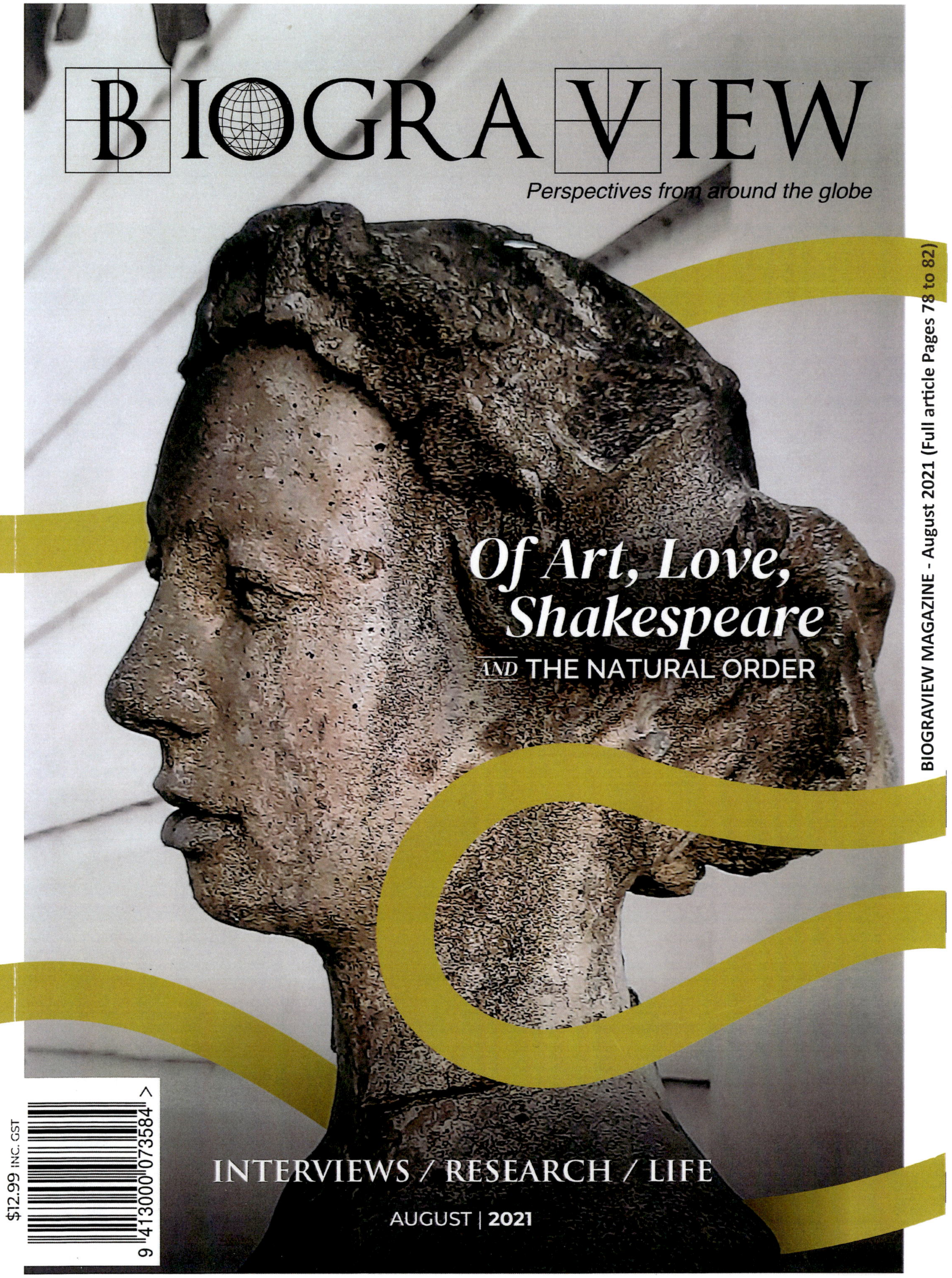
BIOGRA VIEW
Perspectives from around the globe
Of Art, Love, Shakespeare
AND THE NATURAL ORDER
BIOGRAVIEW MAGAZINE - August 2021 (Full article Pages 78 to 82)
INTERVIEWS / RESEARCH / LIFE
AUGUST | 2021
$12.99 INC. GST
9 413000 073584

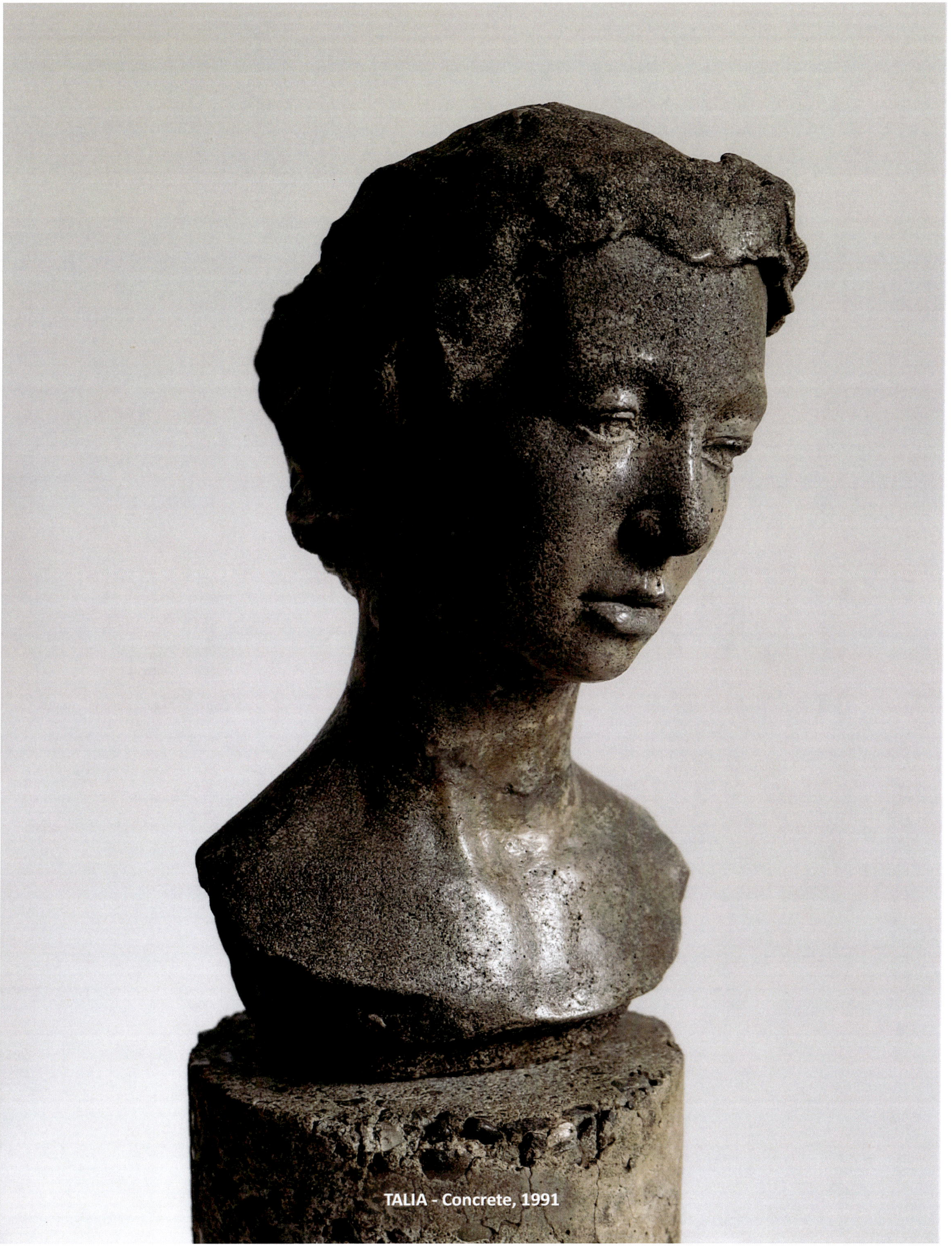
TALIA - Concrete, 1991

Songs of the earth strangely unearthly

It's out of it, fascinating. We live in such a sheltered life unless we go and explore things, it's so different was Dorothy Symes enthusiastic comment on viewing an exhibition at Pihama Lavender.

Entitled Songs of the Earth, the exhibition by Roger Peters from Kaponga is both a sensory and intellectual experience.

A graduate of Elam School of Fine Arts in Auckland, as a second year student Roger won an Air New Zealand Art Award open to students in tertiary institutions nationwide and judged by none other than Colin McCahon, widely recognised as New Zealand's foremost painter.

Roger majored in sculpture and the exhibition encompasses five decades of his work.

He cites conceptual artist Marcel Duchamp as a major influence. The French-American painter and sculptor rejected what he termed 'retinal' art (intended to please the eye) in favour of work that was conceived in the mind.

At Elam Roger came into contact with visiting overseas artists who encouraged experimenting using industrial materials and also everyday items using various froms of energy. The 28 diverse exhibits include passive displays of inert objects which contrast with energised ones using gas light and heat.

"I'm playing around with the senses," Roger explains invoking light, hearing and smell.

Ultimately the aim is to intellectually, aesthetically and emotionally engage the person.

"An artwork captures something – it brings life into that thing," he says. It encourages us to feel connected; it satisfies those cravings we have and gives us something to look at.

One work in particular he also amuses and confuses with a work entitled Fish which I depict in neon pink a shape which symbolises both a penis and a vagina.

Roger Peters has exhibited in Auckland.

Before leaving I noted Dorothy's husband had a different, reaction to the works questioning Roger on what voltage he used in some of the exhibits. Art is subjective.

Prepare to have your horizons widened.

The exhibition is open daily till Friday May 28 between 10am and 4:00 pm or after hours by appointment.

Bernice McKellar

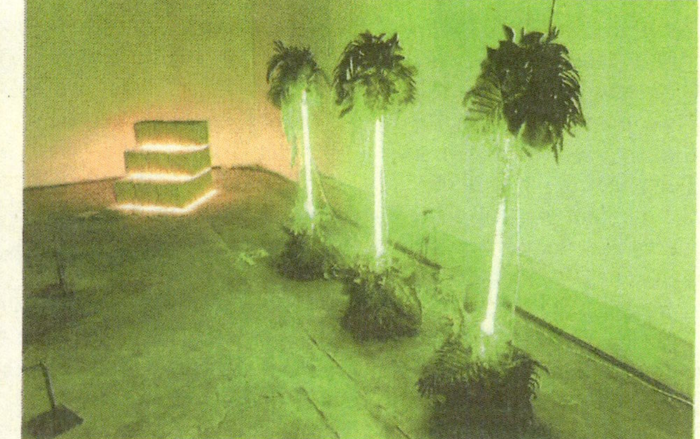

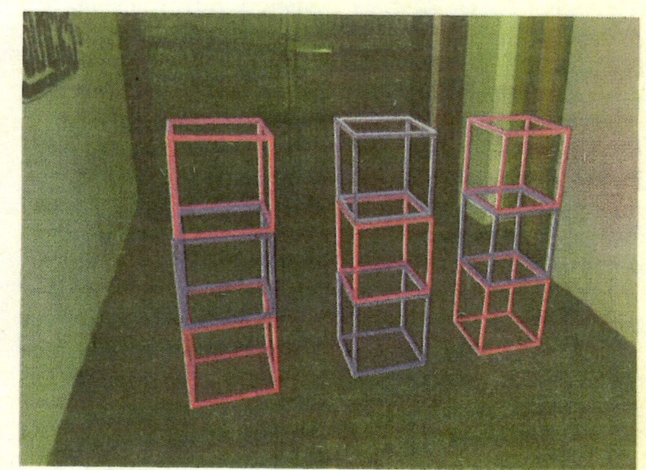

Above left: Roger Peters.
Above top: Leaves and steps.
Above: Cubes.

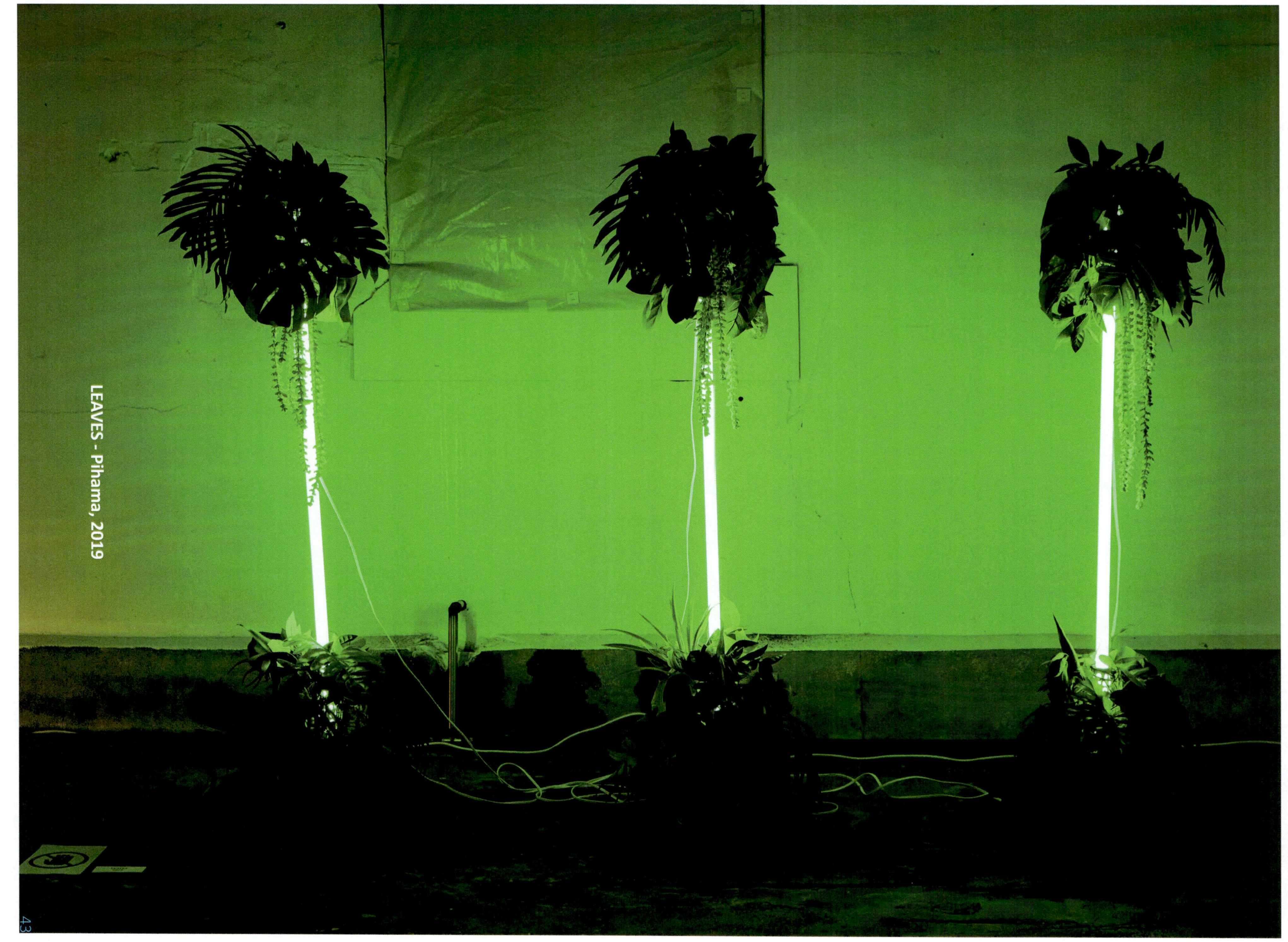

LEAVES - Pihama, 2019

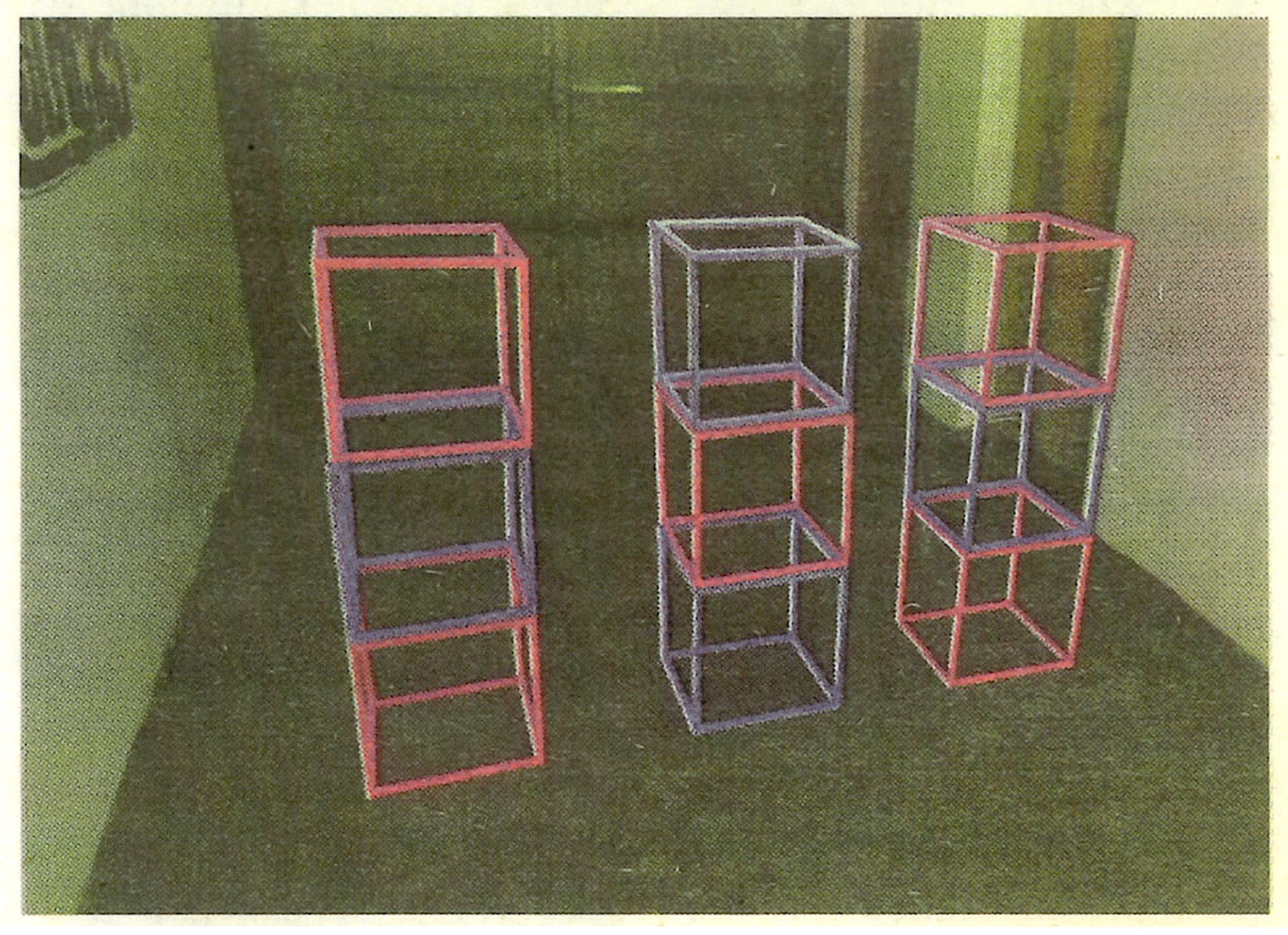

NOTEBOOK 4 Fri 22nd June '84

It's never occurred quite so strongly to me before as it has just now as to how crucial to a sense of ongoing life is the unit of male and female. While it is possible to think in terms of the death of the body and the seeming finality of it such a possibility isn't true in terms of male and female indivisibility. All ideas of the soul leaving the body or the life force ebbing away are phantasms that deny the ongoing function of reproduction. A dead plant like a dead body seems to have lost that vital force that sustains it in life.

Yet we seem to recognise more readily that through its seeds the plant is able to live on. It seems much more difficult for us to accept that the only way we live on is by passing on our seeds — by the combination of the male seed and female seed. Like plant bodies our dead bodies, deprived of our electricity, magnetism and other natural factors that sustain life, become part of the living earth. In these ways both our uniqueness and commonness with all else is preserved.

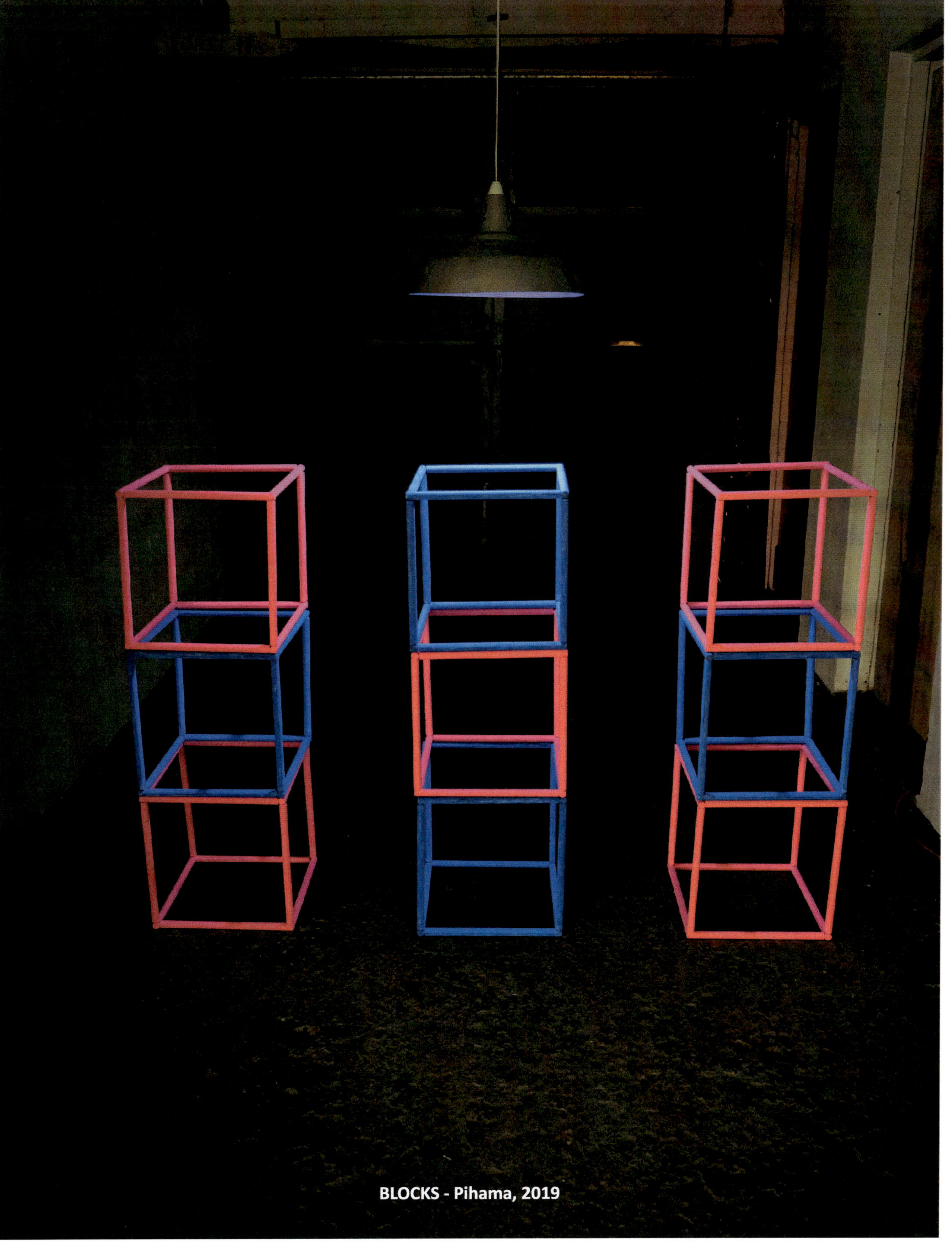

BLOCKS - Pihama, 2019

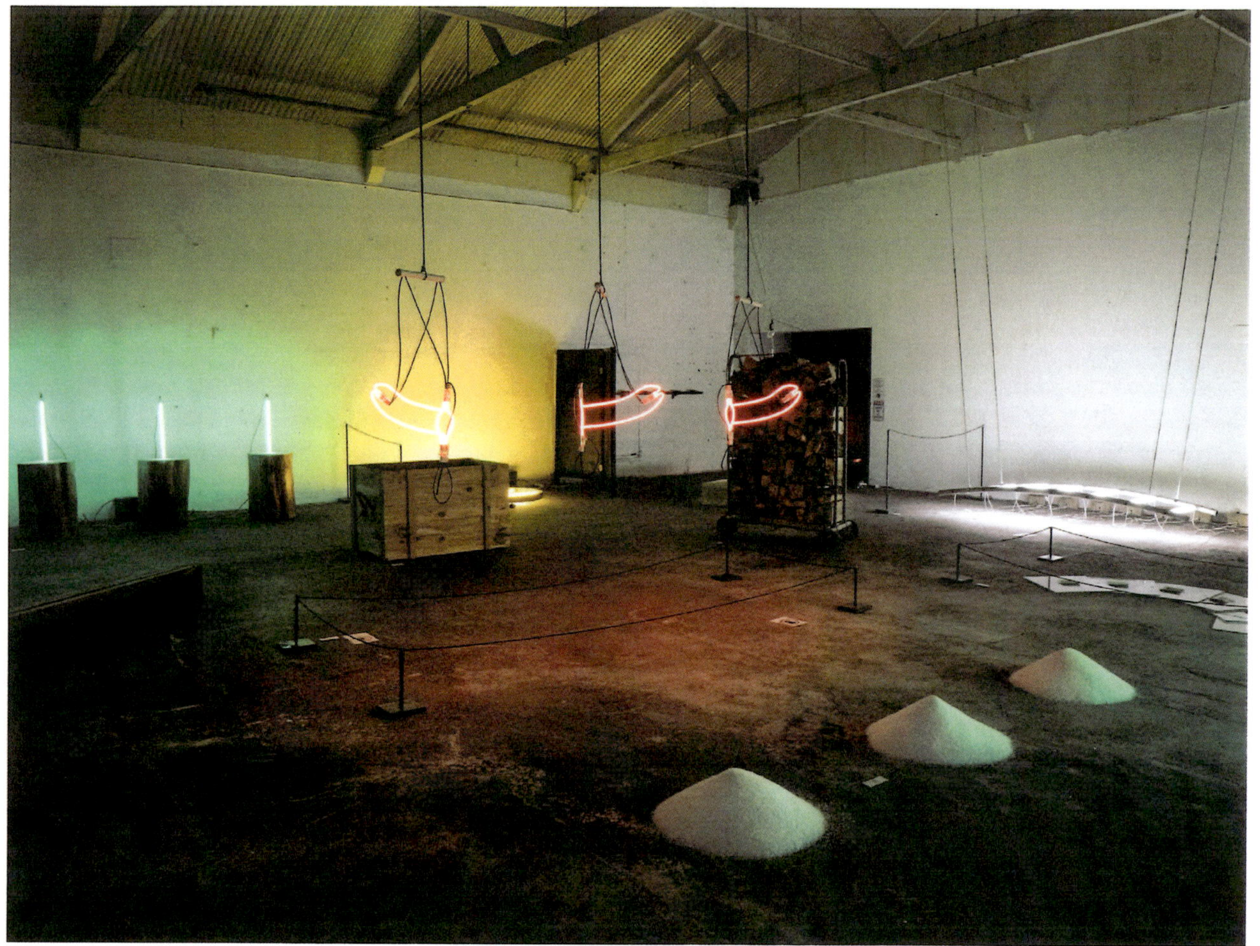

ART NEW ZEALAND - Spring edition 179, P98, 2021

Blink and You'll See It

Songs of the Earth at Pihama

DON ABBOTT

It could be said that the plains of South Taranaki are just that. Unfussy. Pragmatic. Cows get milked; bread gets baked; rugby gets played. The people might grumble, but they get on with the task at hand anyway.

It was a stretch of belief then, when Pihama Lavender started production inside an abandoned dairy factory in 2013. Under the guidance of owner Liz Sinclair, the soil produced not grass—green, thick, lush, milk-producing grass—but lavender and, at a pinch, this place was less the provinces, more Provence. Suddenly the prospect of aromas, oils and propagation introduced a world that was frankly a little fussy, less sensible.

It is a further stretch of belief to enter Pihama Lavender in the month of May, the time around which Roger Peters' *Songs of the Earth* occupies its great hall. It is best to arrive at Pihama driving down the Skeet Road—a long straight flat lane, with a premonition of descent; the horizon expands and the blue ocean swells. For a moment the world is an upturned

saucer, and those who do not slow down will drop off its edge. The venue's grand circular driveway and manicured landscaping surprise the first-time visitor; a foyer leads to a door that opens, magically, and here is a looking glass through which every Alice can enter to see what they can find.

Songs of the Earth is a collection of 28 artworks that Roger Peters has made over 50 or so years. Many of them date from his Elam shows of the early 1970s, and a 1975 Auckland City Art Gallery exhibition of the same name.

Upon entering the other-world of *Songs of the Earth*, it is immediately clear that Peters is a sculptor of light. Moreover, he manipulates, moulds and uses light, revelling in its possibilities. What he does with light he also does with the dark (I think he may be secretly thrilled to be called a prince of darkness). The hall may be chilly, but it is also a parade of highlights and recesses, and the eyeballs and brain lurch into self-pleasuring hyperactivity.

Fish is the first work to be seen, and the newest in the show, completed this year. Three pink neon penises hang in mid-air in the middle of the room,

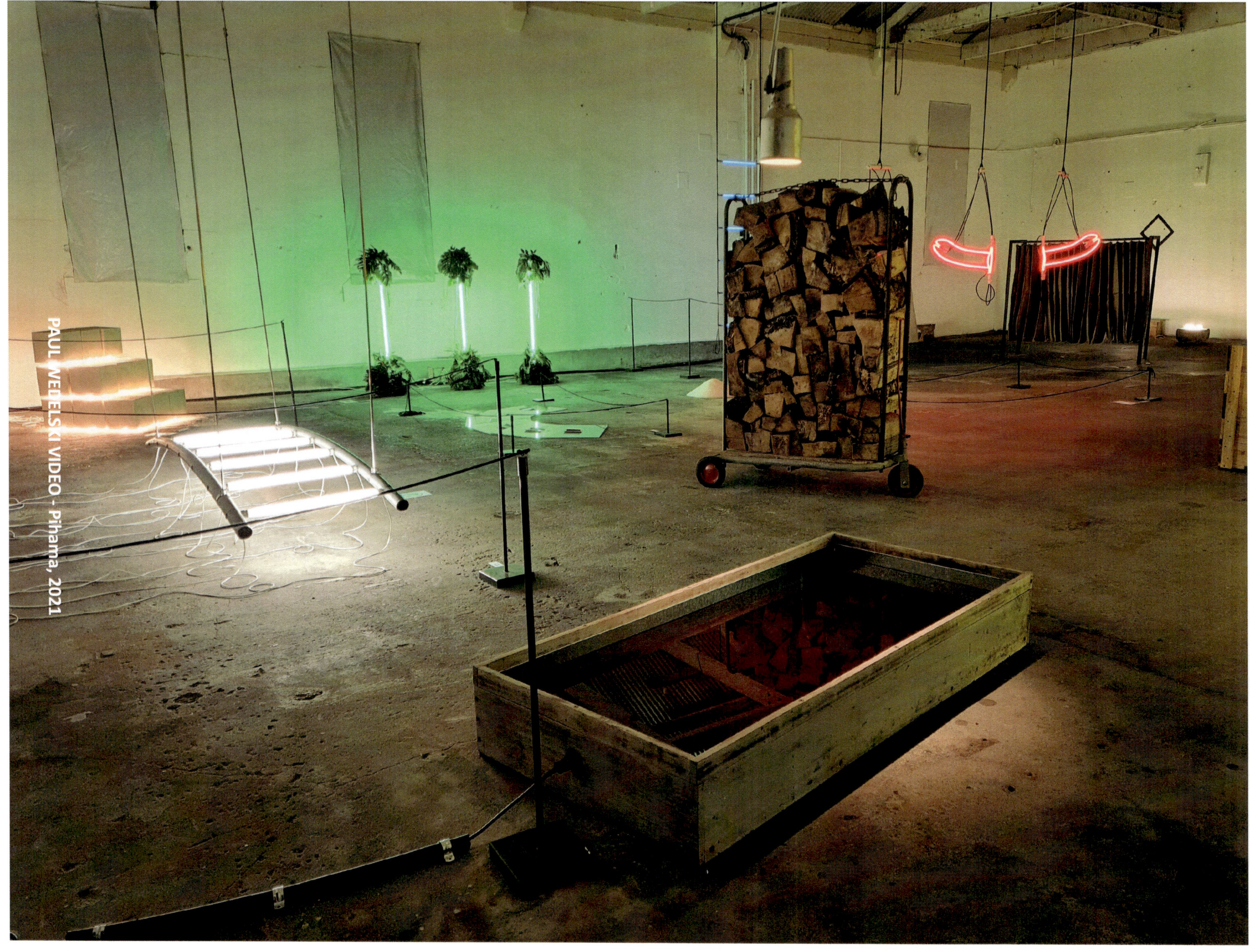

PAUL WEDELSKI VIDEO - Pihama, 2021

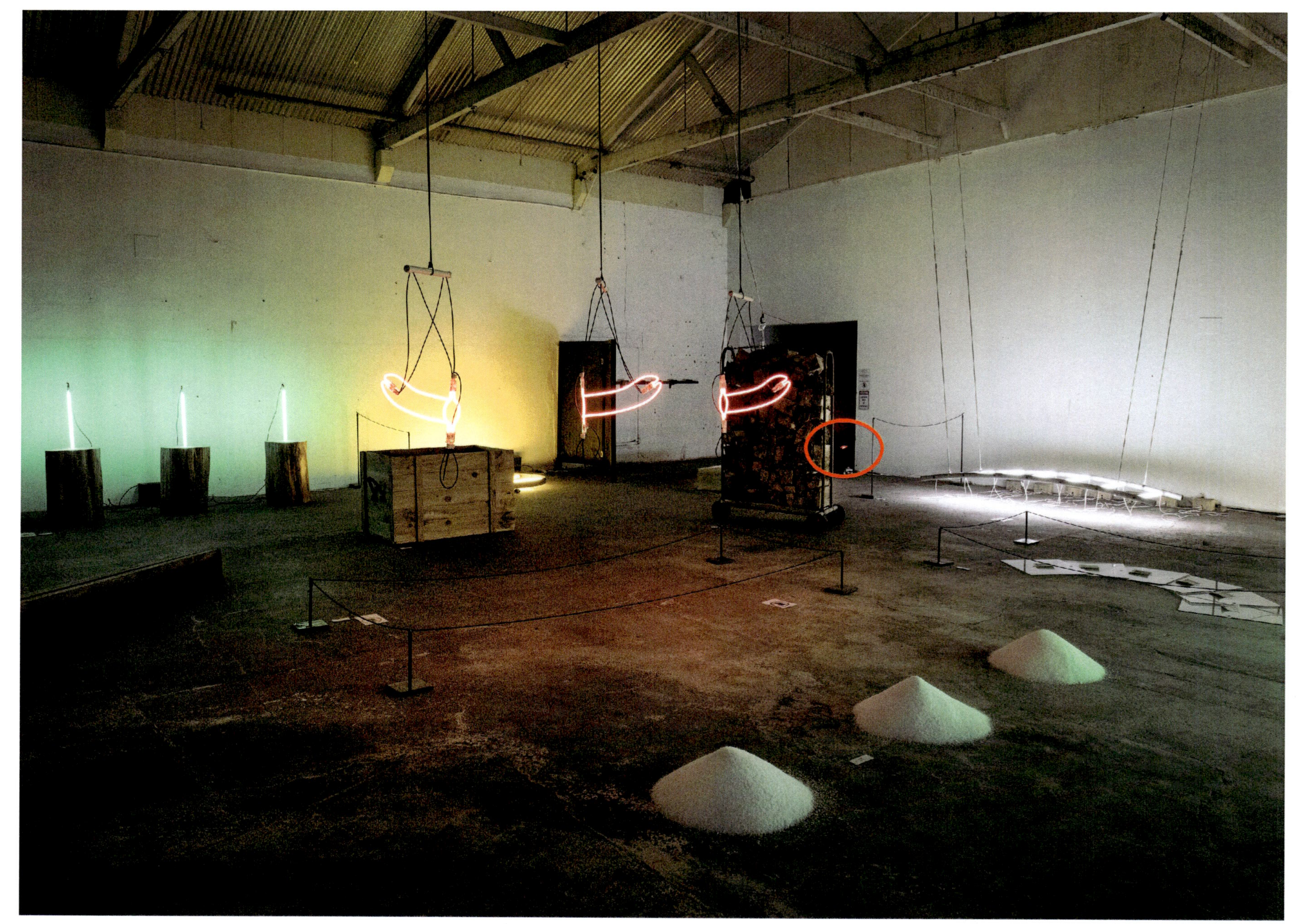

ART NEW ZEALAND - Spring edition 179, P98, 2021

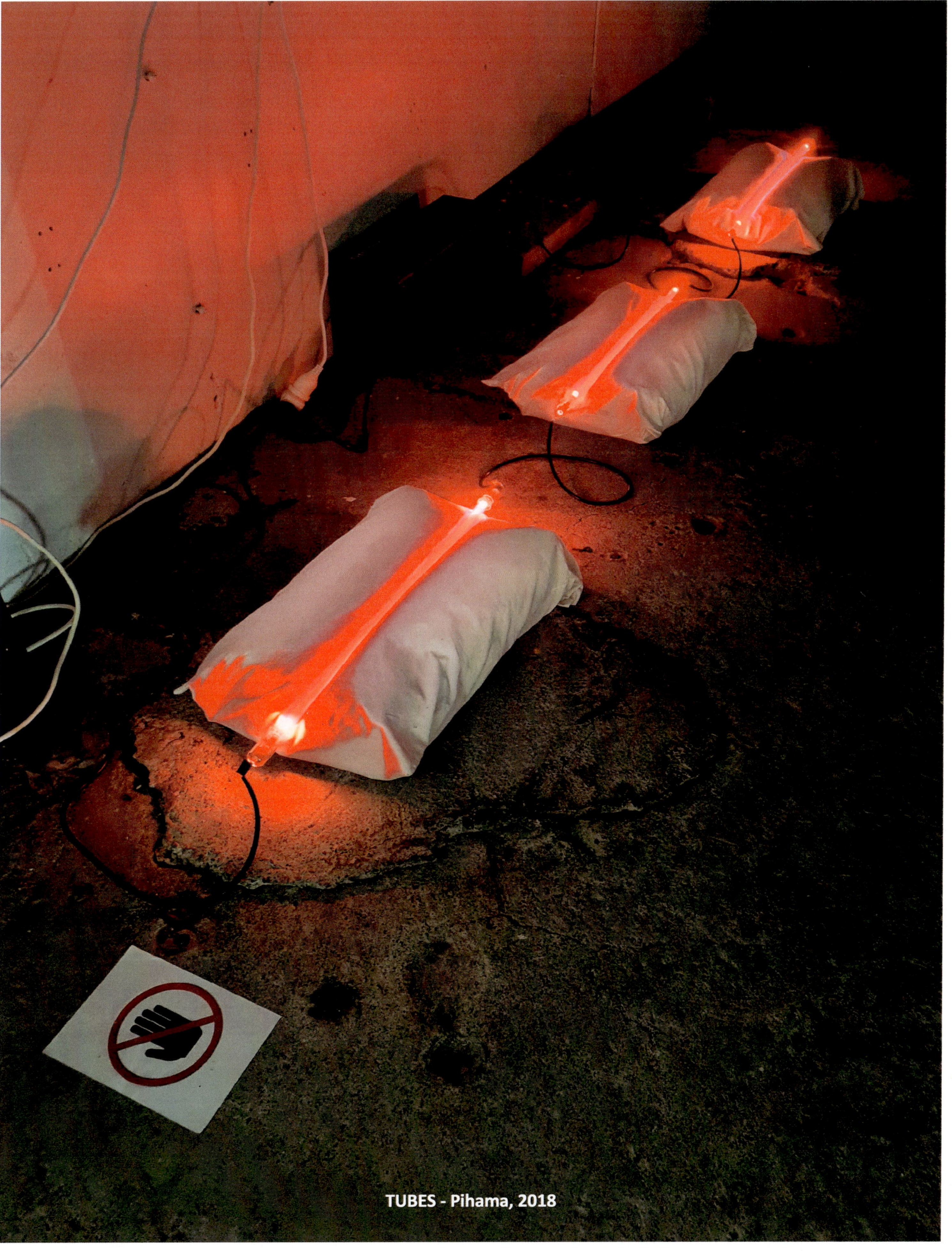

TUBES - Pihama, 2018

(opposite) Roger Peters' *Songs of the Earth* at Pihama Lavender,
May 2021
(Photograph: Maree Horner)

(right) ROGER PETERS *Steps* 2018
Concrete blocks & lightbulbs, 800 x 800 x 800 mm.
(Photograph: Maree Horner)

(below) ROGER PETERS *Wheel* 1976
Metal & fluorescent tubes, 130 x 1580 x 1580 mm.
(Photograph: Maree Horner)

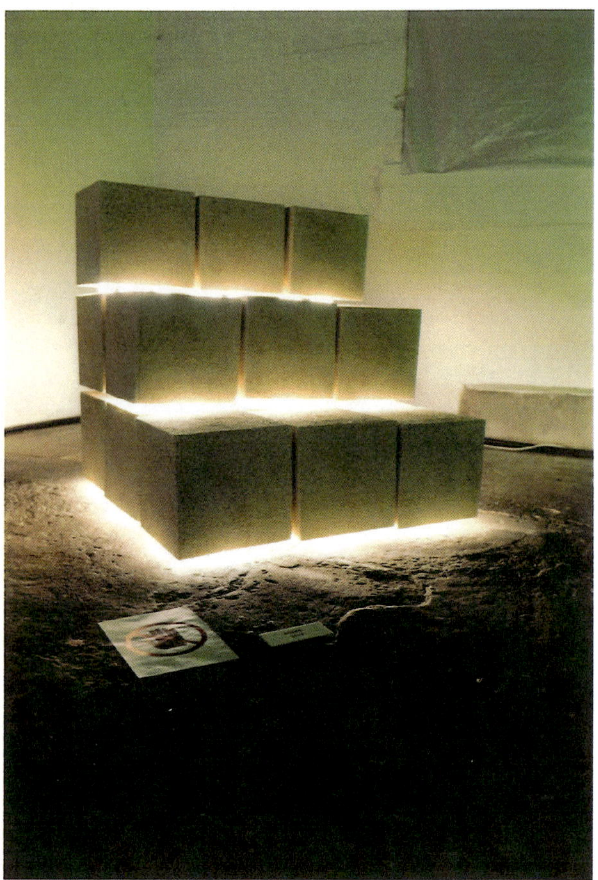

pointing randomly and obscenely at their artistic
bedfellows. End on, however, the neon shape becomes
a vagina and, all of a sudden, the puerile becomes
universal, philosophical and fundamental, evoking
Adam and Eve, the war of the sexes, reproduction,
evolution, and so on. This later Peters is proving to be
a fine successor of the younger.

Next door is *Trees* (1977), three short vertical green
neon strips that could be an arboreal equivalent to
the anthropomorphising vertical fluorescent lights
of Dan Flavin. If you are unsure of which is human
and which is tree, however, Peters has planted his
in wood, quite literally—each neon tube disappears
rather tightly into a hole in a roughly hewn log. Tree
comes of tree, it seems. A companion piece, *Leaves*
(2019), puts artificial foliage at the top and bottom of
three green tubes, like pompoms, asking duplicitously,
what is real? *Steps* (2018) is dangerously playful, an
assemblage of concrete blocks that rest on lightbulbs
to form a short glowing staircase that leads only
to the precipice of its own creation. Its architecture
is exposed, in a perfectly aligned, Busby Berkeley
kind of way. *Bridge* (2019) and *Wheel* (1976) are
structures that use tubes of light, neither destined to
go anywhere at all. *Bridge* is suspended, *Wheel* is lying
down. (Geddit? Suspension bridge, waggin' wheel.)

By now it should be clear that Roger Peters gives
titles to his works that are pithy, to the point, and
preferably monosyllabic. His use of language is as
economical as the execution of his artworks. This
focus heightens and condenses the impact of the
word and, by extension, the work. *Salt* (1973) is three
mounds of sodium chloride on the ground. Say it
three times as you walk by, out loud and to yourself,
and the word expands, its consonants abutting and
stretching out. The word loses, then gains, meaning
and import. Semantics crumble; visiting *Songs of
the Earth* is a linguistic trip, as much as it is a visual,
visceral and intellectual one.

By now it should also be clear that Peters works
in series. A good idea becomes a great one when you
repeat it. There are so many sets of objects in this dim
cavern of discovery that it is safe to call him a serial
artist. Alongside his partner, artist Maree Horner, he
spends his waking hours attending this exhibition,
hosting, engaging and discussing his work to all who
might visit. He shifts his delivery to suit city-based
curators and collectors, as well as local school groups
and, when I was there, an aircraft engineer from the
nearby township of Kaponga. Peters was deservedly
thrilled with how the work looked and felt in its
location. It could easily occupy a public gallery, and
indeed might benefit from an environment that is

better regulated in terms of temperature and light
levels. However, such a showing would be vastly
different; *Songs of the Earth* gained currency being
away from a gallery and its customary audience,
in the same way that a wind wand transcends its
function as contemporary art when placed on a city
foreshore.

In 1976, responding to Peters' *Songs of the Earth*
at the Auckland City Art Gallery the year before,
Wystan Curnow noted that the works of Peters 'seem
to comprise "things of the world" caught in the act
of being themselves'.[1] It seems he is an artist who
cannot go past the elemental; for all the headplay,
wordplay, artplay and theatrics, the media that Peters
uses are of the elements—fire, water, earth and air. For
all his knowledge and exposition of philosophy, art
and literature, he is grounded in the fundaments and
foundations of life itself.

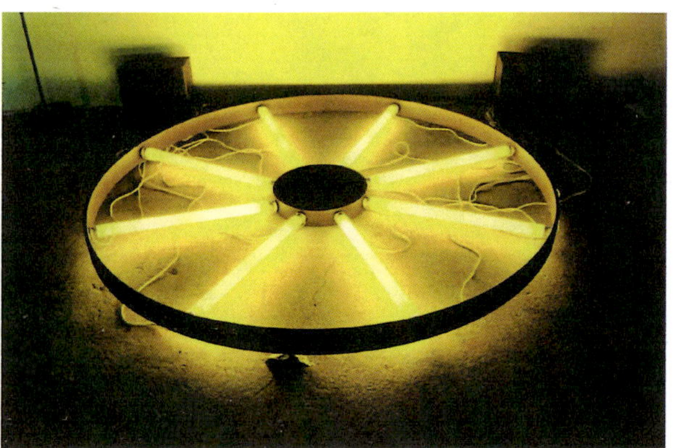

ART NEW ZEALAND - Spring edition 179, P99, 2021

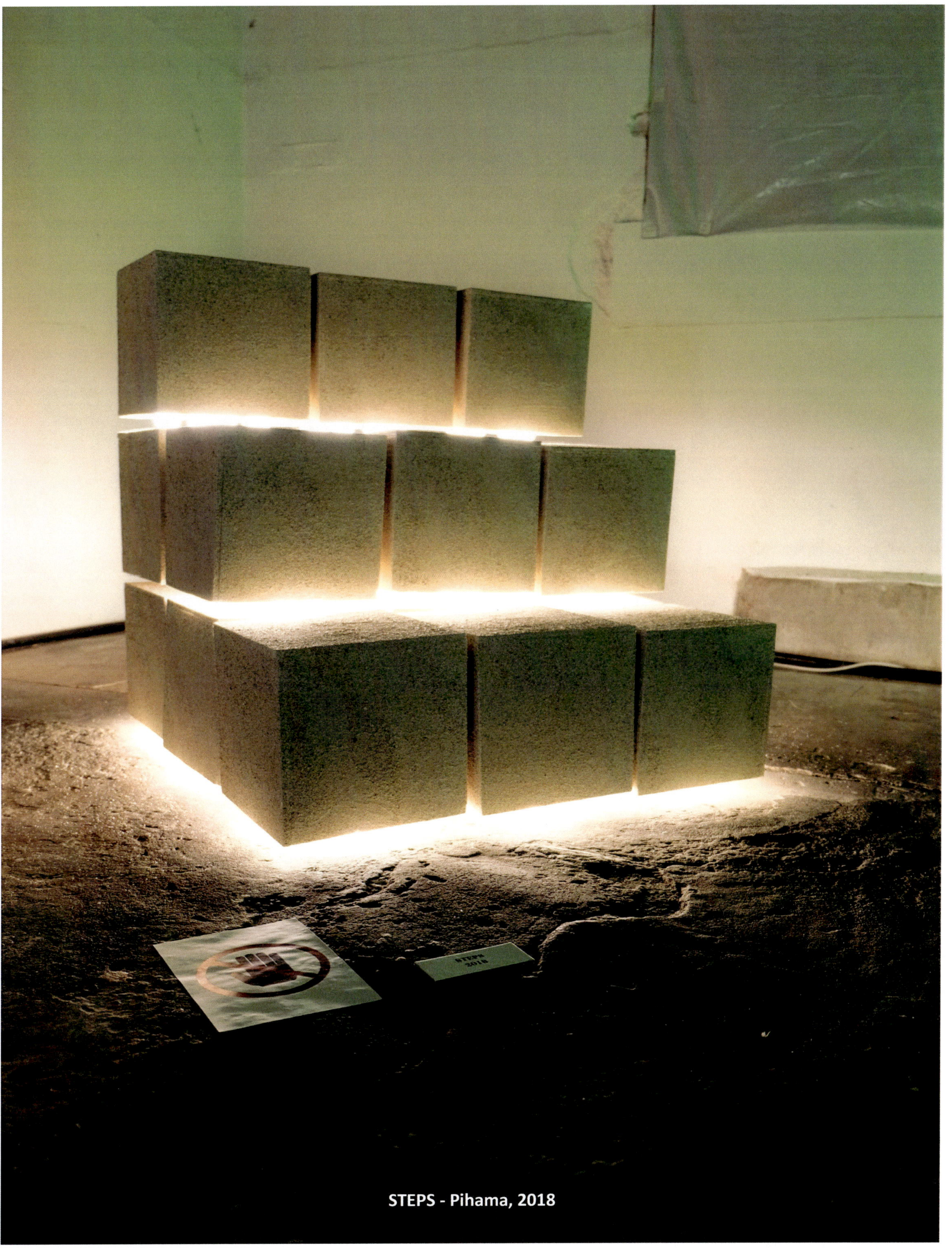

STEPS - Pihama, 2018

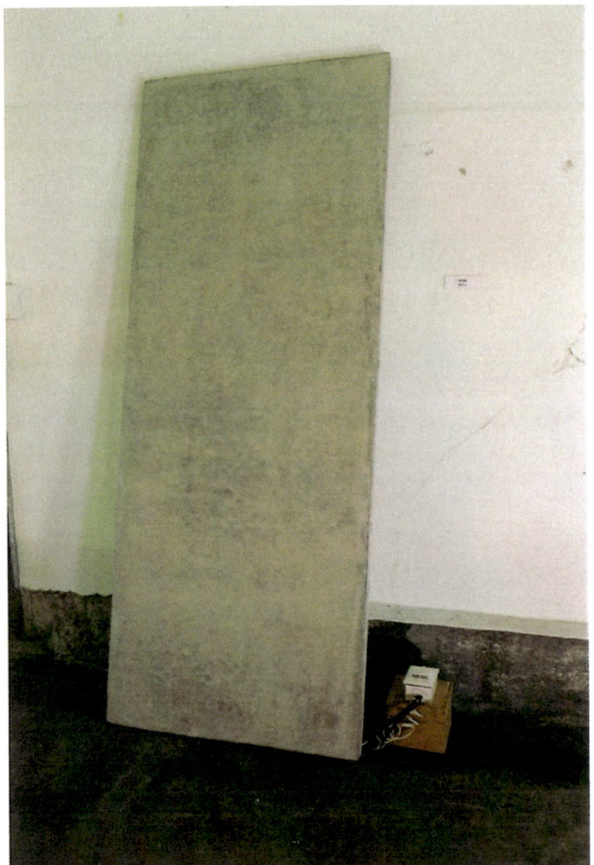

Peters matches the human body to these elemental forces and at times pitches the two against each other. *Coal Box* (1972) is what it says it is, a large box full of coal. The coal is satisfyingly black and organic, glowing with earthy portent; the box is groin-high,

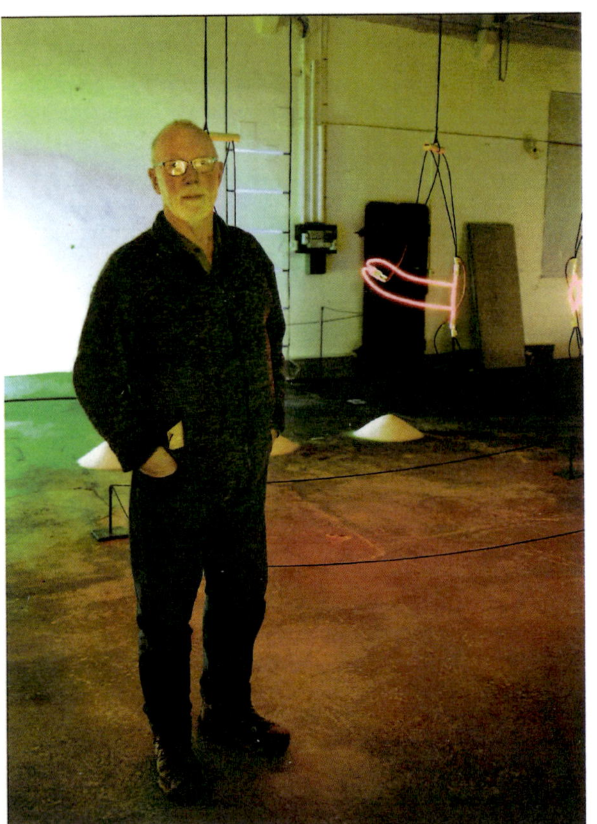

wooden, with a handle on the side that is built for human hands. The box is too heavy to move of course, but the handle hints that it might be possible, and the mind can easily see it happening. *Red Ladder* (1972) and *Blue Ladder* (1974) lean against the wall, and are useless as ladders, but very good catalysts for imagining the act of climbing. This kinaesthesia—the experience of the body through intuition and thought—is a tribute to the venue's history, to the role that labour played inside its walls and beyond, to the prosperity and story of Taranaki.

Peters is fond of the place in which he lives and lets the local feature in *Songs of the Earth. Netting* (1972/2020) is made of chickenwire and could be installed and overlooked in any implement shed on a neighbouring farm. The lamp that illuminates *Oil Bath* (1972) resembles the heat lamps that help to keep fragile newborn lambs and calves from death. The westerlies blow often and hard in this region, so *Wind* (1973) is familiar. It could be a suggested soundtrack for a silent movie, and the pose struck to listen to the suspended speakers brings to mind the bent-over form of Lillian Gish in the 1928 Victor Sjöström film. The element Peters is drawing here is air, evoking what is invisible and intangible by what is itself invisible and intangible—sound. He complicates matters considerably by placing *Wind* next to *Wires* (1973), glowing filaments that move in a convectional equation of their own making; yet they appear to be waving in the wind that you can hear, even though the air around you is still. This is a hall of mirrors that stretches all your senses, and logic too.

With *Slab* (1974) he has made prefabricated concrete—a large door-sized slab of it—feel elemental. Everyone who visits can only agree, as this is one work that viewers are encouraged to touch; the wires and regulators at its base are evidence of the fact that it is heated to body temperature—an electric shock in a building that is so cold. The artist loves the word of the title, and its meatiness is reinforced as you mentally repeat it, feeling the warmth of the concrete, and joining in its defiance of death. Its position, as a lean-to against the wall, ensures that it can be perceived as the lid to a sarcophagus—a jokey-yet-serious reference to millennia of art history (from the ancient Egyptians on), and the fact that it is all dead. If art history is to be a living thing then it is here and now, in Pihama, the flesh on concrete, the flickerings of response and the thrall of art.

1. Wystan Curnow, 'Roger Peters Songs of the Earth 24 November–2 December 1975', in Christina Barton and Robert Leonard (eds), *The Critic's Part: Wystan Curnow Art Writings 1971-2013*, Adam Art Gallery, Wellington, Institute of Modern Art, Brisbane, Victoria University Press, Wellington 2014, p. 76. The review was originally published in 'Project Programme 1975' in the *Auckland City Art Gallery Quarterly*, no. 62-3, December 1976.

ART NEW ZEALAND - Spring edition 179, P100, 2021

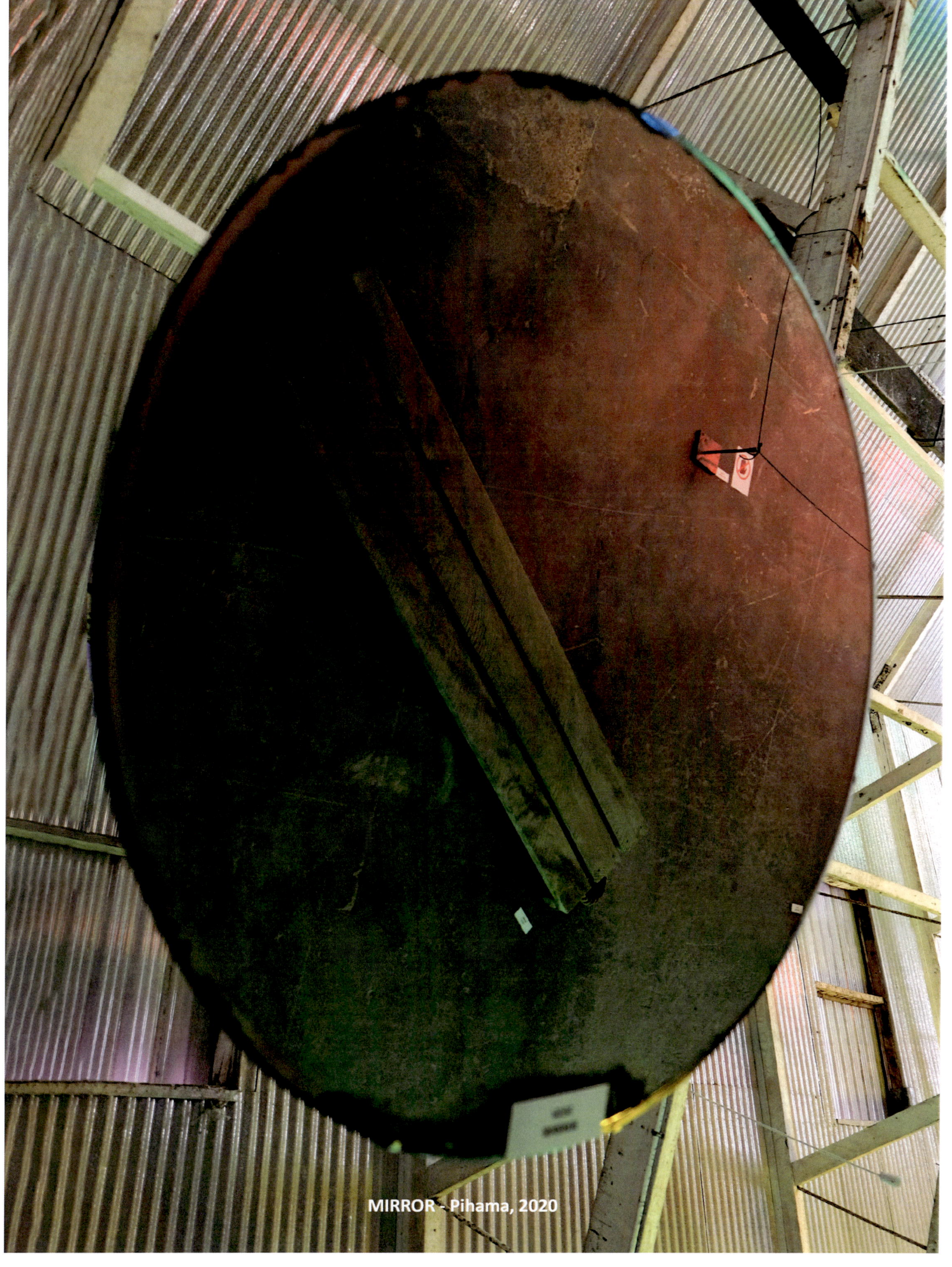

MIRROR - Pihama, 2020

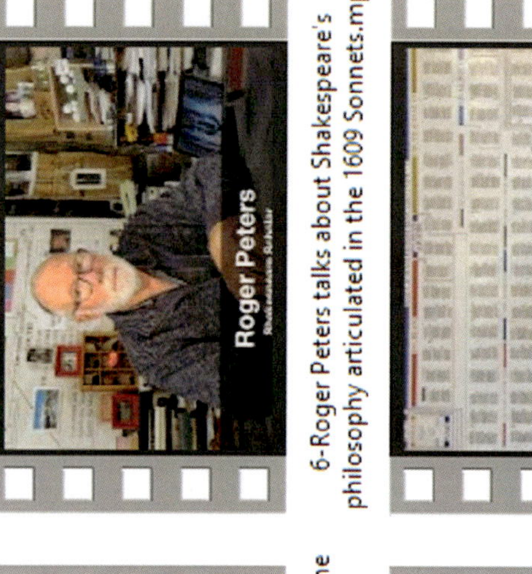

6-Roger Peters talks about Shakespeare's philosophy articulated in the 1609 Sonnets.mp4

8-Revealing the multi faceted natural logic embedded 1609 Sonnet structure No. 1.mov

14-The nine Quaternary Imprint publications detailing Shakespeare's philosophy.mp4

16-Roger Peters' talks about creating his daughter's unique Rainbow Dollshouse.mov

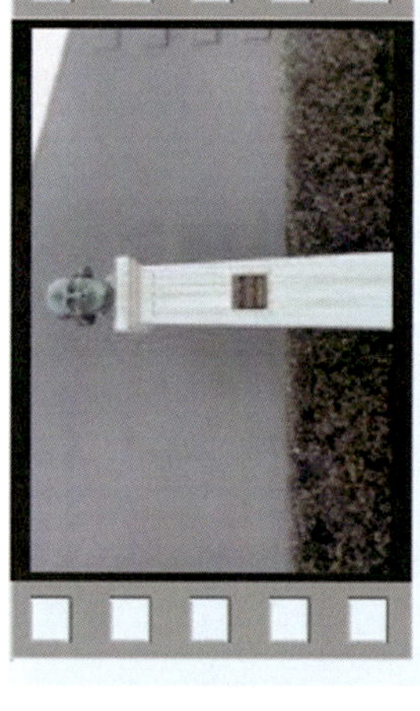

5-Understanding the relationship between Anne Hathaway and William Shakespeare.mov

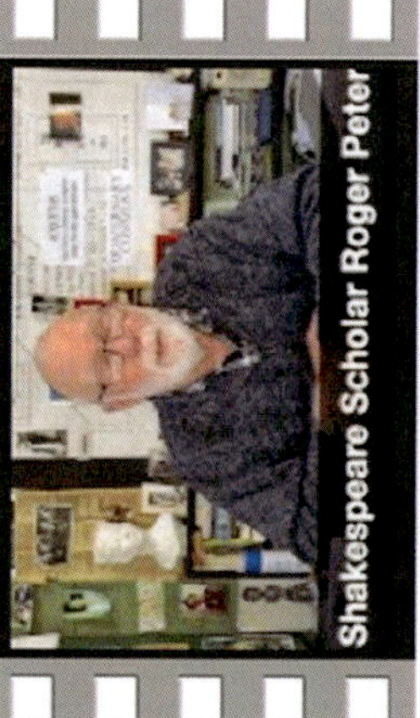

7-The structure of the nature-based philosophy within the 154 Sonnets and two sequences.mp4

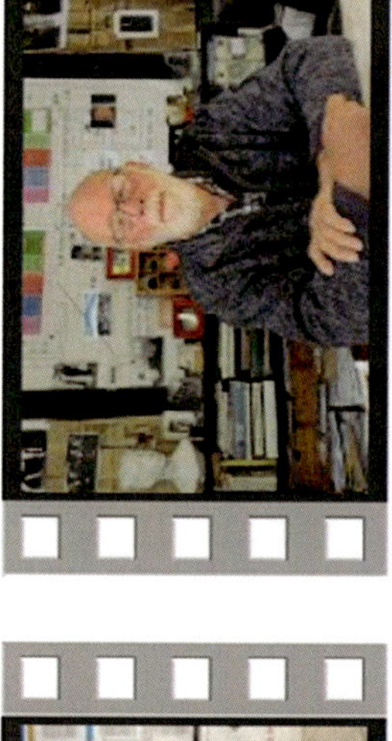

13-How those with mind-based and other prejudices are blind to the philosophy.mp4

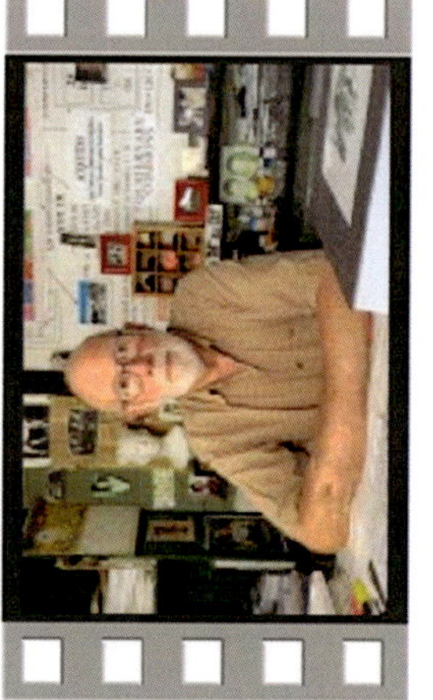

15-Exploring the many-layered Quaternary Institute and Quaternary Imprint Website.mp4

2-Roger Peters' 1998 Shakespeare bust in Prospero Place, Stratford-on-Patea.mov

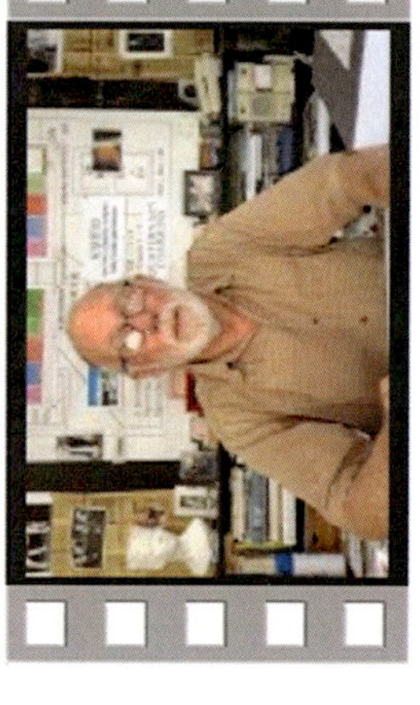

4-Roger Peters, the formation of the Quaternary Institute and the significance of the Globe.mov

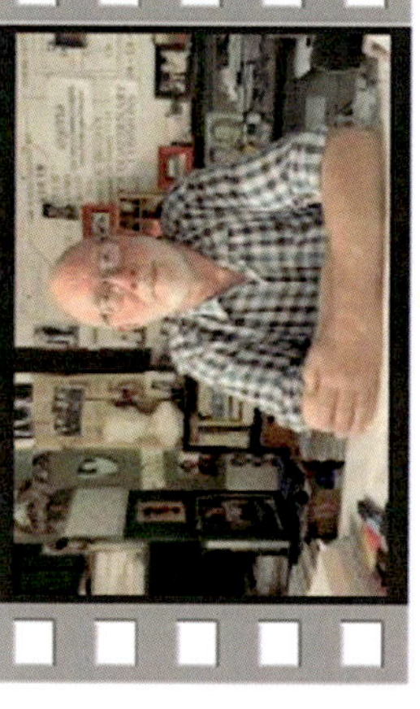

10-The Nature and other Templates derived from the 154 Sonnets and its two sequences.mp4

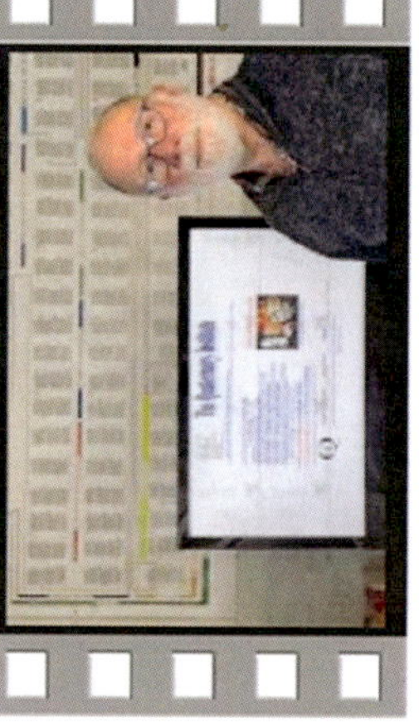

12-Using the 1609 Sonnet philosophy to understand all 36 1623 Folio Plays.mov

1-Roger Peters' Commentaries to the thirty-six plays in Shakespeare's 1623 Folio.mov

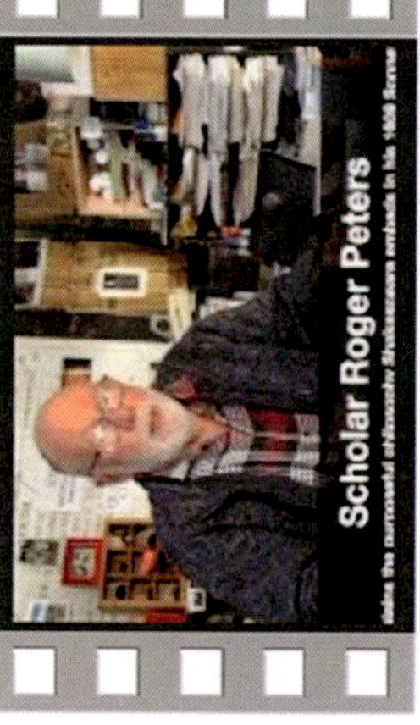

3-Roger Peters' 50-year philosophical journey through seminal art and philosophy.mov

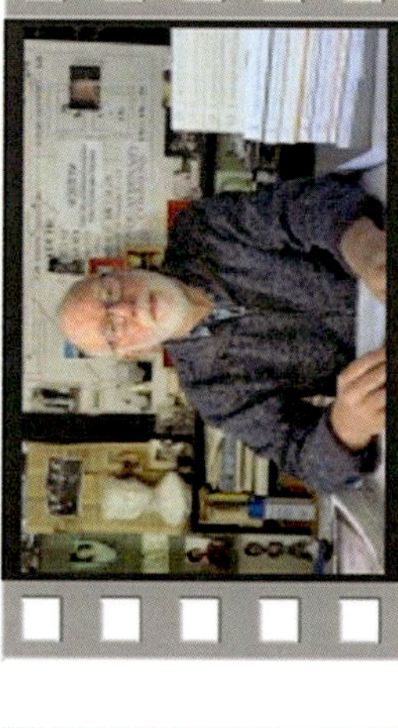

9-Revealing the multi faceted natural logic embedded 1609 Sonnet structure No. 2.mp4

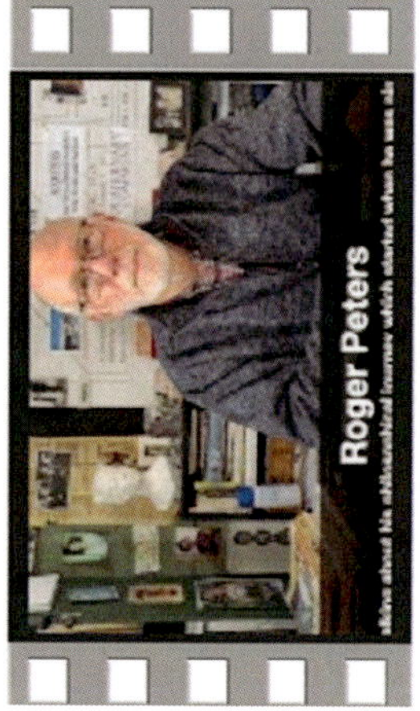

11-Shakespeare's nature-based philosophy is already evident in his Early Poems.mp4

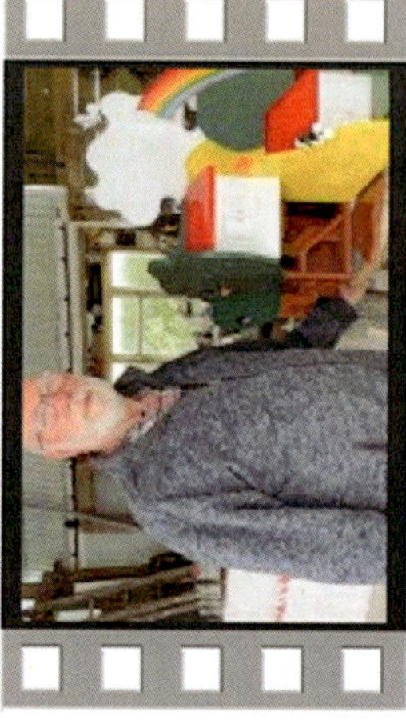

BRYAN VICKERY MEDIA - interviews with Roger Peters

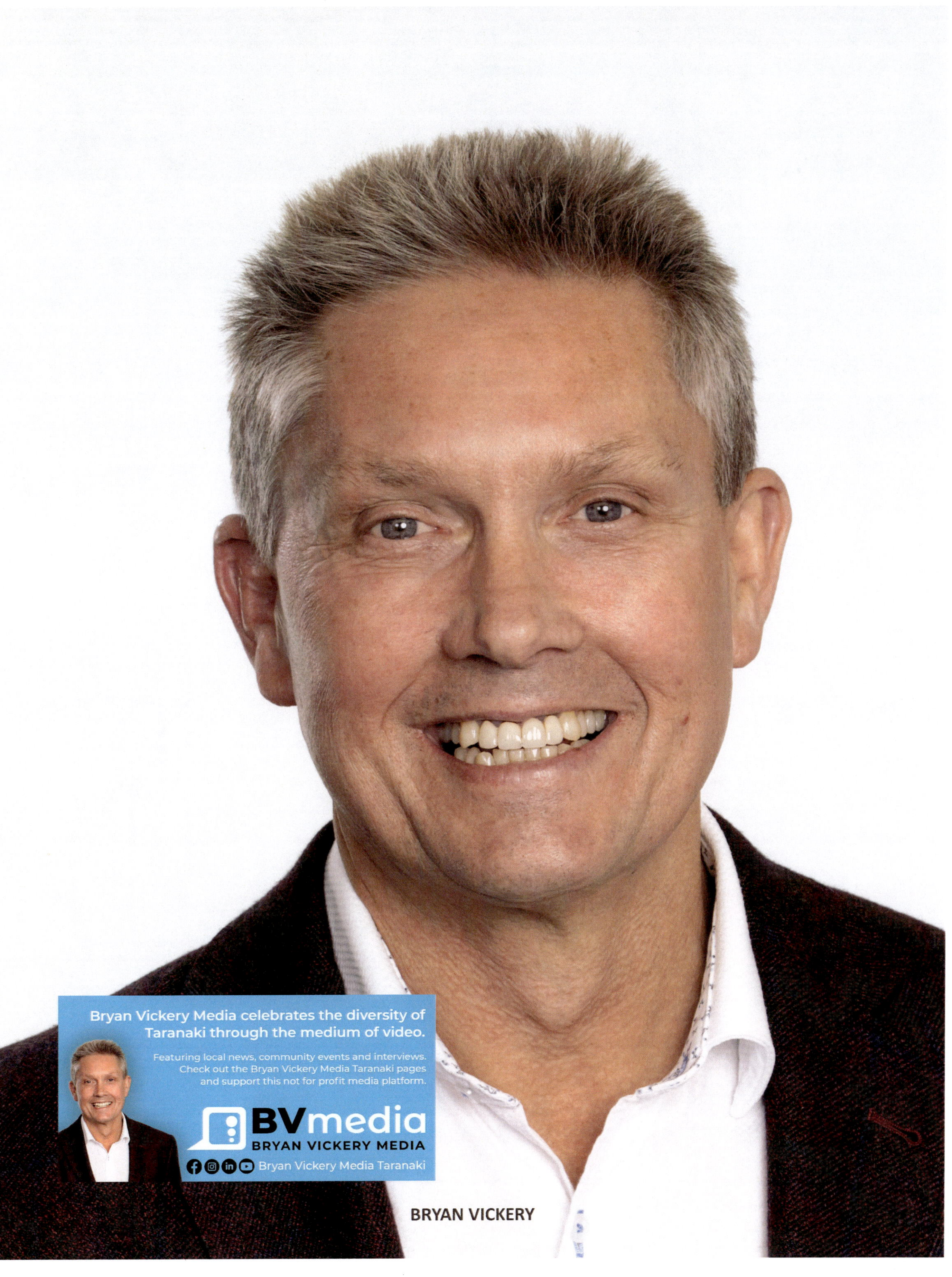

BRYAN VICKERY

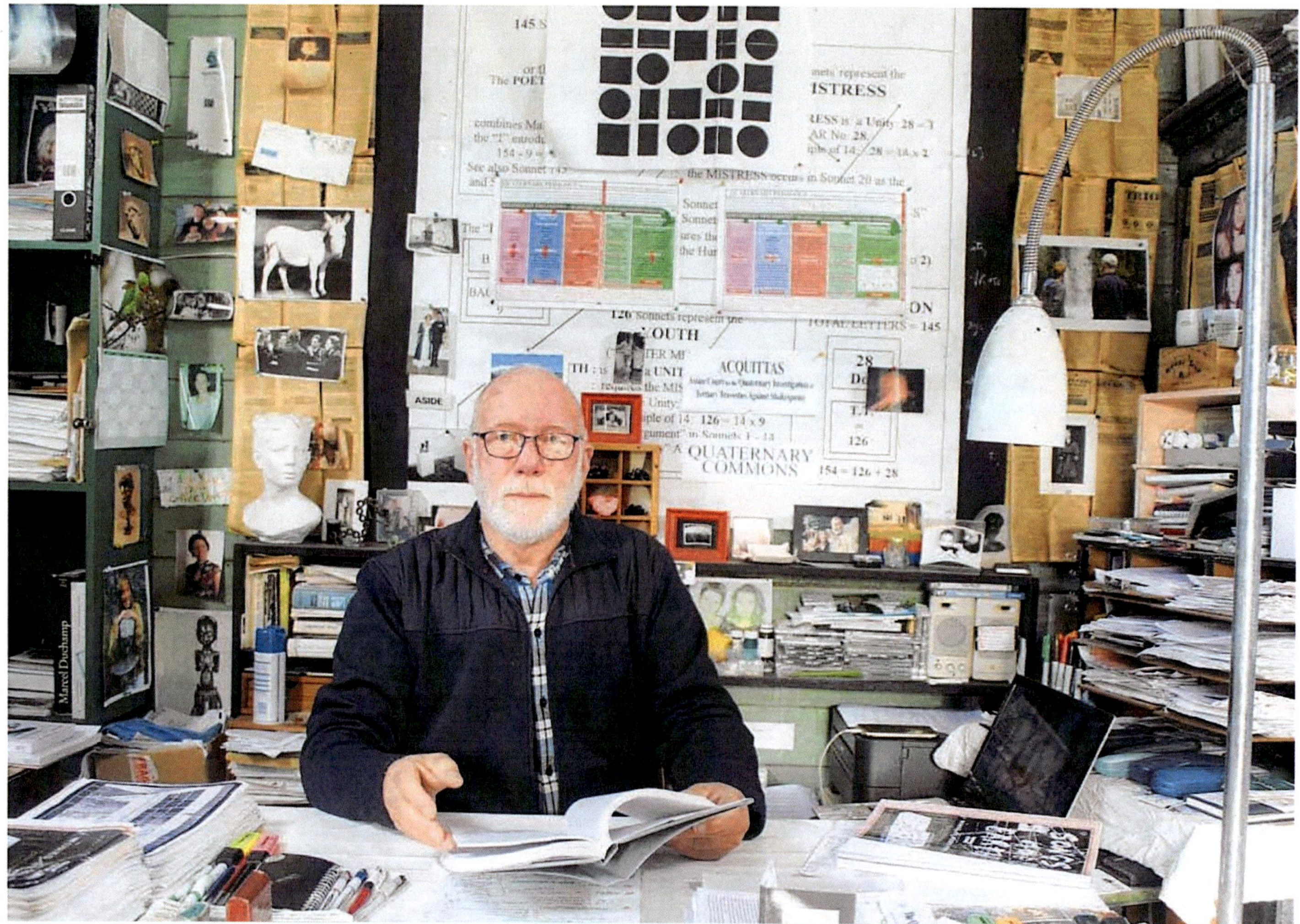

THE WHANGANUI CHRONICLE - June 15th 2024 (Full article on Page 54)

Scholar delves deeply into Bard's philosophy

"When I started investigating Shakespeare, I knew what I had learned about the other critical thinkers overarches and brings them and Shakespeare together."

Roger Peters

Stratford man's Shakespeare studies lead to numerous books

Alyssa Smith

Stratford Shakespeare scholar Roger Peters surrounded by his research and works.

PHOTO / ALYSSA SMITH

NOTEBOOK 21 Mon 27th Feb '95

Getting to know Shakespeare! from out of nowhere. It seems Shakespeare is approaching from the inside out – as any good idea should. First there was Ted Hughes' Mythic Equation as a means of appreciating something of the creative process (S) used to structure his plays and the whole sequence of plays. Then there was a sense of Shakespeare's Ethics out of a speech by Ulysses then comes the possible reading of the Sonnets as exhibiting a philosophy close to 'Human Being' – Early days but very exciting!

Momentous and yet sobering. If this truly is the Key to Shakespeare then the question again is why not before this and why now. And yet it has to be done – there can be no stopping of the process of bringing this out into the open by finding the simplest and most concise expression of its obviousness at the same time not devaluing its wonderful sense of profundity and metaphysical insight.

Whatever it has meant to study Wittgenstein, Duchamp, Mallarme, Darwin esp, then this moment confirms and extends that study into a reality as broad as it has ever been expressed. The next few weeks and months will require the will and temperament I hardly know to ensure the integrity of the insight and the integrity of its presentation.

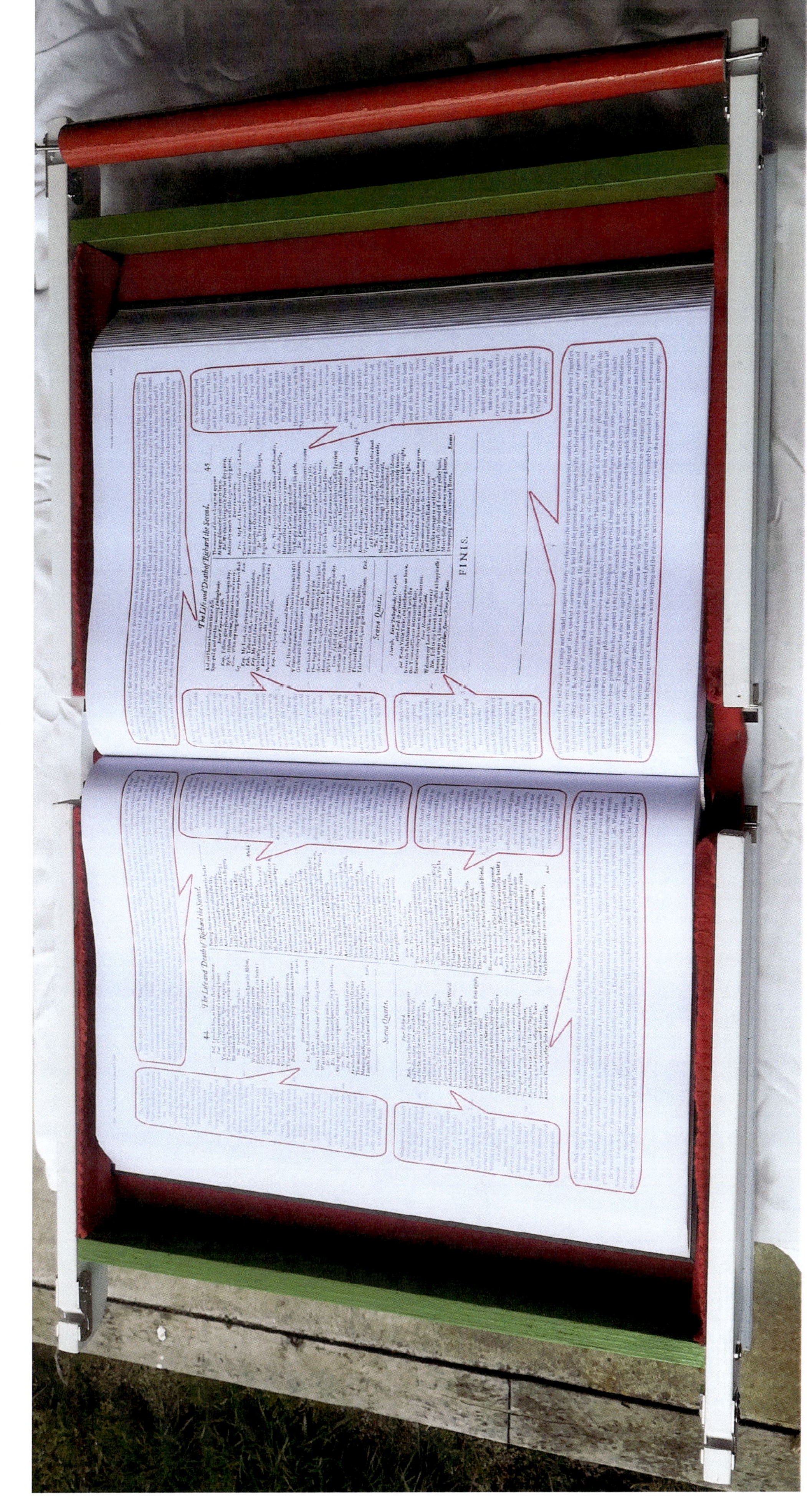

PLAY COMMENTARIES TO WILLIAM SHAKESPEARE'S 1623 FOLIO – with balloon style commentaries, 2022

Scholar delves deeply into Bard's philosophy

A sonnet reading transformed into decades of research and knowledge for Stratford Shakespeare scholar Roger Peters.

Peters has spent decades researching and writing books and essays linking philosophy to Shakespeare's work.

Although Peters was born in Whanganui, it was not where his family lived at the time, he said.

"My dad was a traffic officer so we shifted a lot for his work. My mother had gone to Whanganui to visit family and gave birth to me. She then went back to Kaikohe, and from there we lived in Ohakune briefly, then Raetihi until I was 10. I then lived in Palmerston North before attending architecture [school] and Elam School of Fine Arts in 1974 [before] moving to Eltham in 1981."

After moving around frequently as a child, Peters and his partner, Maree Horner, have spent nearly 40 years at their current home in rural Taranaki.

"All of my reading, research work and dive into deep philosophy started here. The property has been pivotal to it."

While the writing began in Taranaki, he said his interest in Shakespeare started in Whanganui in 1995.

"I had an exhibition there. My friend was part of a Shakespeare group and he encouraged me to go. We spent a weekend reading Shakespeare's sonnets, half on Saturday and the other half on Sunday.

"I spent 25 years studying Austrian philosopher Ludwig Josef Johann Wittgenstein, French painter-writer Marcel Duchamp, geologist and naturist Charles Darwin and French poet Stephane Mallarme. So, when I started investigating Shakespeare, I knew what I had learned about the other critical thinkers overarches and brings them and Shakespeare together."

After thinking about the sonnets, he discovered he was most interested in the philosophy of The Bard, Peters said.

"At the next meeting, we were asked what we thought of the sonnets. My answer focused on philosophy, and from there I started unpacking the works to see what appealed to my investigative and philosophical mind. It was the connections between male and female, nature and the sensations of the mind."

From there, Peters spent five years visiting well-known national scholars, lecturers and philosophers.

At the time he was also writing his first set of books, *Shakespeare's Sonnet Philosophy*, unpacking how The Bard structured his nature-based philosophy into the sonnets.

"I received a grant from the Taranaki Electricity Trust to get 1000 copies printed. This four-volume set is 1760 pages. The series took me 10 years to complete."

After publishing his first series, he set up the Quaternary Institute.

"It's representative of the fourth level of education, going from primary, secondary, tertiary and then quaternary. The studies I have done and the works I've published are above the tertiary level. In tertiary, people are taught to stick to their topic but, for me, I delve deeper and cross-examine."

His partner Horner runs Quaternary Imprint, the publishing firm attached to the institute. She helped Peters republish his *Shakespeare's Sonnet Philosophy* series in 2018-2020.

"I learned how to self-publish using Ingram Content Group in America. It has a lot of benefits, including that it's available globally."

Peters then published five more works — *Shakespeare and Mature Love* (2017), *Shakespeare's Global Philosophy* (2017), *Shakespeare's Philosophy Illustrated — Quaternary Teaching Aids* (2018), *Quaternary Essays* (2021) and *Play Commentaries to William Shakespeare's 1623 Folio* (2022).

When Peters and Horner aren't working on research or publishing Peters' work, they create art. Peters' work has been exhibited in the Auckland City Art Gallery (1975) and Whanganui's Sarjeant Gallery (1994).

Peters said both he and Horner graduated from Elam School of Fine Arts. While Horner paints, Peters creates sculptures, dollhouses and other works.

"My current project is a dollhouse I designed while in Auckland for art school. I entered it in a Stratford art competition in 1982 and won first prize. However, I was looking at the original dollhouse and thought that I could expand the dollhouse, creating new components of it. I will create 10 similar to give one each to my grandchildren."

He has also created smaller dollhouses out of aluminium to gift to family members.

"There are 18 to gift to my children, their partners and my seven grandchildren."

One of his artworks is on permanent display at Stratford's Prospero Place. The bronze sculpture was gifted to Stratford District Council and placed on a plinth in 1998.

He said having multiple projects on the go is important with regard to keeping a clear mind.

"It helps keep your mind grounded. You could work on one thing and switch to the other and back again."

He said he planned to shift focus, writing monographs on Duchamp, Mallarme, Wittgenstein and Darwin.

"I'm looking forward to getting those projects under way. I also want to publish a book of Maree's artworks and then another book of my artworks."

He said he had a lot to work on.

"Between my research, writing, art and odd jobs around the property, there's lots to keep me entertained."

> "When I started investigating Shakespeare, I knew what I had learned about the other critical thinkers overarches and brings them and Shakespeare together."
> Roger Peters

...continued from Page 54; THE WHANGANUI CHRONICLE - June 15th 2024

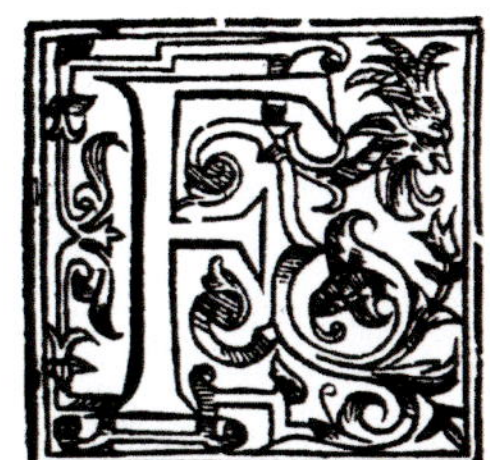

ROM the moſt able, to him that can but ſpell: There you are number'd. We had rather you were weighd. Eſpecially, when the fate of all Bookes depends vpon your capacities : and not of your heads alone, but of your purſes. Well ! It is now publique, & you wil ſtand for your priuiledges wee know : to read, and cenſure. Do ſo, but buy it firſt. That doth beſt commend a Booke, the Stationer ſaies. Then, how odde ſoeuer your braines be, or your wiſedomes, make your licence the ſame, and ſpare.

It had bene a thing, we confeſſe, worthie to haue bene wiſhed, that the Author himſelfe had liu'd to haue ſet forth, and ouerſeen his owne writings ; But ſince it hath bin ordain'd otherwiſe, and he by death departed from that right, we pray you do not envie his Friends, the office of their care, and paine, to haue collected & publiſh'd them ; and ſo to haue publiſh'd them, as where (before) you were abuſ'd with diuerſe ſtolne, and ſurreptitious copies, maimed, and deformed by the frauds and ſtealthes of iniurious impoſtors, that expoſ'd them : euen thoſe, are now offer'd to your view cur'd, and perfect of their limbes ; and all the reſt, abſolute in their numbers, as he conceiued thē. Who, as he was a happie imitator of Nature, was a moſt gentle expreſſer of it. His mind and hand went together : And what he thought, he vttered with that eaſineſſe, that wee haue ſcarſe receiued from him a blot in his papers. But it is not our prouince, who onely gather his works, and giue them you, to praiſe him. It is yours that reade him. And there we hope, to your diuers capacities, you will finde enough, both to draw, and hold you : for his wit can no more lie hid, then it could be loſt. Reade him, therefore ; and againe, and againe : And if then you doe not like him, ſurely you are in ſome manifeſt danger, not to vnderſtand him. And ſo we leaue you to other of his Friends, whom if you need, can bee your guides : if you neede them not, you can leade your ſelues, and others. And ſuch Readers we wiſh him.

A 3

Iohn Heminge.
Henrie Condell.

WILLIAM SHAKESPEARE'S 1623 FOLIO, Preface

NOTEBOOK 22 Tues 22nd Aug '95

Do not mind, it doesn't matter, of course there is time· If it's a fact then be happy that it might have been otherwise· Why Hurry the world is all around, the world already knows· It merely requires exquisite timing to remind it· What a waste of energy if the time is not right· Just because in 1989 what seems central is overlooked then maybe in 1998 the lights will shine· Meantime use the space to refine refine refine·

NOTEBOOK 23 Sat 28th Sept '96

Patience, thoroughness, incisiveness, persistence === Last night I came to realise why Mac Jackson treated me so badly last year· Now that I have seen the 1996 Edition of Cambridge 'Sonnets' in which his theory of compositors is used in justifying Emendations in the discussion of textual matters·
I can only surmise that at that time last year at least the CUP Edition was being edited or even prepared for Press· His extraordinary behaviour of cutting short the time he had originally allowed for our meeting in Nov '95 and a total unwillingness to assist and a need to want to 'Agree to differ' suggest to me that something else was indeed the case·
My response now must be measured but decisive· As the philosophical aspects of my position are becoming clearer and as the Number and Symbol system seems so evident even to others and as my understanding of Duchamp and Wittgenstein and Darwin seems to be acknowledged as fair and appropriate there is but this matter of emendations and that is but a factual concern in that Mac J's work has no basis in other than that dimension·
A first task will be to analyse his suppositions now they are exposed in the CUP Edition to see their internal consistency i·e· to see if they are even consistent in their own terms· From my point of view they have no answer for the philosophical critique and numerological consistency this understanding seems to have,
So ease out and work to put in place all the necessary components to present to some form of publication·

NOTEBOOK 22 Wed 20th Oct '95

Towards the end of an analysis of the alterations to the Sonnets· Out of the 60 or so from Modern Editions I find only 2 are at all justified or justifiable· That is extraordinary· Not only is there a thematic scheme in the Sonnets consistent with my understanding developed in 'Human Being' and not only do I have a numerology consistent with that understanding and the sequence of Sonnets as published in 'Q' in 1609 now there is possible a critique of past changes in the same basis and it shows that all past editors have been too ready to alter the Sonnets basically because they have misunderstood them·
And happening at the same time over the last month or so Ruapehu has been erupting· What magic is it not necessary to imagine or conjure by spurious means·

NOTEBOOK 23 Wed 28th Aug '96

However is it possible to communicate an understanding that is at once so obvious and at the same time so rare· Nowhere in the annuals of Philosophy is there a mention of that of Shakespeare because, it seems, no one really suspects it is there· That means that even an insight as that of the last Sunday regarding the importance of Sn 14 must wait for an audience educated in even the possibility of such an event·

ART
ARTIST
ARTICLES

(1972-2024)

STRATFORD
DISTRICT
LIBRARY

Bridget Roper

Librarian

Dolls house wins exhibition prize

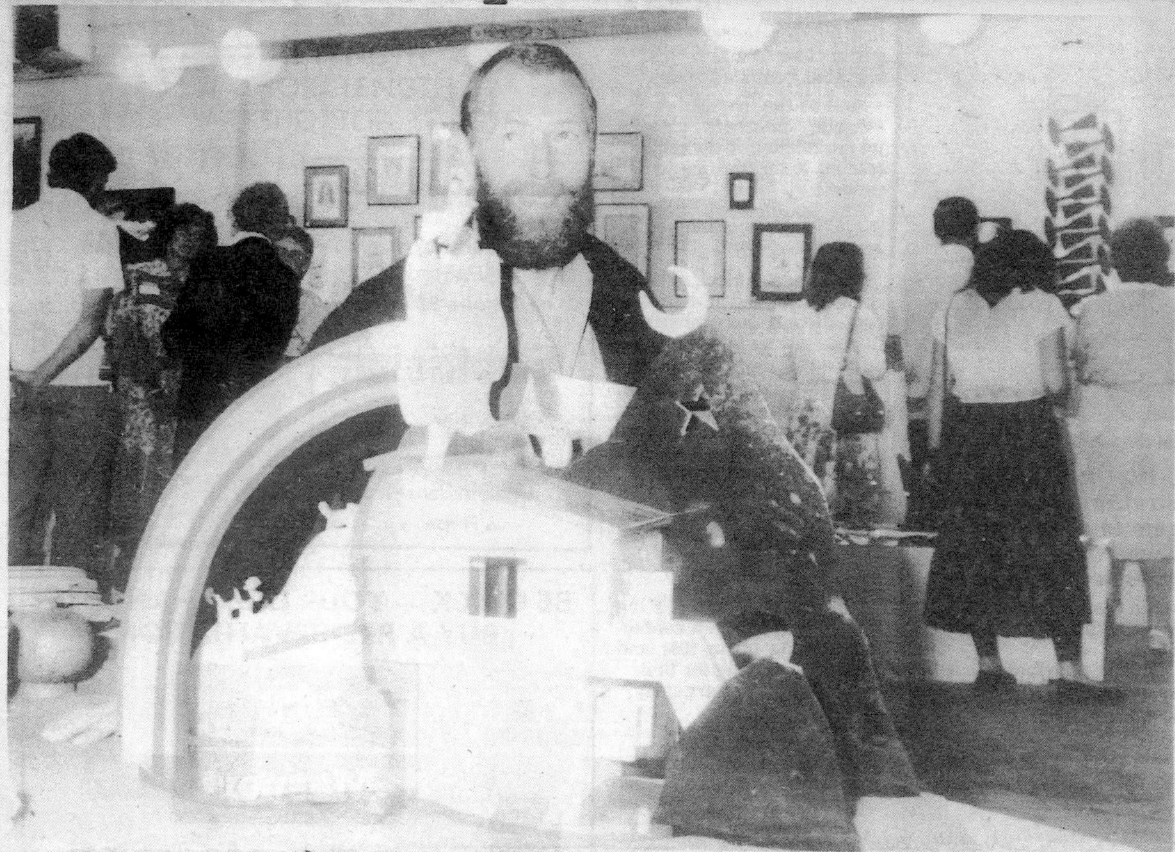

Roger Peters and his dolls house (pictured), won the major award at the Introduction to the Arts exhibition which opened in Stratford last week.

Judges Rusty Ritchie, potter, Ann Smith, an art teacher from New Plymouth and Joan Comer, Registrar from the Govett-Brewster gave Mr Peters the award for the most original, colourful and visually exciting piece on display.

Ms Smith said the house, painted in bright colours, attracted attention and the colours worked well.

"It's designed for its purpose - for children."

Mr Peters said he has made dolls houses for about eight years, starting with some fairly ordinary designs.

But gradually he has changed them to produce the colourful and different house on display.

"It started off as a very ordinary dolls house and I just pushed it around," he said.

"That's what I do - push ideas as far as they can go because in the end you get something that is quite unique."

The judges awarded five merit awards to exhibitors Sue and Herb Spannagl, Fergus Power, Irene Major, Lis Morton and Marrianne Muggeridge.

Mr Ritchie said the Spannagl pots were good honest pots - "something which appeals to me personally."

Fergus Power worked in a very different medium, Ms Smith said, and the judges felt his underwater photography mastered the technique.

"We feel his photographs are quite magnificent," Ms Smith said.

Ms Smith said Irene Major's patchwork and embroidery showed her skill and fine technique.

"We love the subtle colours in the quilt and the effect."

Lis Morton's quilts were very original, bright and quite witty, she said. "We loved them very much."

And Marrianne Muggeridge's oil paintings showed her skill as an artist.

"She's got an eye for the unusual," Ms Smith said.

Introduction to the arts has been going very well, said organisers Lis Morton and Kirsty Callaghan.

About 200 people visited it every day and many pieces had been sold.

Kaponga musician Alan Muggeridge was there on Saturday and many people had commented on how good the music was, Lis said.

Alan may return for the open day this Saturday, but several artists will definitely be there.

Potters, painters and screen printers will demonstrate their art and members of the public will be able to try their hands at various art forms.

Kirsty said the demonstrations were popular on Saturday, particularly with the children.

The exhibition will open late nights, including the Wednesday before Christmas, and Saturday mornings.

Introduction to the Arts is in the Prestige building in Fenton Street daily from 10 am to 4 pm. It closes on December 21.

THE STRATFORD PRESS - December 1984

NOTEBOOK 6 Mon 14th Oct '85

I have a mere pond here that has no depth and knows no limits. I try to regulate my fantasies within the physicality of a droplet. Like a traveller content to stay at home I want the rain to transfigure the ships of my imagination. Last night I died again for the possibilities. The machine guns, the seaside, the obscuring wardrobe, the painting of death, the gallery of concern threw me sleepless in front of our apprehension for disaster in the marriage bed. Tired but catalysed we dragged ourselves through the conversations of the small hours. Maybe only those bodyless thoughts have the power to heal for today I can once again accept the union of differing souls cast together in love and procreation.

That bond is a 'given', a salvation in its finiteness. That is our craft, our future direction sealed forever in a moment irrevocable. My own boat, my personal voyage is laden with stone anchors that seek a draught within the play of my line. Every moment I would lie down with an easy grace if this constant evocation gave me the measure at will. The droplet though has no dimensions except in a fleeting way. The constant renewal of that way echoes the uncertainty of our end.

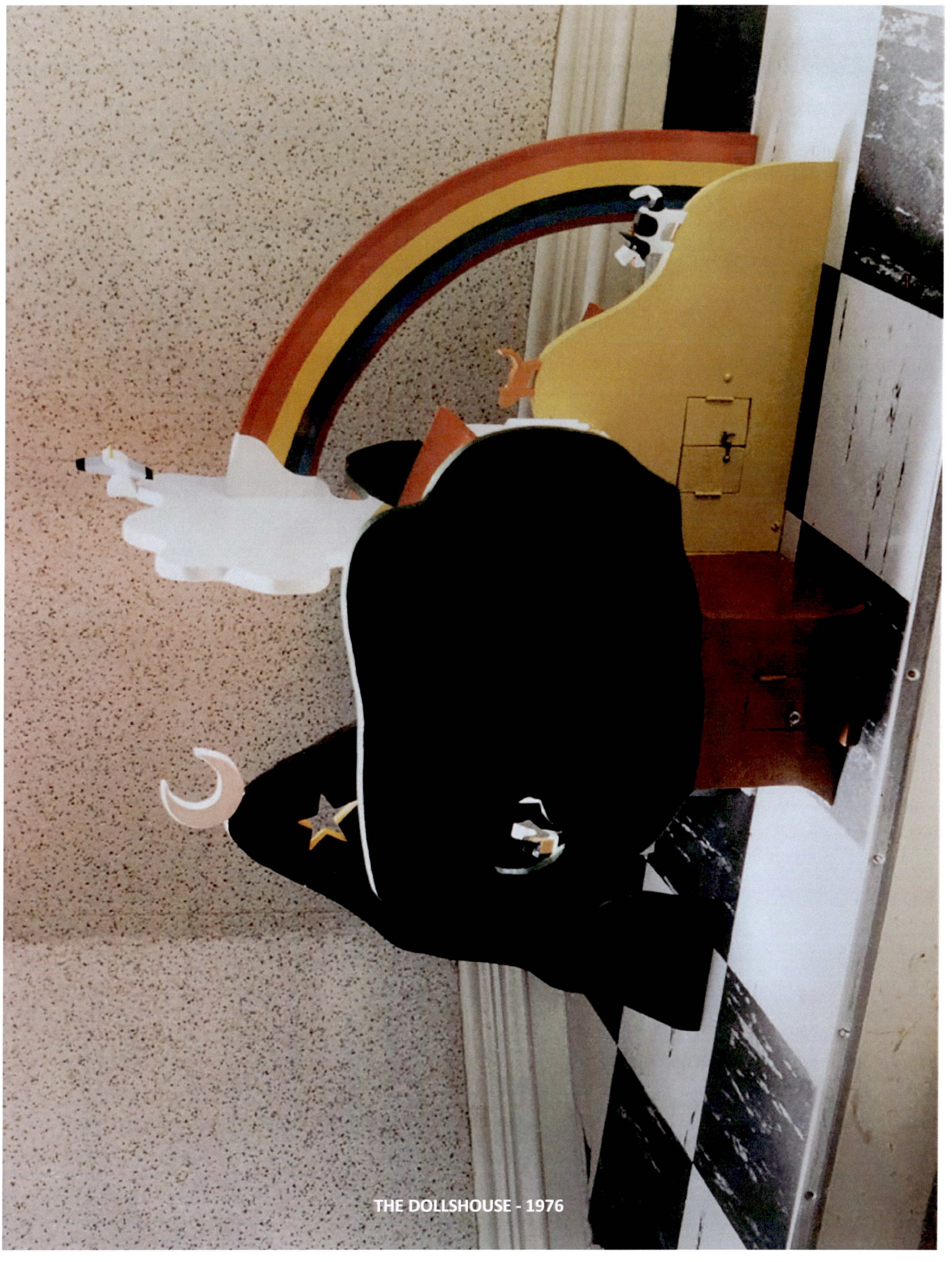

THE DOLLSHOUSE - 1976

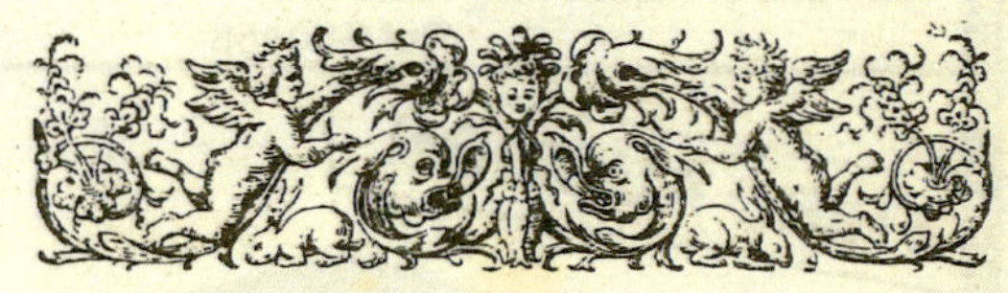

SHAKE-SPEARES
S O N N E T S

Kindly sponsored by:
Maree, Talia, Teresa,
Katie and Lucy
for the year 2000

This is the 79th in a series of presentations of "Shake-speare's Sonnets" featuring a Sonnet with a commentary by Roger Peters of the Stratford Shakespeare Society.

Sonnet 91
Some glory in their birth, some in their skill,
Some in their wealth, some in their bodies force,
Some in their garments though new-fangled ill:
Some in their Hawks and Hounds, some in their Horse.
And every humor hath his adjunct pleasure,
Wherein it finds a joy above the rest,
But these particulars are not my measure,
All these I better in one general best.
Thy love is better than high birth to me,
Richer than wealth, prouder than garments cost,
Of more delight than Hawks or Horses be:
And having thee, of all men's pride I boast.
Wretched in this alone, that thou may'st take
All this away, and me most wretched make.

Sonnet 92
But do thy worst to steal thy self away,
For term of life thou art assured mine,
And life no longer than thy love will stay,
For it depends upon that love of thine.
Then need I not to fear the worst of wrongs,
When in the least of them my life hath end,
I see, a better state to me belongs
Than that, which on thy humour doth depend.
Thou can'st not vex me with inconstant mind,
Since that my life on thy revolt doth lie,
Oh what a happy title do I find,
Happy to have thy love, happy to die!
But what's so blessed fair that fears no blot,
Thou may'st be false, and yet I know it not.

Sonnets 91, 92, and 93, are logically connected by a "but" and then a "so". They need to be considered together, but space allows that 91 and 92 be considered here and 93 in the next column.

In the first 8 lines of 91, the Poet regards "birth (rank), skill, wealth, bodies force, garments, Hawks Hounds and Horse," as being of less value than the "love" of the youth. The love of the youth is "better" because it provides the key to "all men's pride" (91.12). The sexual pun on "pride", suggests the youth possesses an attribute essential to "all men". From the beginning, the Sonnets have represented the logical need to increase as prior to every other attribute. The couplet concludes, that "this alone", if "taken away" by the youth, would make the Poet "most wretched"

Sonnet 92, reveals the reason the Poet does not need "to fear the worst of wrongs" (92.5). The youth cannot "steal away" (92.1) because, consistent with the philosophy of the Sonnets, the condition of youth, and so the Poet's own youth, is a part of life. The state of youth, and the consequences of being young, remain with the Poet (and so all men) for the "term of life" (92.2). The Poet is "happy" to acknowledge the "love" of youth as a necessary part of his life just as he is "happy to die" (92.12). The couplet notes, ironically, that while there is nothing so "blessed" that it cannot also be "false", philosophically the role of the youth's love in life cannot be false.

The Stratford Poetry Group meets monthly. Phone: 06-764 6497.

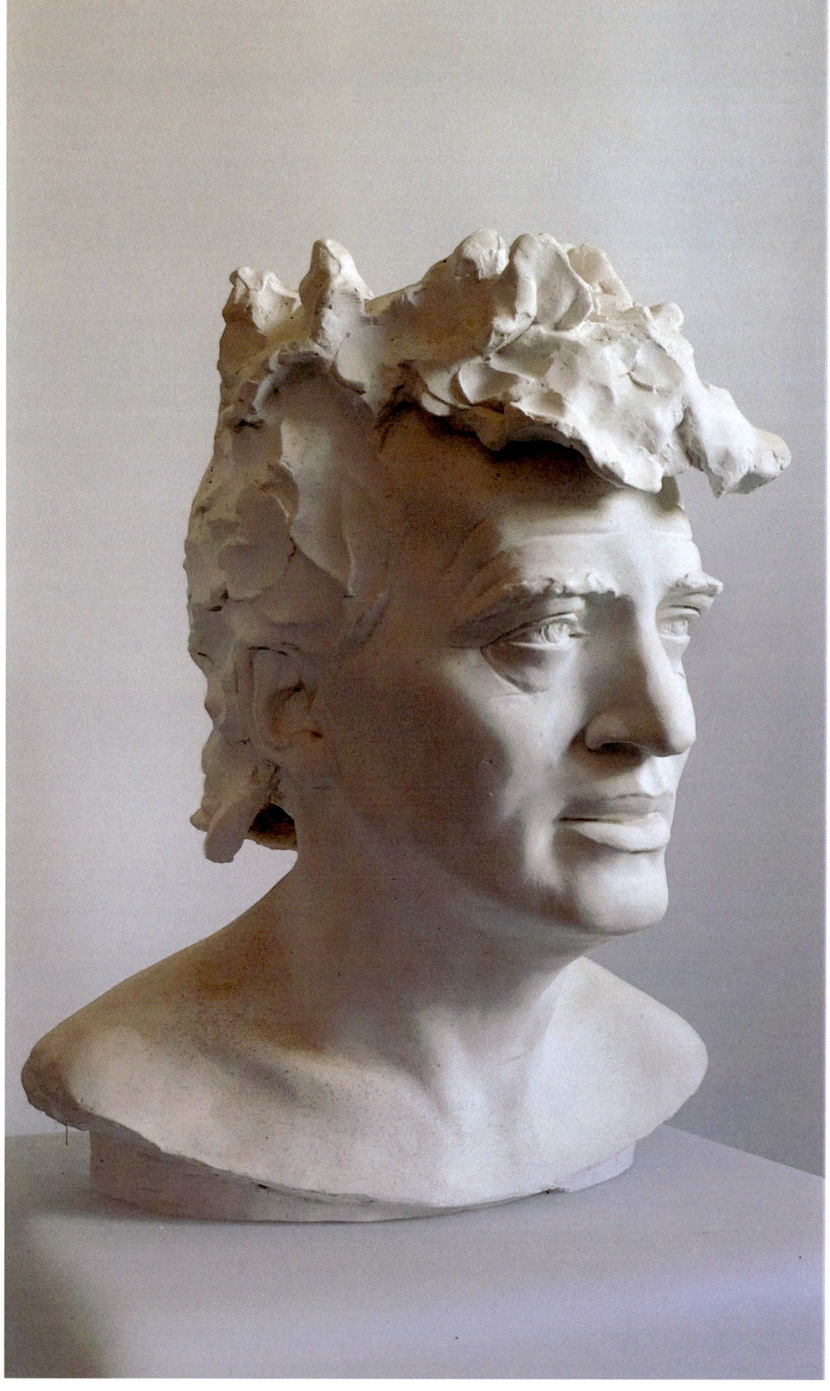

ABOVE: RAY CLEAVER, Plaster, 1992
The Stratford Press Editor

LEFT: THE STRATFORD PRESS,
January 17th 2000

RIGHT: SHAKESPEARE SONNET COLUMN
Business & Other Sponsors 1996 to 2002

BUSINESS *& Other* SPONSORS *Shakespeare Sonnet Column*
STRATFORD PRESS 1996 – 2002 (Editor Ray Cleaver)

Perera's Topline Bookshop Stratford	Crown Limousines Stratford
Backstage Café Stratford	Roger Hignett Chairmen Community Arts Council
O.Neill's Brewing Company Ngaere	Riverlands Eltham
Axemans Tavern Stratford	DesignNZ Stratford
Moss Rocard & Smith Chemists Stratford	Lithgow and Associates Chartered Accountants Stratford
Cottage Pottery & Craft Eltham	Stratford Engineering
Crossroads Music & Computer Centre Stratford	Broadway Motels Stratford
Eltham BP	Johnson & Webber Optometrists Stratford
Shakespeare's Trading Centre Stratford	Dr M. Smith Page St Medical Centre Stratford
Ashton Projects Services Ltd Hamilton	Stallard Farm Bed & Breakfast Stratford
Connell Creative Photography Eltham	Firth Certified Concrete Stratford
Stratford Auto Electrical Ltd	Taranaki Medlab Pathologists Stratford
Joe Bros Fruiterers Stratford	Dean Cameron's Tyre Centre Stratford
Dimock's Retravision Stratford	Egmont Tanneries Ltd Stratford
Rosen-Argus Printing Co Ltd Eltham	LansNZ Stratford
Standard Machinery & Hire Stratford	Perera's Topline Bookshop Stratford
Unichem Mackays Pharmacy Stratford	Taranaki Steelformers Stratford
Campbell's Holiday Shoppe Stratford	Urban Attitude Café & Bar Stratford
Lazer 1 Hour Photo & Copy Centre Stratford	Pioneer Village Villa Café Stratford
Stratford Timber & Hammer Hardware Stratford	Gordon & Mooney Barristers & Solicitors Stratford
Penniall & Jordan Stratford	Challenge! Stratford
Eltham Major Decorating	Central Taranaki Veterinary Services
Stratford Shakespeare Society	Dawson Falls Mountain Lodge
Dippa Strippa Midhurst	Silhouette Bar Stratford
Graham Jordan Electrical Eltham	Mike Childs Builder Stratford
McDonald Real Estate Stratford	London Car Sales Stratford & Eltham
Excelsior House The Bike Shop Stratford	Central House Movers Stratford
Contemporary Art Foundry Fielding	Eltham Apiaries
Stratford District Veterinary Services	Kevin Davis Panelbeater Stratford
Stratford Office Furniture	Jordan Horton & Co Ltd Chartered Accountants Stratford
Soundvision Stratford	Sayer Bros Stratford
Eagers Furnishing Centre Stratford	Eltham District Veterinary Services
Stratford Décor & Lighting	Mountain House Mount Egmont
Taranaki Pump & Filtration Stratford	Oak Wood House & Antiques Stratford
Toyworld Stratford	Graeme Goble Motors Stratford
Taranaki Fresh Fruit & Vege Stratford	Eltham Pharmacy
Norwood Farm Machinery Centre Stratford	World-Wide Sires Midhurst
Clive Cullen Architects Hawera	Mary Anne Costello Dentist Stratford
Mike Radich Wine Merchant Stratford	Jamieson Motors Stratford
No Name Computer Shop Stratford	Harvey World Travel Eltham
P & C Hilford Panelbeating Hawera	St Mary's Diocesan School English Department Stratford
Mountain Motors Stratford Ltd	Ken Maul Automotive
Austco Communications (NZ) Ltd Auckland	Stratford Table Tennis Club
National Mutual Stratford	Eltham Four Square
Thomson O'Neil & Co Solicitors Stratford	Heavy Machinery Services Stratford
Taranaki Farmers Stratford	The Windmill Café & Catering Stratford
Selectrix 100% Stratford	Sovereign Life Insurance Midhurst
Caltex Stratford	Thomson O'Neil & Co Solicitors Stratford
J. A. Reed Joinery Ltd Stratford	Globe Stratford
Central Alfa Laval Agri Stratford	Paperplus Stratford
Lobbs Craftsmen Plumbers Stratford	Taranaki Galvanisers Stratford
TSB Bank Stratford	Cottage Antiques Eltham
The Mill Liquor Save Stratford	Stratford High School
TSB Reality Stratford	Taranaki Electricity trust Kings Theatre Stratford
Eagers Funeral Services Stratford	Stratford Shakespeare Society
Sheehy's Clothing Ltd Eltham	Past President Stratford Shakespeare Society
Ralph Vosseler Barrister & Solicitor Stratford	Inter-University Drama Weekend
Maree, Talia, Teresa, Katie and Lucy for the year 2000	*For Mary Kelly Greaves (1918-2001)*
In Memory of Ellen Martha Peters	*Maureen for All Librarians*
Mrs Bernadette Peters for Husband Bob (1920-2001)	*Mrs B Peters for Son's Birthday*
Clarice Blyde Horner	*Natalia Peters*
Lesley Dowding	*The Bullen Family for Sally and Michael's Wedding*

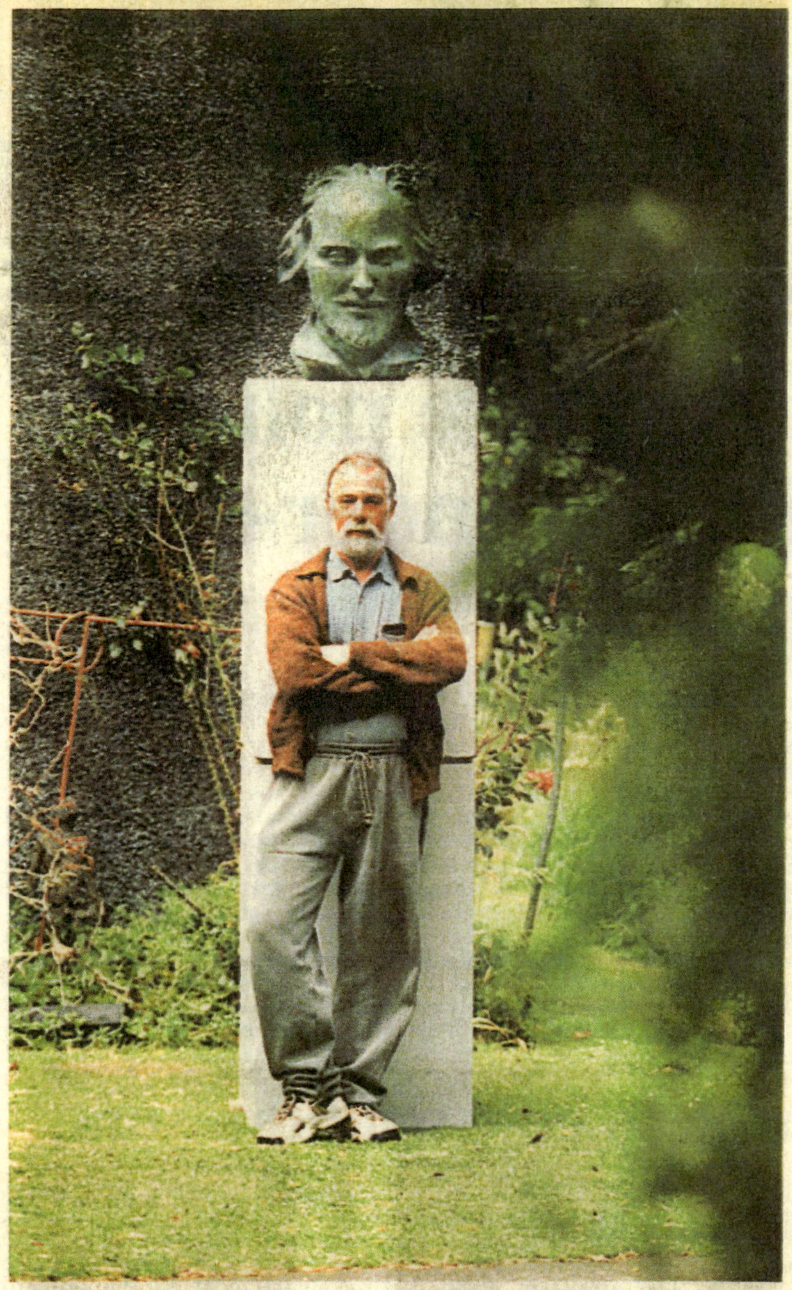

Larger than life

BRONZE BARD: Eltham sculptor Roger Peters admires his latest creation — a twice-lifesize bronze bust of the Bard of Avon, William Shakespeare.

Recently cast in Feilding, the bust will go on show during the Stratford Shakespeare Festival, which will run from February 14 to March 18. After the festival, the bust will have a permanent place in some place of honour as yet undecided.

Peters said he might also produce various additional versions of the bust in either concrete-and-marble-dust or concrete-and-white-sand; they would be displayed at locations which might include the information centre, the Fletcher Challenge Energy King's Theatre and a festival sponsor's shop.

Entries will close on February 1 for a sonnet-writing contest organised by Peters. There will be two divisions in the Perera's Topline Bookshop Sonnet Competition — a secondary schools class and an open class. Judging will be done by Gwen Smith, who will be in New Zealand as a member of a visiting Shakespearean group.

Photo: SCOTT BARBOUR
Story: MARK BIRCH

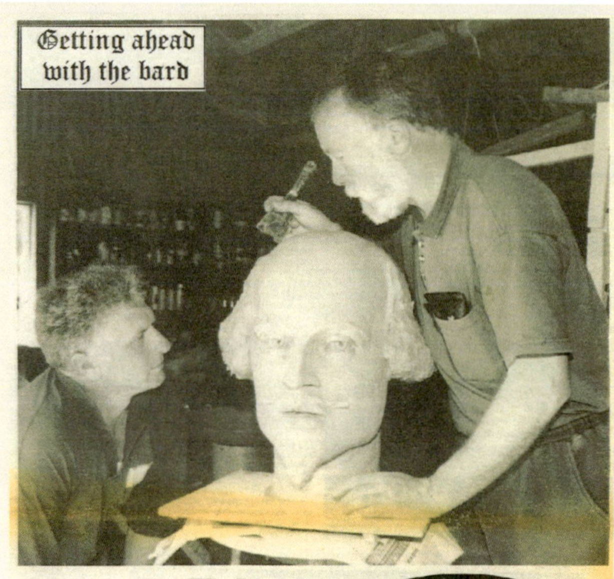

Working on a clay sculpture of William Shakespeare is Kaponga artist Roger Peters, watched closely by Stratford Shakespeare Society president Mike Radich. The making of the head is a Shakespeare Society project and it will be cast in bronze and placed in a prominent place in Stratford.

ABOVE: THE DAILY NEWS - October 9th 1997

NOTEBOOK 21 Thurs 23rd Mar '95

Don't presume too much nor presume too little. When it comes to the Sonnets of (S) see only what is there and see everything that is there. It seems that historically the objectivity brought to bear upon them has been woeful esp in regard to aesthetic appreciation — as if all other modes of understanding have created a blindness for the actual artistic accomplishment and what seems to be the explicit poetic exposition of that achievement. The whole has yet to be seem but the part is nearly whole enough!

NOTEBOOK 21 Tues 11th Apr '95

Who's to say. And if they could say so what would it come to. Why introduce a possibility into consciousness when consciousness will reject it like a gob of spit. Common sense has a poor public and worse even a poor place in the History of Wisdom. If indeed there is a Key to the Sonnets and it is the one I suspect then it will need the labours of 9 muscles at least to ensure its reception and its promoters sanity.

LEFT: THE DAILY NEWS - January 13th 1998

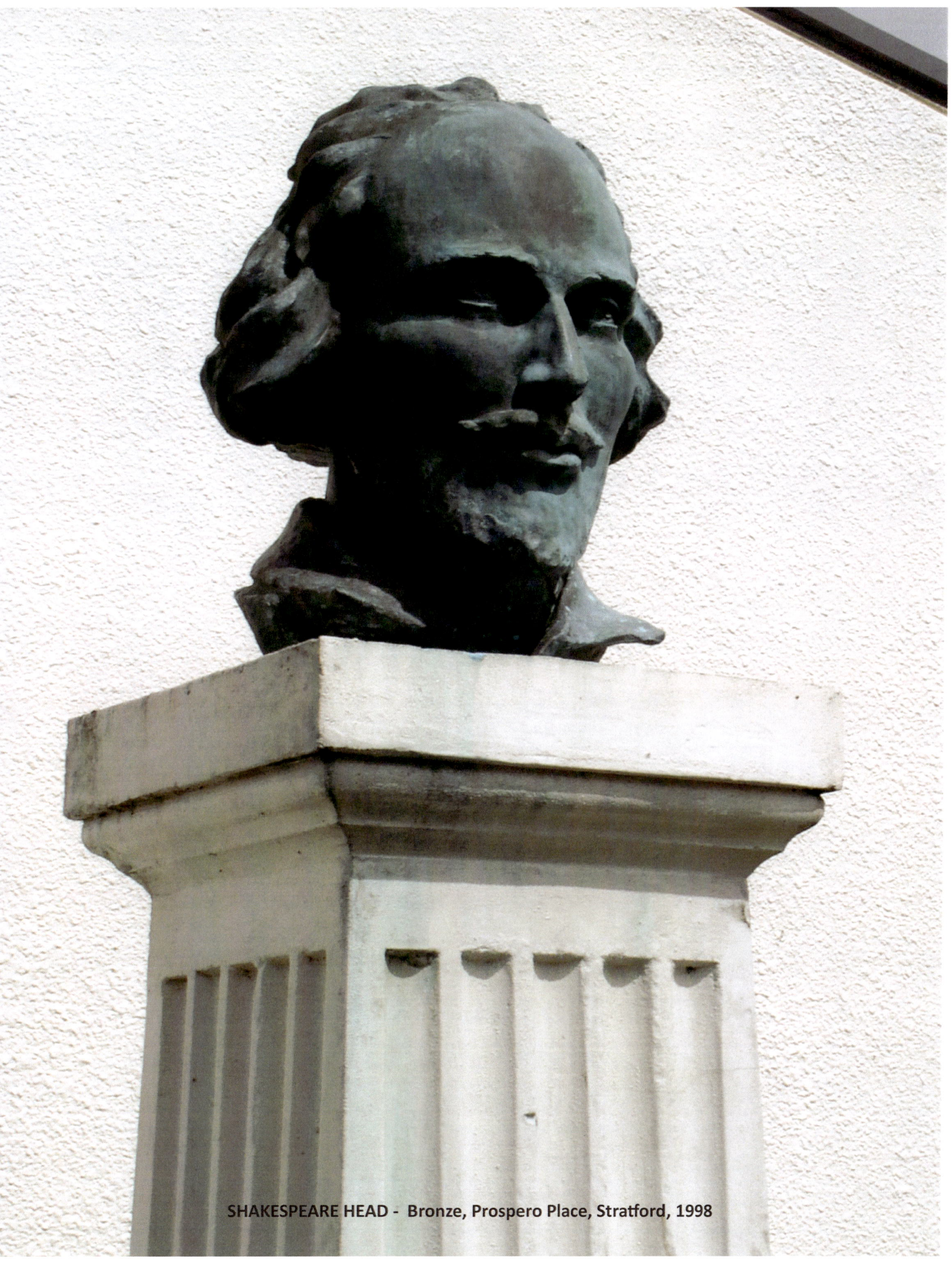

SHAKESPEARE HEAD - Bronze, Prospero Place, Stratford, 1998

Stratford sonneteers sought

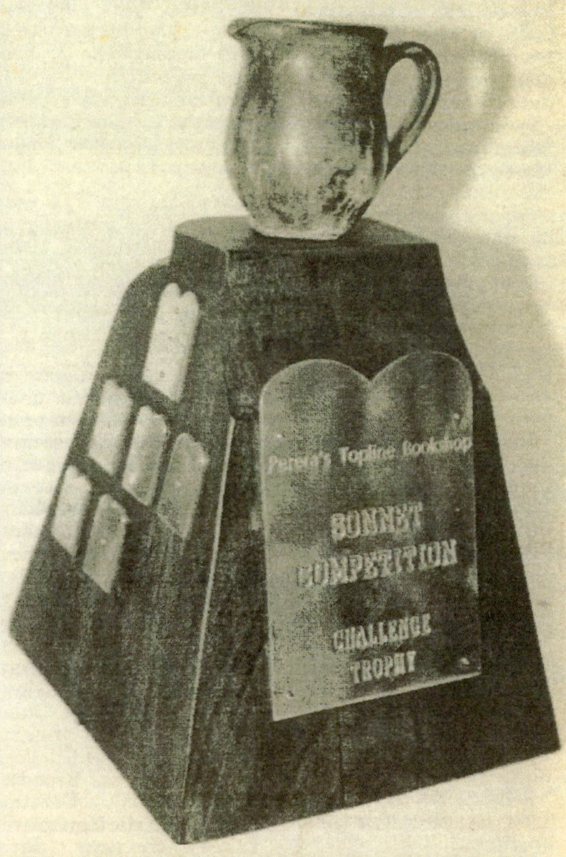

THE STRATFORD PRESS - November 26 1997

The trophy for the national sonnet competition, designed and made by Roger Peters, is displayed at Perera's Topline Bookshop, Stratford.

The second national sonnet writing competition is being organised and any hopeful sonneteers need to start putting pen to paper.

Organiser, Roger Peters said that the format for the Perera's Topline Bookshop Sonnet Competition would be much the same as last year, with two categories for entries - the young poets (under 20 years old) and senior (20 and over).

However this year the competition will have its own website on htpp://members.xoom.com/stratfordnz/sonnet.html.

"Last year we had 20 entrants from Taumarunui to Wanganui and almost every centre in Taranaki, and 50 sonnets were entered," he said.

The competition, which closes on February 1, 1999, will be judged by Michael Farmer who is the Mayor of Stratford, Prince Edward Island, Canada. He will be travelling to Stratford for the biennial meeting of the five sister Stratfords in the world in March. Mr Farmer is a lawyer, but has interests in many fields of endeavour.

"He says he can draw on the expertise of his fellow Prince Edward Islanders, and will present the results of the competition during the March celebrations," said Mr Peters.

Sonnets, which will be judged on their content and their use or development of the traditional sonnet form of 14 lines with set syllables and rhymes, must be presented one per page. Up to 14 entries are permitted per person. They must be clearly typed or printed.

Perera's Topline Bookshop Sonnets Competition 1999 must be written on a separate sheet of paper, along with entrant's name, age, address and phone number.

The winners, to be announced in the week of March 16-23, will have their names inscribed on the trophy that is installed in Perera's Bookshop, Stratford. They will also receive a small replica of the trophy and a $50 book voucher. Certificates will be presented to runners-up. The winning sonnets will appear in the Stratford Press during the festival.

Sonnets can be sent to the Stratford Shakespeare Society, c/o 979 Eltham Rd, RD 29, Kaponga.

Search for sonneteers

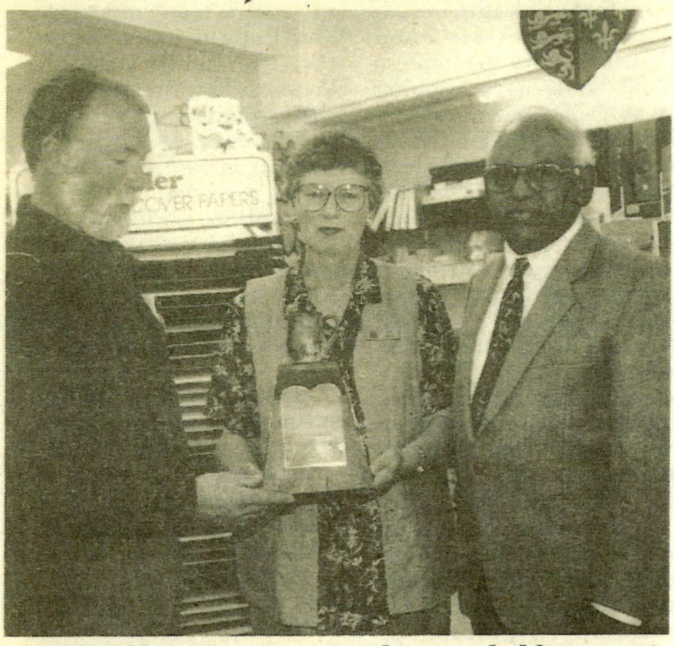

National honours are now to be awarded for sonnet writing. Raymond and Pam Perera of Perera's Topline Bookshop, Stratford, have donated a trophy for the winner of the new annual sonnet competition. On left is organiser Roger Peters.

THE STRATFORD PRESS - October 28 1998

Those who like to dabble in poetry have a golden opportunity to indulge themselves in the new nationwide annual Perera's Topline Bookshop Sonnet Competition.

The competition, sponsored by Pam and Raymond Perera and run by the Stratford Shakespeare Society, will allow entrants to submit up to 14 entries of their own sonnets in one of two categories. Entries close on February 1, 1998 and winners will be announced during the Stratford Shakespeare Society Festival which begins on February 14, 1998.

Roger Peters, a member of the organising committee, said that the competition would be judged by Gwen Smith of Stratford-on-Avon, England, who would be attending the festival as part of the visiting Shakespearean Theatre Group. She has a Master of Philosophy degree from the Shakespeare Institute (part of Birmingham University). She teaches English and is currently doing a PhD in Shakespearean studies.

The winners' names will be inscribed on a trophy, donated by the Pereras, which will be installed in Perera's Topline Bookshop, Broadway. Winners will receive a small inscribed replica of the trophy and a $50 book voucher.

The sonnets will be judged on both their content, and their use or development of the traditional sonnet forms of 14 lines with set syllables and rhythms.

The first category will be for secondary school and younger students and under 20 year olds, and the second for tertiary students and poets 20 years old and over. Entry is $2 for younger entrants and $5 for older entrants.

Each sonnet must be presented one per page, clearly printed or typed. The words 'Perera's Topline Bookshop Sonnet Competition, 1998', entrant's name, age, address and phone number should be written on a separate page and attached to the entry. Also a stamped, addressed envelope must be included if entrants require their sonnets to be returned.

Sonnets are to be sent to The Stratford Shakespeare Society, PO Box 401, Stratford. Entry forms will be available shortly from the Stratford Press, Perera's Topline Bookshop, libraries and schools.

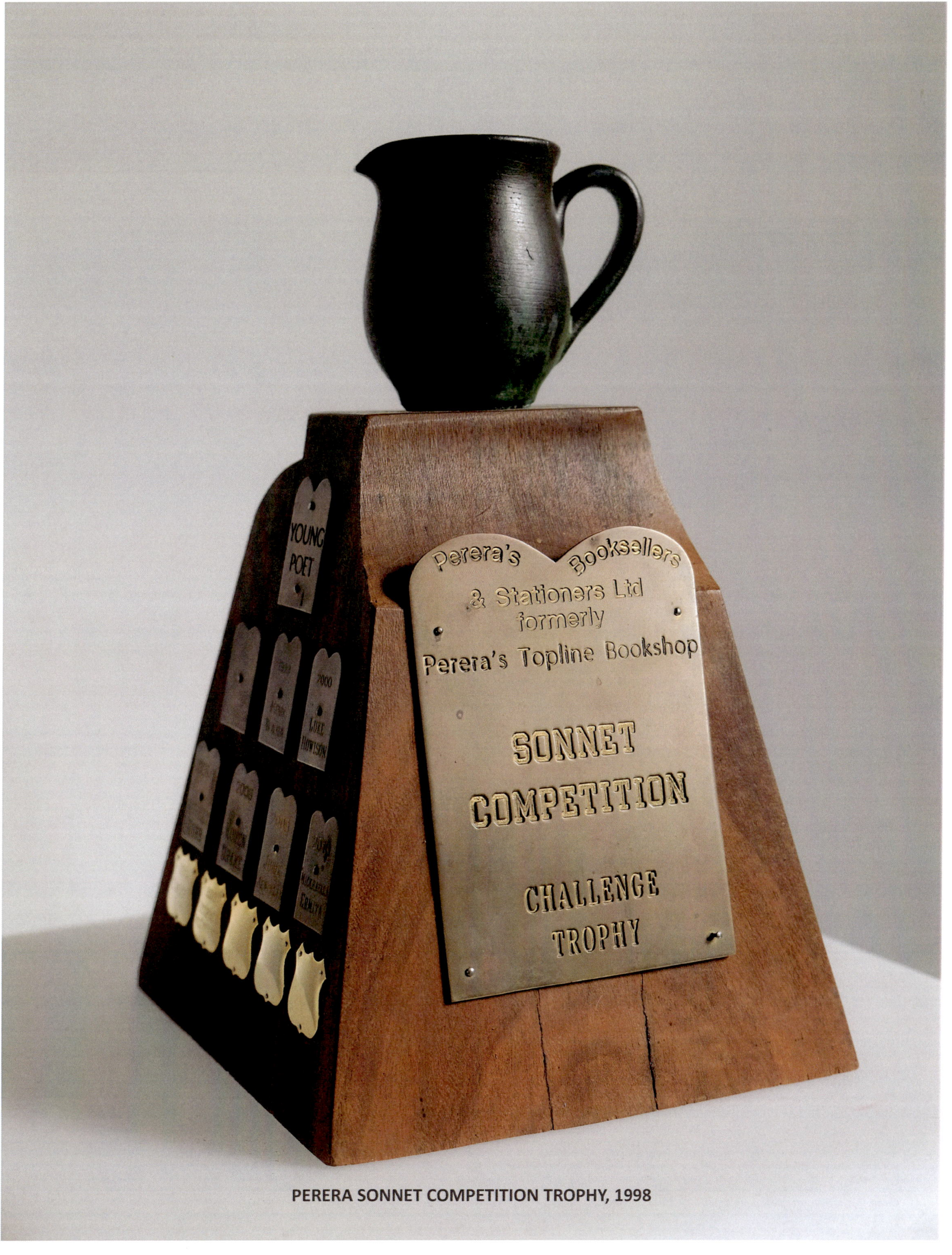

PERERA SONNET COMPETITION TROPHY, 1998

Secrets of the Sonnets

SHAKESPEARE SCHOLAR: Roger Peters in his Kaponga writing room.

Photos: TREVOR READ

BREAK TIME: Roger Peters takes a break from his work, wandering and fossicking in the Kapuni River by his home.

Shakespeare's 154 sonnets do not share the same acclaim as his plays do. But they are just as important, if not more so, says Shakespearephile and artist Roger Peters. Peters lives in a farmhouse in the shadow of Mt Taranaki and has almost completed a book about Shakespeare's philosophy encompassing the sonnets. He is taking a radically different approach from traditional scholars. **JULIET SMITH** visits Peters at his home

THE DAILY NEWS - Magazine Section, Saturday March 17th 2001 (Full artcile continued on Page 70 & 71)

NOTEBOOK 21 Sun 15th May '94

I sail a plank with a stolen brassiere as a sail. Blinded by inordinate desires I can only feel for the truth – and at the moment I seem to have my course set around a desert island. I have no means of distinguishing between a compulsion and a genuine inspiration until all doubt is reduced by a moment of forgetfulness when the process has, by then, reduced myself to shambles. This body cannot last. Rather than toss it over an edge I am constrained to wring out of it a moment or two of clarity.

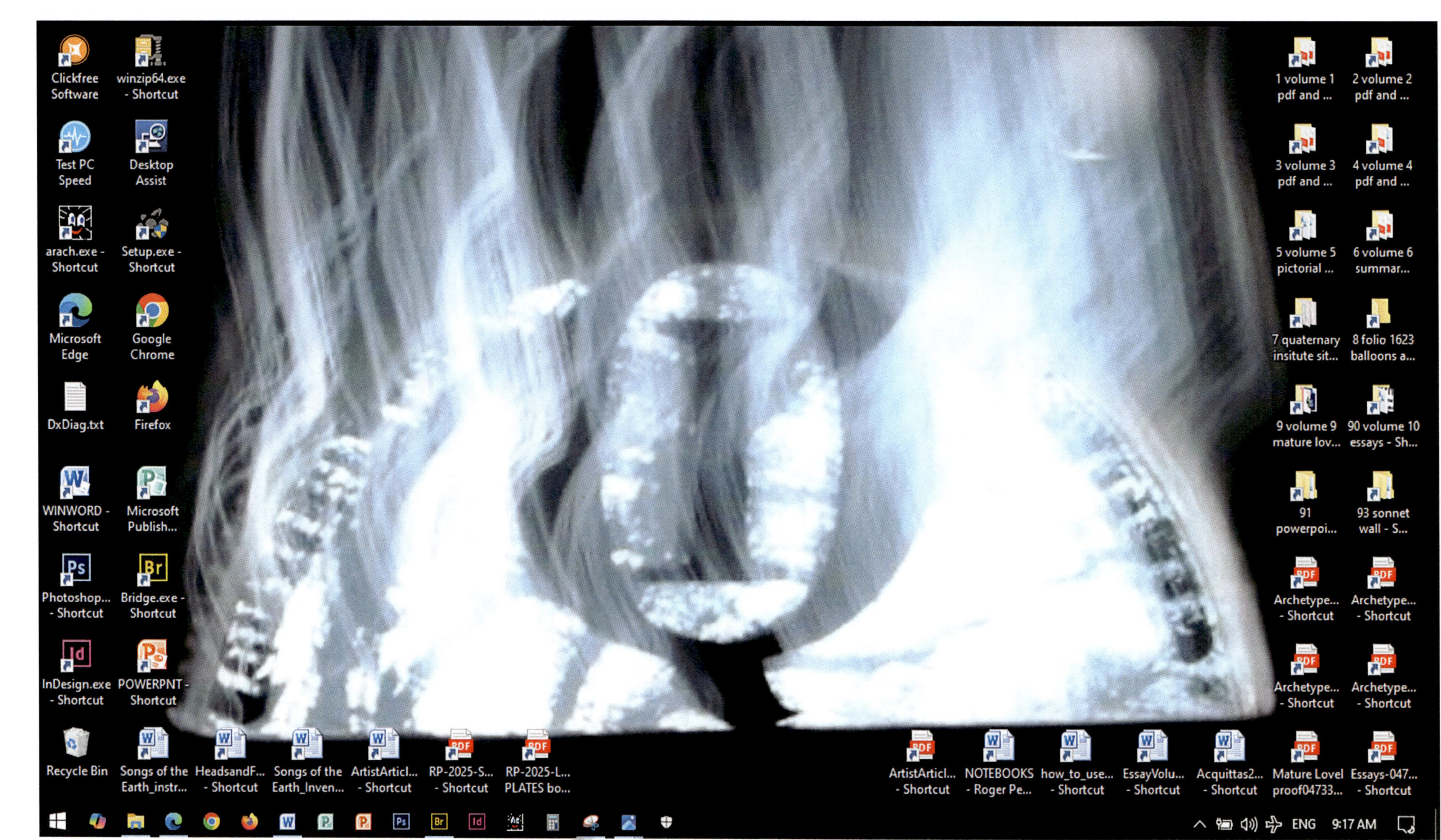

THE QUATERNARY INSTITUTE DESKTOP

PICTURES of Shakespeare, newspaper cuttings and large, complicated-looking diagrams line the walls.

Books are stacked in meticulous piles.

Sculpted heads are on display and a sense of being in another world is heightened by bushy vines growing through walls and the open doorway.

This is the workroom of artist, Shakespeare expert and serious thinker Roger Peters.

Over the past few years in this room, Peters has plotted out a comprehensive and unique theory of William Shakespeare's philosophies.

"I'm in and out of here all day, continually plodding away," he says. "It came to be my writing space when I was kicked out of the side room of the house as my daughters were getting older."

Life models used to be sketched here, with the burner cranked up in winter during a different artistic stage.

Peters, who has intense eyes and a beard not unlike that of Shakespeare, meets visitors at the gate of his farmhouse near Kaponga. He shares the house with his art-teacher wife, Maree, and one of his four daughters.

The garden, which overlooks the Kapuni River, is littered with Peters' classical sculpted heads.

Inside the house, Maree Peters' painting room is filled with large abstract paintings. Elsewhere, knee-high figures are stuck to the ceiling, adding a quirky touch to an already creative household.

"They have stayed up since a party and I haven't taken them down since then," Peters says. The plasticine, resin and sand figures were part of an exhibition in Wanganui and are slowly deteriorating.

"I'm still waiting for one to fall off," he jokes.

In the 1970s, Peters studied architecture and then changed tack to major in sculpture at Elam Art School in Auckland.

His early works were conceptual and experimental, such as a series of installation works with heated light rods, some of which were re-exhibited in a retro exhibition at Auckland's Art Space two years ago. He then made traditional figurative sculpture and classical bronze-cast heads, teaching himself the lengthy modelling process.

But for now Peters' sculpture work is on the back-burner as he devotes himself full-time to the study of Shakespeare's sonnets.

Peters' obsession dates back to 1995. When giving a talk about his sculpture exhibition at Wanganui's Sarjeant Gallery, he met a woman who was into the sonnets.

"We were introduced and struck up a mutual interest society. I read all the sonnets with a group of three other people over two weekends. I sensed something was in the sonnets that I had come to through my own work."

Readers of the Stratford Press will be familiar with Peters' column, published every two weeks. In it the sonnets, which were written between 1590 and 1610, are steadily dissected, decoding

what comes across to most of us as a foreign language.

He is up to sonnet 120.

Peters says the columns are a labour of love because he has to find a sponsor to get each one published.

"I think they were trying to put me off doing it."

He took on the challenge and says some people only read it to get a kick from seeing Stratford businesses, which would normally have nothing to do with the arts, sponsor the column.

Peters' book is taking shape as the columns progress, nearing the final stages before publication is sought.

WHILE it sounds slightly bizarre to spend several years of your life writing about Shakespeare in a country house near Kaponga, New Zealand, it makes sense to him.

"Nothing else has been written like this. It deserves to be out there. What I am doing is looking at each sonnet individually and applying his philosophy."

Peters says where he differs from other scholars is in taking a systematic approach to each sonnet.

"Most scholars pick out sonnets but say virtually nothing on others. They have been coming at it from a completely wrong angle for the last 400 years. Most people misunderstand him. They are coming to him from a Christian or Greek expectation."

Peters says the sonnets are basically approached as love poems to a young man rather than as a form Shakespeare used to systematically set out his life philosophy. The sonnets are crucial, he says, because the underlining philosophy also forms the basis for all his plays and other poems.

He credits Shakespeare with sorting-out the logic of the mind, on a par with Galileo sorting out the planetary system and Darwin doing the same for evolution.

Despite not yet having a publisher, Peters is confident the book will be published and sees it as a life-long study with three more volumes planned. He proposes that Shakespeare's works all embody an overriding philosophy on a mythic level of truth and beauty based in nature, one he says has been overlooked by academics.

"He bases his understanding in nature. The way in which we think and understand things is determined by the way we understand male and female."

This philosophy explains areas academics have grappled with, such as the strange dedication at the start of the original book of sonnets, loaded with punctuation and making little sense.

Peters says any book on the sonnets will dedicate at least 10 pages to explaining the dedication.

According to Peters' theory, which uses numbering principles of male, female and nature, the logic of the sonnets falls perfectly into place.

Shakespeare's ideas even surpass that of the Bible, he says.

❑ **Continued on next page**

... continued from P66; THE DAILY NEWS - Magazine Section P1, Saturday March 17th 2001

I take my cue from the perseverance of my own stupidity· If there is a destiny in the revelations of the last few years it is not one I have been aligned with· Rather there is more a sense of tracking backwards and forwards across the path that reveals the glimpses of insight· Otherwise why indulge in so many ancillary activities even to the point of desiring closure when there is nothing but work to be done· I accept that· I accept the need not to know most of the time as to why this process is not more forthcoming and the response to it is not more tumultuous· The faintest echo of a vehicle on the road or an unopened letter seems to augur the reception that I think these insights deserve – yet nothing happens·

The small gestures of interest fade quickly in this quietness of mountain, river, and trees so that what is left is the accolades of silence that steel the heart and steal the flame leaving pure resolution and cold winter's day·

Shakespeare passion drives Kaponga artist

☐ **Continued from previous page**

To allow easier digestion of his theoretical discourse, Peters takes this visitor to his favourite walking spot down by the river.

"I'm constantly addressing people. Most people burn out after half an hour," he says.

Discussions take place with artists, English teachers and academics. He engages in lengthy e-mail debates with overseas scholars about his ideas and where he sees failings in theirs. His large wall diagrams attest to a seminar he gave at Massey University last year.

While Roger Peters does not consider himself an academic, he has read widely across disciplines to develop his ideas, from Plato and Homer to theorists such as Duchamp and Wittgenstein. His appetite for such heavy reading must have come from his childhood, when he took to reading the encyclopedia, one of the few books his parents kept.

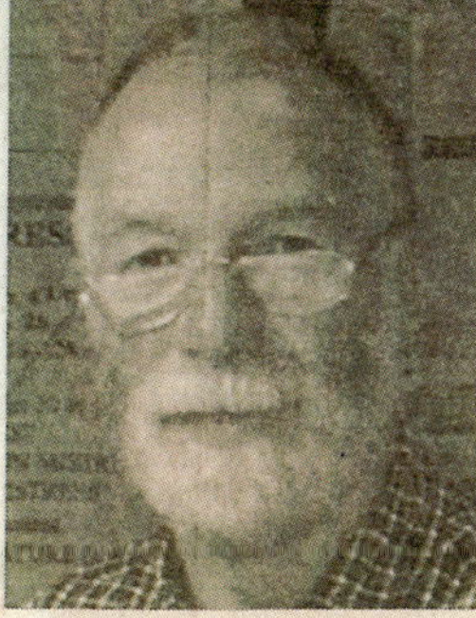

ROGER PETERS: Some experts disagree.

For light relief he sometimes works on what he calls his side projects, in a small room between his modelling studio and writing room.

The latest project is a miniature book that sits snugly in the palm, containing a reduced set of images of the "history of madness". The handbound books are placed in crafted wooden boxes and given to special friends and family.

Other projects have included his larger-than-life Shakespeare heads, on display at the Stratford library and council buildings.

Peters considers himself an artist, with no writing pretensions.

"My wife told me my writing was terrible. I still write in a deliberate way but that is not necessarily a bad thing."

He credits his wife as being a driving force behind his work and says her art also comes from a similar ethos.

"Basically it's where Shakespeare is coming from, too. Ann Hathaway, Shakespeare's wife, was crucial to his experiences."

Retired English teacher and Stratford school principal Richard Habershon says Peters approaches Shakespeare in a revolutionary way that collides with existing theories.

"He has delved so deeply it staggers me. He sees illusions and connections and creativity that I have never seen. It is certainly innovative and remarkable and it hangs together. He has a profoundly different point of view that goes against the traditional views of Shakespeare."

For that reason, he says, Shakespeare scholars will and do react vigorously against his ideas.

Shakespeare authority Ida Gaskin, of New Plymouth, says Peters' theory is very interesting but she believes it is impossible to know what the truth is and exactly what Shakespeare's thoughts were.

Regardless of what others think, Peters knows he is on to something.

His cheap and idyllic country lifestyle gives him the luxury of space and time, if need be his whole lifetime, to continue to pursue his theories.

And he will continue working with the driving singularity that is his hallmark. ☐

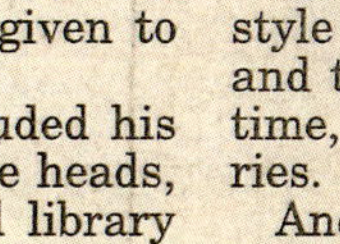

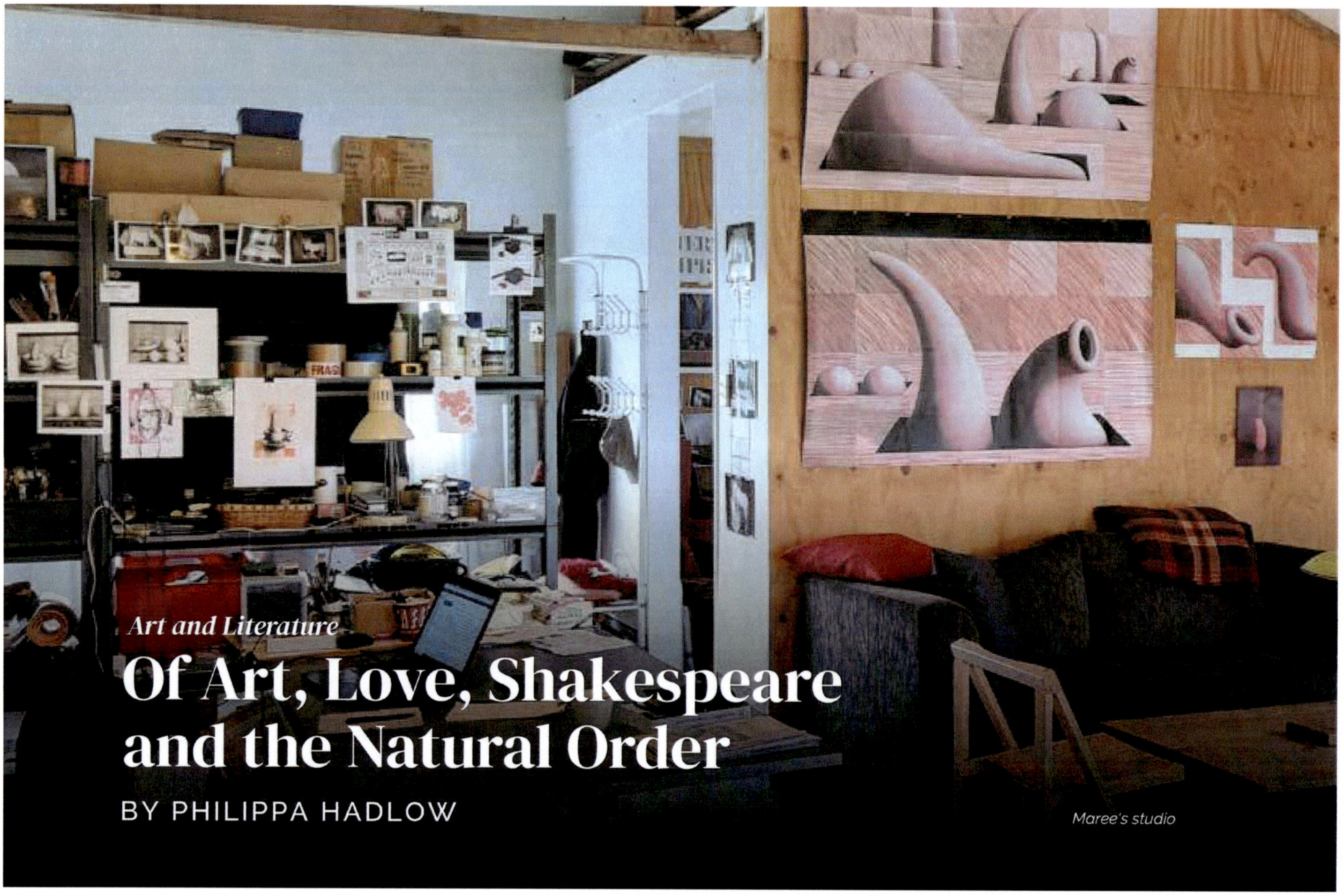

Art and Literature

Of Art, Love, Shakespeare and the Natural Order

BY PHILIPPA HADLOW

Maree's studio

BIOGRAVIEW MAGAZINE - August 2021 (Full article Pages 78 to 82)

A journey to Kaponga one sunny Saturday morning led me to the one hundred-year-old villa of Roger Peters and Maree Horner. Cordial greetings welcomed me and as I replied in kind, those salutations marked the beginning and end of my social equilibrium.

Expecting a simple chat about art – Roger and Maree are both Elam School of Fine Arts-graduated (1974) artists – I was instead led down a garden path to discover real-life erudite, surreal, creative brilliance.

The exposé begins innocently enough with a wander to Roger's writing shed. Here, for the last twenty-five years, he has delved into the nuances of Shakespeare's sonnets, all 154 of them, line by line. Not only delved, but analysed, interpreted, translated, and equated to what Roger describes as the meaning of life. Roger believes that Shakespeare's sonnets are indicative of a nature-based philosophy encapsulated by the edict that "articulates the natural logic between the sexual dynamic of the body with its potential to increase, and the erotic dynamic of the mind with its capacity for truth and beauty".

Some of Maree's work echoes Shakespeare too. Shylock's 'pound of flesh' comes macabrely alive in her 2011 *Furniture of the World* digital art display of cut-away bellies, no less. They're tidily stuffed into tin pails, wooden boxes, suitcases, and sinks; complete with insy or outsy belly buttons evocative of umbilical nurturing and the toil of childrearing.

Eminent art writer and curator Bruce Phillips described Maree's work in 2012: "These works sit on a tenuous line being both comfortably homely or horrifically debauched – a betwixt and elusive conclusion that reveals more about the animal within us and how little we understand our suppressed psyche."

Maree's explorations of sculpture, installation, and digital photography reflect a surreal expression of humanity and relationships, randomly poised upon a contrasting assortment of objects. Her work has occasionally moved in tandem with Roger's art, albeit in mediums juxtaposed with his.

Roger's latest exhibition, *Songs of the Earth (1972-2021)* at Pihama Lavender brought together a collection of works conceived over the 50-odd years bracketed - some of which were originally exhibited in Auckland Art Gallery's *Project Programme 1975*. *Songs of the Earth* comprised a flow-through walk on the elemental side of life, with salt, fire, and oil; roughly hewed materials like sacking, and the more base: mildly phallic/yonic floating fish. The exhibition smacked of sensory naturist symbolism at its best.

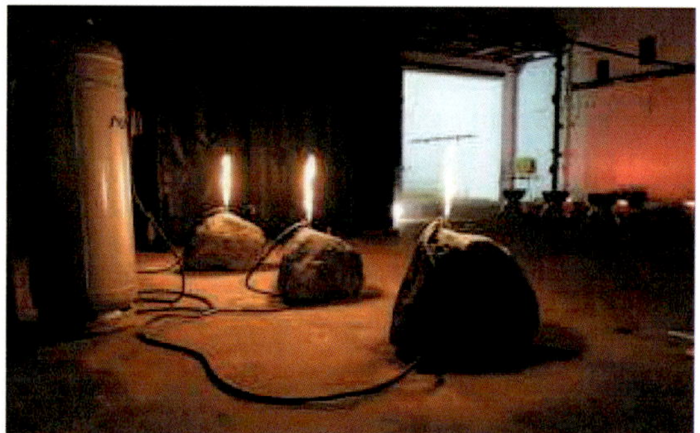

Songs of the Earth-Space2

Over the last 20 years, Roger developed the 'Quaternary Institute' – a unique teaching and learning facility designed to disseminate what he has gleaned from his intensive years' studying Shakespeare's sonnets. By unravelling the intent of said sonnets, Roger feels he has created a clear-field, logical explanation for the rest of Shakespeare's writings, and indeed, a guiding philosophy for life per se.

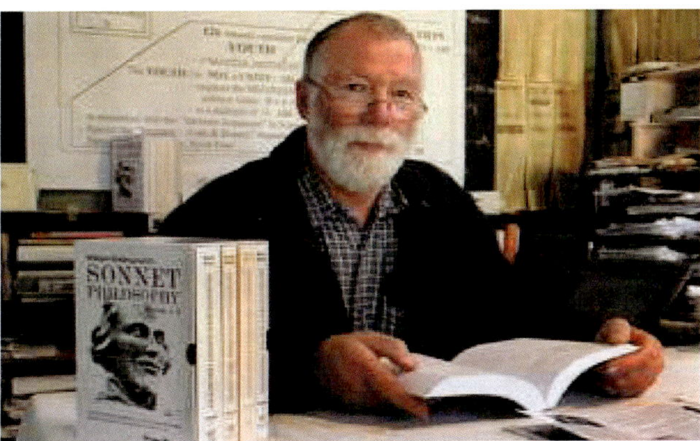

Roger Peters

He is sure that the establishment of the Quaternary Institute was imperative to formalise a first-of-its-kind forum to take students beyond tertiary level, to quaternary level. Roger has since written four weighty tomes: *William Shakespeare's Sonnet Philosophy, Volumes 1-4,* and another four volumes looking at Shakespeare's global philosophy and the 21st-century relevance of the Globe Theatre; Shakespeare's portrayal of mature love; a pictorial volume on his philosophies, and a set of commentaries on his plays have either been published or soon will be.

Roger and Maree's work is idealistically symbiotic. Both reveal entrenched primordial human traits and habits: Roger's sonnet analysis recovers the natural priority of the female over the male, subverted by three to 4,000 years of male-based religions; Maree explores the relationship between male and female and creates overt images that contextualise the male within the female.

Roger believes Shakespeare's nature-based philosophy complements Galileo and Darwin's and supersedes thinker-philosophers, Duchamp, Mallarmé, and Wittgenstein. Maree's work investigates the feminine and the masculine; the mind and the body; eroticism and fantasy.

As we discuss these enlightened concepts, we are seated on a revolving deck of Roger's own making. He gently turns a handle that slowly spins us to face the sun, or to enjoy some shady relief. "See what happens on this deck? You just get out here, and you stay here," says Roger. "You create a space in which somehow or other you are put at ease."

Am I at ease? Perhaps I am, but my drop-jawed expressions, upside-down sensations, and mind-altering observations make me wonder. I look above my head and see the letters QI (for Quaternary Institute) carved out in steel, hanging, glinting in the light. Another etching is carved deep into the wooden table before us. We laugh (a trifle cautiously) at the idea of subliminal QI persuasion.

The deck is one of Roger's many engineering feats. A platform reaching out towards the Kapuni River (which hosts trout 'That Big') is suspended only by a cantilever, though the user is falsely reassured by the optical illusion of a supporting timber strut diving downwards. In reality, it goes nowhere.

There's another deck over by the house, erected by steel pipes and, Alice in Wonderland-like, shaded by a trampoline mat - which, of course, kids wish they could bounce on! Each side of the shade mat can be elevated or lowered according to the heat of the day.

Sculptures are scattered everywhere: figures moulded from wax then bronze cast, fine-featured faces, and way up high on a shelf in a shed are five busts of local men. While modelling, one of them kept fidgeting, then finally relaxed, and fell asleep; his countenance is sublime in repose.

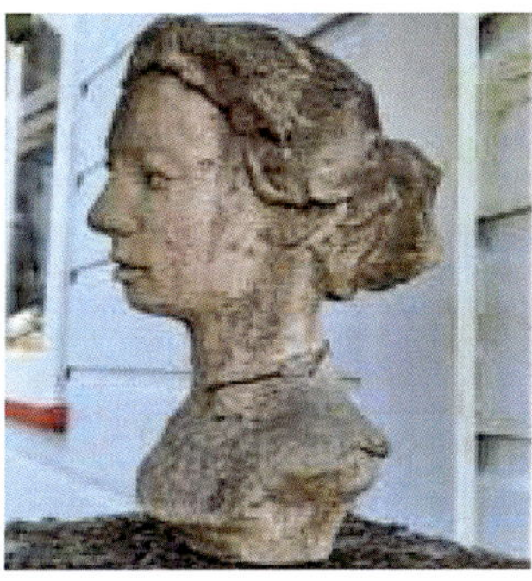

A bust

The 70s saw Roger living in a warehouse space in Parnell for $10 a week after leaving Elam art school. During this time, he "sublimated all his influences" and went deep into Self. In time, Roger began an investigative journey towards anthropomorphism; instead of creating inanimate objects like ladders and rocks, he felt a pulling towards body shapes.

So, mid-to-late 80s, Roger began studying Rodin and Michelangelo to figure out how they imbued their work with such depth of meaning. He wanted to fathom why a shape orchestrated in a certain manner affected your mind oppositely to another shape, made differently.

During the 1990s, he sculpted dozens of little figures and exhibited them in Hawera, Manawatu, and Whanganui. He inadvertently invited controversy by extending them to the exterior of the Sarjeant Gallery (Whanganui) in his 1994 Dome show called *The Wrestler's Ball.* The embellishments were called a desecration of the historic building by a district court judge, who in turn was mocked by media commentator Bill Ralston on the evening news.

Roger became involved with the Shakespeare Group in Whanganui, run by poet and artist Joanna Margaret Paul (now deceased). The group read Shakespeare's plays, then his sonnets.

Upon reading the sonnets, "I intuitively and immediately saw that there was this incredible philosophy that no one had seen before. I call it our birth right philosophy; a nature-based philosophy that respects the default status of the female over the male then delves into the mind and reveals how biology affects the mind," says Roger.

It was an uncanny and strangely déjà vu kind of realisation because Roger had already written a rudimentary outline of his concept of life in 1987 called *Human Being* that reflected the philosophy contained within Shakespeare's sonnets. Human Being evolved from his studies of proto-quaternary philosopher Ludwig Wittgenstein (1889-1951), artist/writer Marcel Duchamp (1887-1968), poet Stéphane Mallarmé (1842-1898), and naturalist Charles Darwin (1809-1882). Roger believes that Shakespeare's sonnets - pre-dating these philosophers - over-arches their beliefs and yet, brings them all together.

Maree is both Roger's inspiration and support. She administers the Quaternary Imprint that structures the publishing of his books, and secretly organises the marketing for Luddite Roger. The Quaternary Institute targets 5% of 5% of the world's population. The intensely specialist subject matter means it's a narrow market because today, Maree says, the majority of people like to digest small soundbites, the size of which are reducing steadily year by year.

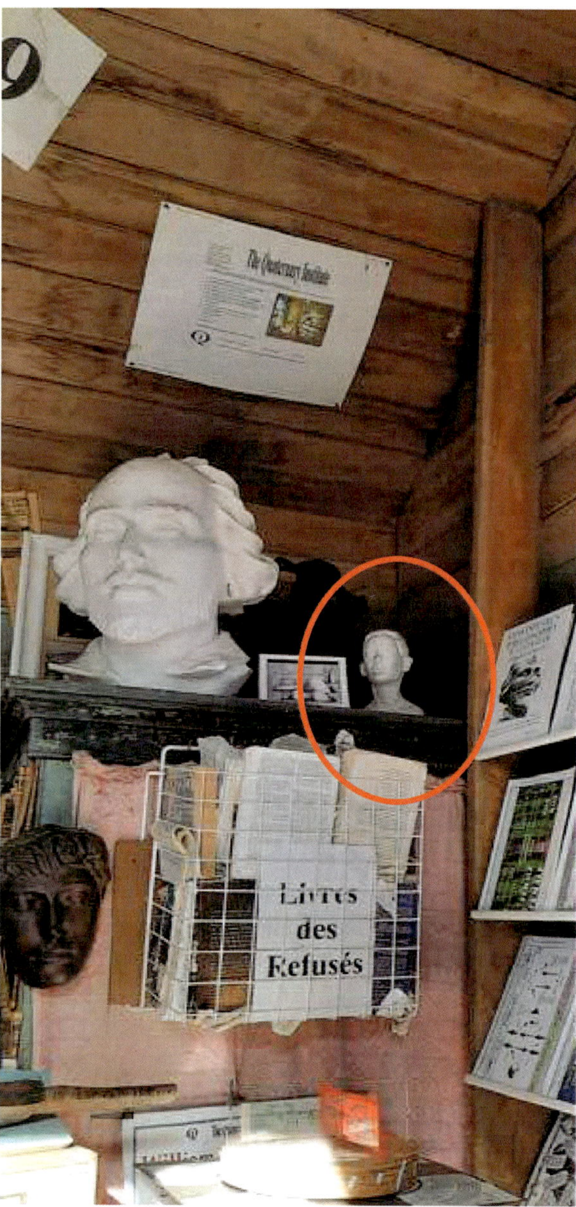

QI headquarters

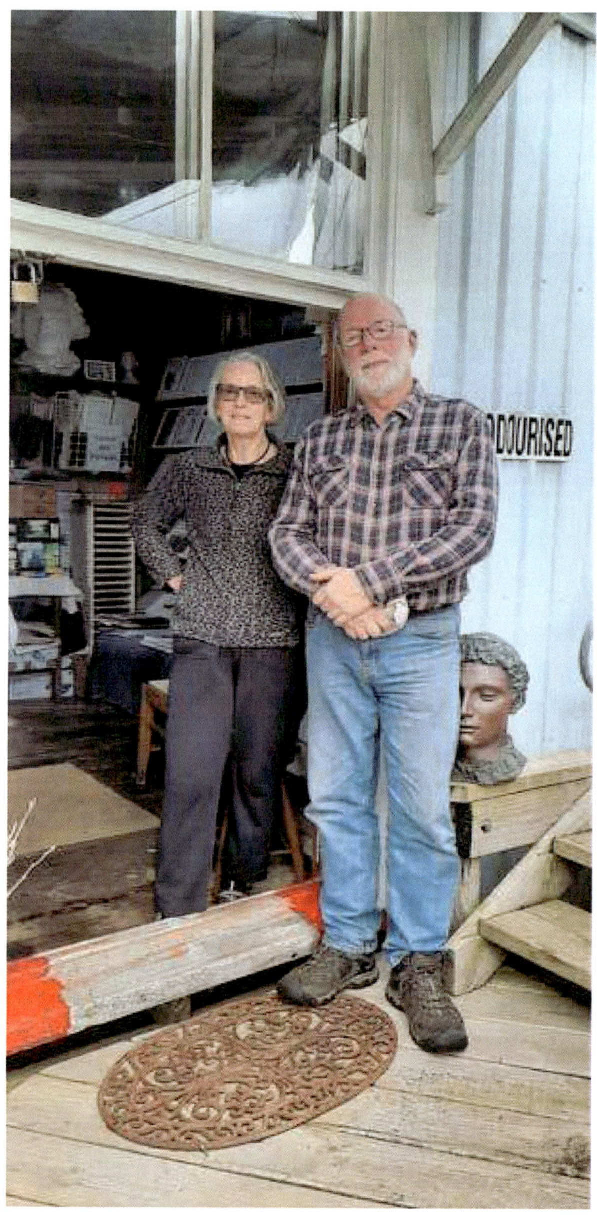

Maree and Roger outside QI headquarters

When he discovered that once understood, Shakespeare's sonnets confirmed Roger's own theories, he was gobsmacked. "In terms of human rights, women's rights, our ways of understanding each other – all utterly significant. The sonnets presented the philosophy behind Shakespeare's plays written twenty years prior. I had to pursue this! And thus, the Quaternary Institute (QI) was born," says Roger.

So the couple work in unison; together then apart; pushing forward then pulling back; working and resting. It's a pattern - like waves breaking in a natural rhythm, each receding wave enabling them to reenergise to regain productivity.

Part of that momentum is living the Philosophy through their creative endeavour. Maree takes me to her converted

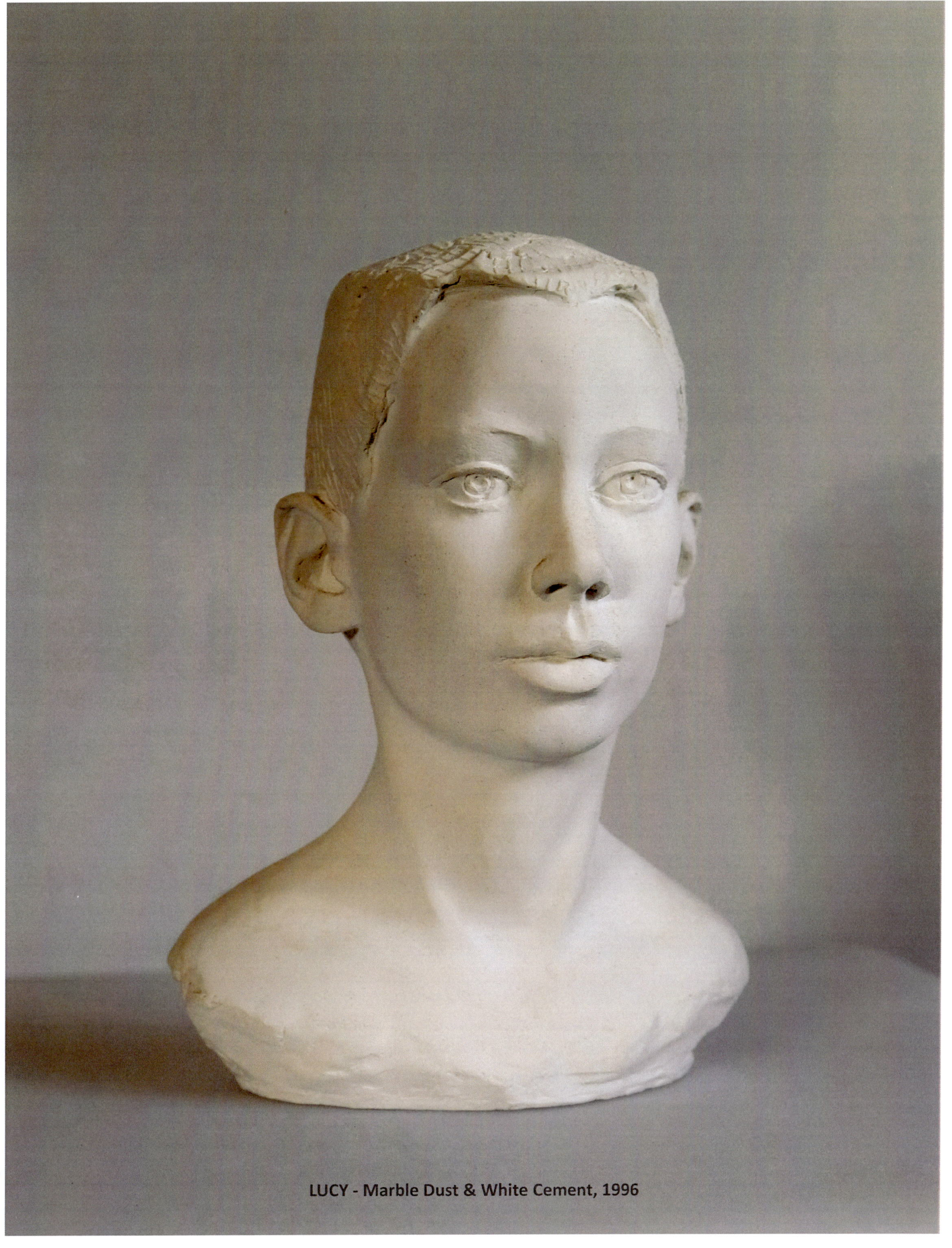

LUCY - Marble Dust & White Cement, 1996

implement shed studio space. I stop to admire the recycled hundred-year-old timber beams and the original cobbling floor at the back entrance where the work drays were stored in the 1900s.

Maree has exhibited professionally since 1970. Over that time, her art has been collected by such esteemed outfits as the Govett Brewster Art Gallery and the Auckland City Art Gallery. She's sold a few pieces through various galleries (for a pretty penny) and contributed to many exhibitions, some reclaiming lost art from the early days.

There was a time when Maree was feeling a little lost, too. When the couple left Auckland and ended up in this big ol' farmhouse in 1987, they paid $30 a week to rent it. "After art school, I was feeling a bit disorientated; I paused and decided I just wanted to do Life," she says. Having children was the turning point, giving her a base to investigate the continual balancing/rebalancing of the female and male relationship within her artwork.

> **"When you hear famous people talking about their lives, they say that the most significant thing was family: not career. The funny, ironic thing is that the kids all go off and do their own thing and don't 'get you' anyway! After living Motherhood, most of my work became about the male-female relationship and 'increase'; the same as what Roger articulates," says Maree.**

In 1990, Maree trained as an art teacher to help sustain their lifestyle. She taught at Patea and Hawera until semi-retiring in 2016. "A brilliant, devoted teacher, who got almost all her students through their art assessments," says Roger.

In 2004, she proffered her *Monumental Obsessions* to the Bath Street Gallery in Parnell; in 2011, *Furniture of the World* exhibited at the Bledisloe Walkway Lightbox Project. In 2012, *Monumental Obsessions*, and Eternal Realities were exhibited at Christchurch's City Art Depot with Necessary Substratum in 2019 at the Anderson Rhodes Gallery.

In 2018, both she and Roger exhibited in Groundswell: Avant-Garde Auckland 1971-79 (Auckland Art Gallery) with installations representing the 70s as an era of experimental, conceptual art-making. That exhibition brought together works produced, then largely lost in time. Maree's *Diving Board* installation is in the permanent collection of the Govett Brewster Art Gallery in New Plymouth.

Digital photography, print-based media work, and publishing keep Maree busy these days. We look at the walls of her studio, adorned with more of her recent stuff; a gigantic, gorgeous, cryptic, pastel-hued, organic, and mildly erotic/animalistic series of shapes – another perfect foil for her take on the nature-based philosophy that suffuses, and quite literally, sustains her and Roger.

Roger and Maree make a perfect foil for each other, too. Roger: meticulously groomed beard; intense, prolonged eye contact; diction clear and fast-spoken. Maree: quietly reticent, sweetly-spoken but no less ardent; her body curves and moves like willow, supple as its name.

I leave their property slightly bemused by surreal overload but full of excellent coffee and peach muffin; my arms are laden with books, postcards, QI literature. I've just spent the afternoon with two people who could take star roles in Lewis Carroll's *Through the Looking-Glass* and I'm utterly rapt.　　　　　✳

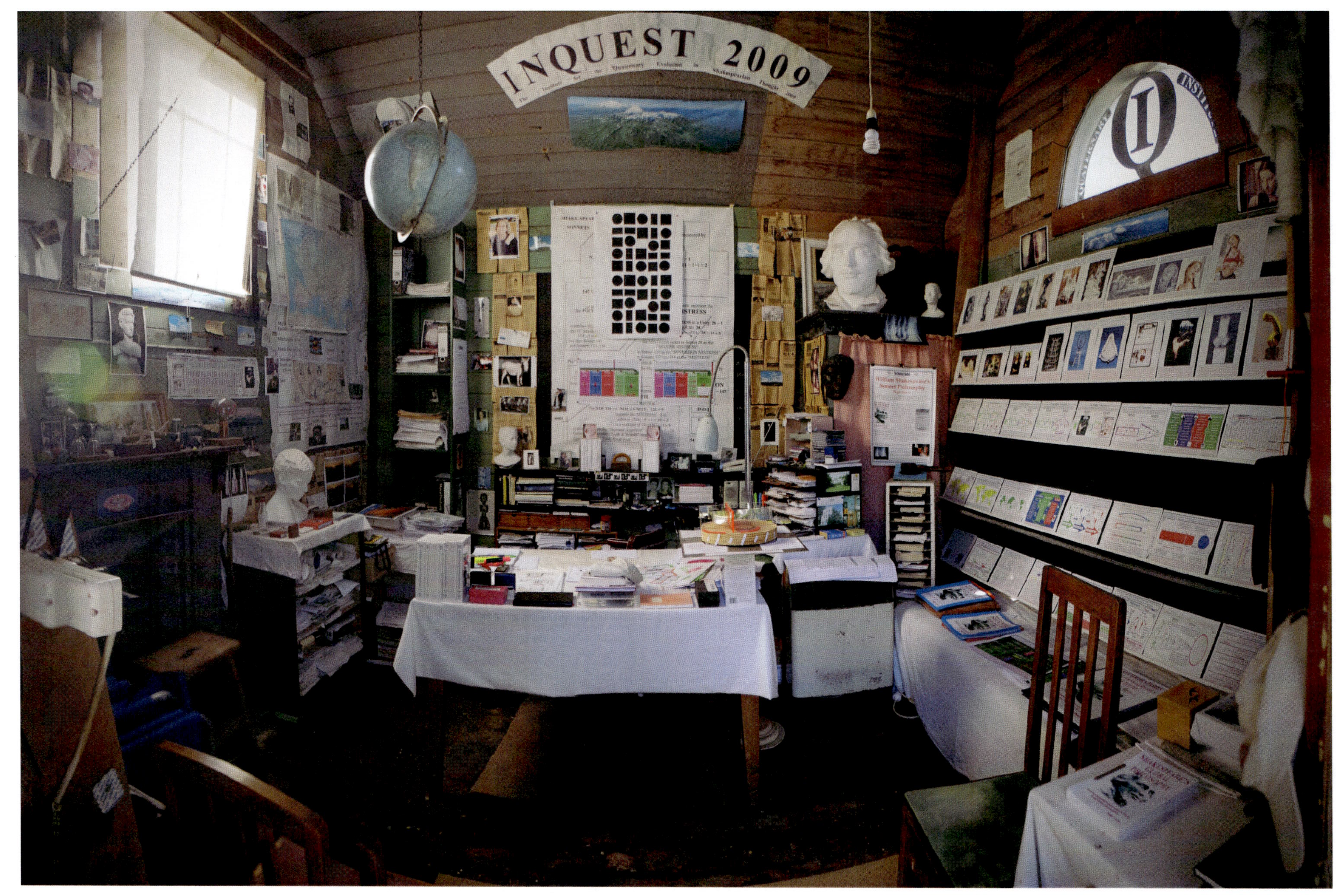

THE QUATERNARY INSITUTUE

The artist, the Bard and the philosophy no one else can see

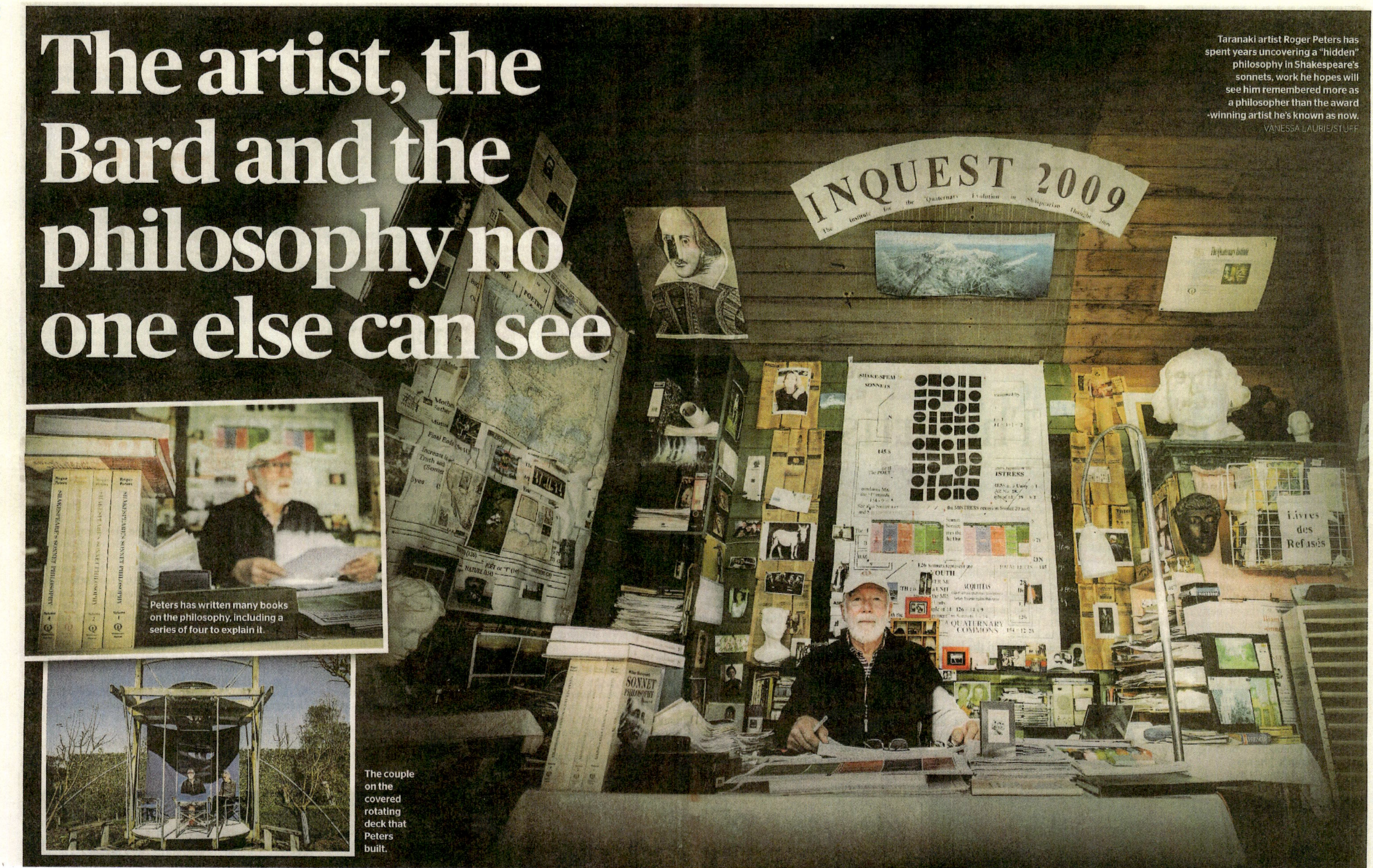

Taranaki artist Roger Peters has spent years uncovering a "hidden" philosophy in Shakespeare's sonnets, work he hopes will see him remembered more as a philosopher than the award-winning artist he's known as now.
VANESSA LAURIE/STUFF

Peters has written many books on the philosophy, including a series of four to explain it.

The couple on the covered rotating deck that Peters built.

THE DAILY NEWS - Saturday July 27th 2024, Front Page and continued on P2 (Full article on Page 74)

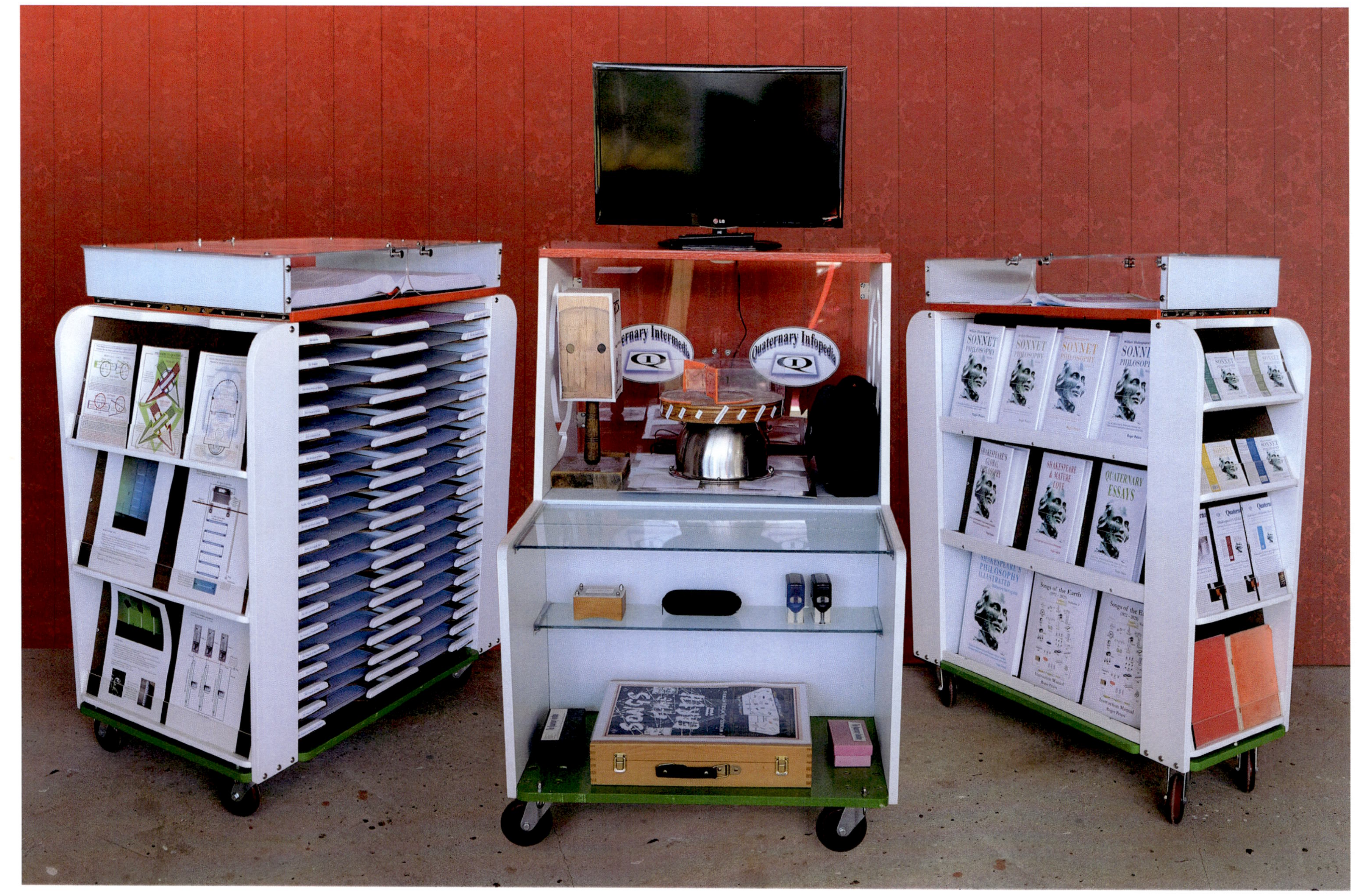

THE QUATERNARY INSITUTUE DISPLAY CARTS

Catherine Groenestein

Despite being known for his sculptures, Taranaki artist Roger Peters would like to be remembered as a philosopher.

It's how he views the world's most revered playwright William Shakespeare - after "uncovering" what he considers a profound philosophy to live by, woven through the famous writer's work.

The insight into the bard's work came nearly 30 years ago and the task of documenting it has consumed him ever since.

However, even after all that time, the philosophy he believes is embedded into the 154 sonnets Shakespeare wrote is almost impossible to explain succinctly.

The philosophy Peters can see in these works "articulates the logic between the sexual dynamic of the body with its potential for increase, and the erotic dynamic of the mind with its capacity for truth and beauty".

To the layman the meaning is almost impossible to access, the work could be a work of genius, or its opposite.

Indeed, despite "casting around in academia and elsewhere worldwide", Peters has found no one else in 400 years had come anywhere near appreciating what he calls Shakespeare's incredible achievement.

The discovery has been dismissed by the academics at universities where he's presented it, but Peters isn't deterred.

After all, his work included founding a new level of education above tertiary learning, which he calls Quarternary.

He's confident his discovery will be recognised one day, even if it is years after his own life ends.

Before his Shakespeare awakening, Peters spent years studying the thinking of great minds including artist Marcel Duchamp (1887-1968), philosopher Ludwig Wittgenstein (1889-1951), Charles Darwin and others.

Then in 1995 he was part of a Shakespeare group in Whanganui who read all 154 of the sonnets over two weekends.

After hearing them all at once, he realised that Shakespeare had perfected what he had been looking for within the other thinkers' work.

Peters' fervour for the topic comes across as almost religious in nature.

Yet, although this "serious" work has consumed him for decades, his often humorous "distractions" are evident all around the garden of his home near Kaponga.

He turns to lighter projects when he needs a break from the philosophy work, he says.

Peters and his artist partner Maree Horner, live in a farmhouse painted duck egg blue with red trim, beside a stream, surrounded by farms.

Horner taught art at Hāwera High School for many years while Peters was a stay-at-home dad with their children, alongside doing his art.

Sculptures in bronze, concrete and resin, are scattered around the couple's house and garden.

Wire figurines, some of 130 that annoyed the establishment in Whanganui when he set them up on the roof of the Sarjeant Gallery in 1994 as part of an exhibition, scramble up wires on a roof, while others dangle off the ceiling in their dining room.

Peters grew up in Whanganui and was studying to become an architect, but switched to fine arts after three years.

He spent seven years teaching himself modelling and casting, and has exhibited

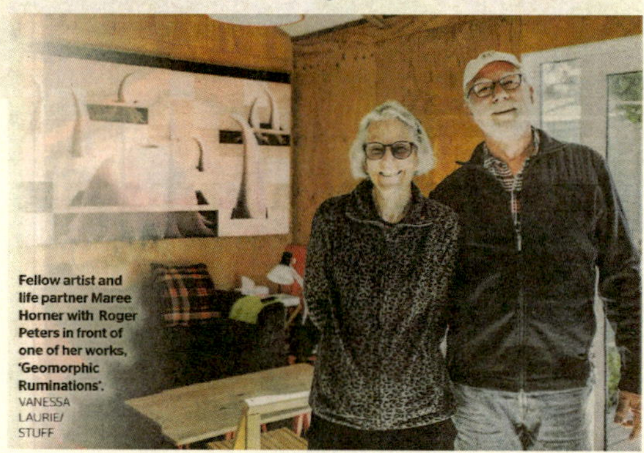

Fellow artist and life partner Maree Horner with Roger Peters in front of one of her works, 'Geomorphic Ruminations'.
VANESSA LAURIE/ STUFF

The artist, the Bard and the philosophy

his work from time to time.

In 2021, he created an installation at Pihama spanning 50 years of his career, Songs of the Earth, including recreated works using neon lights, rock and even oil, from earlier exhibitions.

Peters is the creator of the Shakespeare bust outside Stratford's library.

He's also a self-taught engineer, and the architecture knowledge comes in handy when he's creating what he calls "jokitecture" projects around the property.

He's used a lot of steel pipe from cowsheds, selecting lengths with just the right amount of bendiness for what he has in mind.

The sides of a narrow viewing platform that juts out from their lawn over a stream are made from bunk-bed wire bases, with trampoline frames and more milking shed pipes.

"I just like finding things that work, that you wouldn't imagine would be used in that circumstance," he says.

Horner took a bit of convincing when he wanted to build a revolving sun deck (it has a crank handle so you can move around into the sun or shade from your chair) in her newly planted orchard, he said. But when he saw her having lunch on it with her friends, he knew she had come around.

She has supported him with his work on Shakespeare, which has stretched over years.

And though his philosophy itself is too vast and complex for him to explain in a few sentences, all of his work is freely available on his website, he says.

Or it can be found for sale in the books on their website.

His first four books explain the philosophy, while others cover different aspects, including a complicated numerical system that is part of its structure.

Peters' years of toil on the project, all carefully thought out and meticulously detailed, could be regarded as his ultimate artistic creation as well as a philosophical

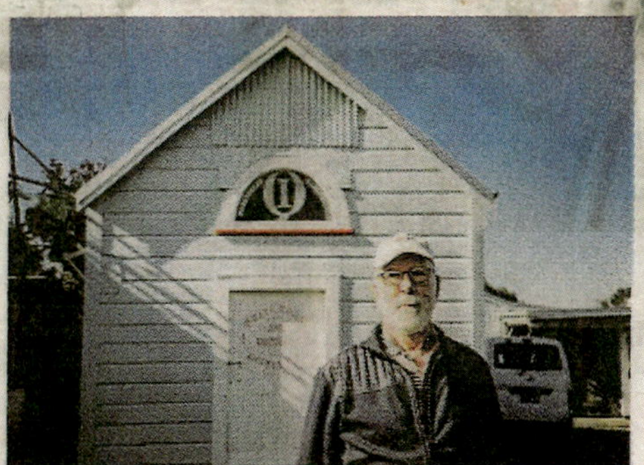

Peters' studio is the HQ for the Quarternary Institute. VANESSA LAURIE/STUFF

work. Alongside the books, he has created large charts, brochures and other teaching materials, all works of art in their own right.

As well as normal-sized volumes that are available for sale on their website, QuarternaryInstitute.com, he has three tomes bigger than an old-style family Bible.

These cost $2000 each to print, and he has crafted timber carry cases and library

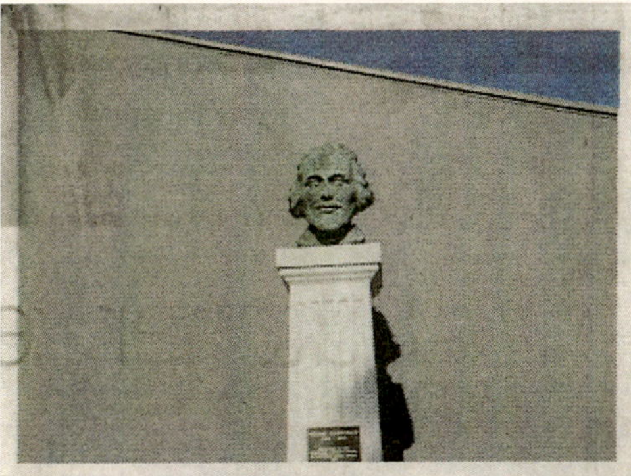

Peters created the bust of Shakespeare that sits outside the library in Stratford.

trolleys for displaying them.

Horner handles the publishing side of the work through the Quarternary Imprint, as well as their social media accounts.

They sell a few, she says, with most customers in the United States and the UK.

The couple's house is awash with art – including several of Horner's paintings of Alf, a white donkey they had for years.

In the lounge, Peters' mapping of the overall structure of the philosophy covers a wall.

A faded photograph of the couple in another room carries an inscription by Peters: "Not every boy gets a girl who is awake to his dreams."

They each have an art studio in the garden.

Horner's is new, with insulation and double-glazed windows that make it a haven on a chilly winter's day.

Now retired from teaching, she is currently exhibiting work in Home Work Maunga Auaha: Taranaki Art 2024 at Puke Ariki.

Peters' studio is in a little building that used to be part of a church.

The QI symbol on the outside signifies it as the headquarters of the Quarternary Institute.

Above the deck outside the studio, a trampoline mat he bought for $20 serves as an awning. "The grandkids always want to

get up on it, but the idea is to bounce ideas around, not to bounce people around," he says.

Inside the room, heated by a log burner, the walls are a tapestry of words, mathematical equations and photographs.

Now that he has written and published his books, he has moved on to ACQUITTAS, the Assize Court for the Quarternary Investigation of Tertiary Travesties Against Shakespeare, challenging 37 authors for their "literary crimes" against the works of William Shakespeare over the past 400 years.

"I'm not interested in tertiary people, but I find it's necessary to make some comment on the state of Shakespearean understanding," he says.

"I thought people would see what was happening, but the Shakespeare world is so tertiary, they dumb it down and make changes to the text.

"But I know it will get out eventually," he says.

THE DAILY NEWS - Saturday July 27th 2024, section on Page 2 TDN (continued from Page 76)

GENIUS or madman — that is the question.

It is difficult to decipher the truth — if there is one — about Kaponga-based scholar Roger Peters.

For the past 10 years he has dedicated himself to studying William Shakespeare's 154 sonnets.

Now he has published his four-volume work — 1760 pages — revealing Shakespeare's Sonnet Philosophy. He has been able to do this with help from a $30,000 Taranaki Electricity Trust grant.

"Shakespeare published the philosophy of the sonnets in 1609, a full 20 years after writing his first play, to present the philosophy behind all his plays and longer poems," Peters says.

The story of how Peters got to this place is a long and winding one. But first, let's go to the end, to his place of work and profound thought.

On Eltham Rd near Kaponga is a letterbox marked Peters and Horner, which heralds a house of unusual and amazing thoughts.

Up the long farm track, past a field being grazed by a white donkey called Alf, stands a church-like building. There is a high window emblazoned with a large Q, an I standing to attention inside the one-legged circle. It looks like a religious symbol, a Latin-like letter with some higher meaning.

In this case it stands for the Quaternary Institute or its publishing arm, Quaternary Imprint. The literal definition of quaternary is "having four parts" and in geological terms it refers to the most recent part of the Cenozoic period, which is this era.

In Peters' world it stands for study beyond tertiary level, but the institute doesn't exist beyond the boundaries of the Kaponga home he shares with artist-teacher wife Maree Horner.

"It's my space," he says. "It's a really nice space to be in. It's like you've gone to this new land. It's like Shakespeare did the surveying."

Entering his place is a surreal experience. The door to the Q-marked building is softened by a jasmine vine, the flowers beginning to bloom like just-dusk stars.

Peters looms on the doorstep of his workplace, a quiet presence with trimmed white beard and metal-rimmed glasses low on his nose.

The Q space is part of an old church, he says. It does look like a place of worship, not to God or gods, but to academic thought and, of course, the man himself.

A huge plaster head of William Shakespeare holds a lofty position in the institute, a great brain to be looked up to. There are other heads here too — bright-white sculptures of the 58-year-old's now grown-up daughters. Talia (33), Teresa (27), Katie (24) and Lucy (21) have all left home, leaving behind serene artworks moulded by their dad's hands.

The near-sacredness of the stand-alone building is accentuated by the use of a white table-cloth on the desk-table, white cover on bench seat and huge white charts filled with words and numbers.

These depict his weighty ideas about the numerical codes, the life philosophies hidden in the sonnets.

"Shakespeare structured the basic elements of his philosophy into the set of 154 sonnets, with the whole set representing Nature, the 28 sonnets to the Mistress representing the female and 126 sonnets to the Master Mistress representing male," he says.

"The set of sonnets has a numerological structure consistent with the natural logic of the philosophy."

To decipher Peters' Da Vinci Code-like mind, it is necessary to step back in time. Not to 1564, when Shakespeare was born, but to Auckland's Elam Art School in the 1970s. That is where Peters, an architecture student turned art scholar discovered the works of artist Marcel Duchamp (1887-1968) and philosopher Ludwig Wittgenstein (1889-1951). Peters was so affected by them that he set himself a goal of reading everything he could on subjects like biology, philosophy, psychology, poetry, physics and mythology.

"I was trying to create some sort of context to what I was getting out of Marcel Duchamp and Wittgenstein."

So, after art school, when he and Horner moved to Eltham, Peters dedicated himself to reading Dante and Darwin, Homer and Milton. He would get dozens of books from the local library and plunge into the world's greatest minds.

On the art scene, Peters had had a successful show at the Auckland City Art Gallery, which eventually bought his Hot Wires work. That glowing sculptural piece took him about seven months to make.

"I wasn't a natural artist. I could get there but it wasn't easy for me. I was to discover later that I could mould faces."

Meanwhile, he spent three years working for the Taranaki Electricity Board — his only full-time job — until a staff syndicate of five won $100,000 from a Golden Kiwi ticket. In 1983, his $20,000 share was enough to begin a new venture.

"I left the power board and I thought I could make a business out of making these doll's houses," he shows a picture of a many-angled construction.

"I'm not a businessman and I got so stressed I could barely walk."

At the time, Peters and his family were living in the Jenkins House on Conway Rd, also known as Ladies Mile. During his slow recovery (it took about five years), he walked many miles on that path.

"I started having this sense of clarity at that time," he says.

He wrote his thoughts and published them in a thin red book. He holds one of the 10 produced and fans through dust-gritty pages, which hold his early ideas on life, body, mind, will and word.

Next came Peters' foray into the field of figures, which led to a show at the Sarjeant Gallery in Wanganui, the town of his birth.

From 1987 to 1994, he studied the works of sculptors Michelangelo, Rodin and Donatello, and taught himself the techniques of head-making. You can see his bronze head of Shakespeare outside the library in nearby Stratford. For the Sarjeant Gallery outing, he made 130 small figures.

"That was my own graduation show," he said, referring to his personal years of body-building.

There are leftover people hanging about the Kaponga place, including a number crawling upside down across the kitchen ceiling. Other rooms are hung with giant donkey paintings by Horner, who has been inspired by Alf.

Peters' reconnection with his birthplace continued when he joined a friend at monthly readings of Shakespeare in Wanganui. In early 1995, the group decided to read the sonnets over two weekends. Hearing all the sonnets read out, Peters had his Shakespeare awakening.

"I was able to sense that what was in there was what I was looking for in Duchamp," he says, talking quickly, but calmly. "Over the next few months, I was just sparking. I was waking up in the middle of the night."

He also began to see the number patterns in Shakespeare's sonnets.

Like a devoted Christian referring to passages of the Bible, Peters talks about particular sonnets and their meanings.

"Shakespeare nails down the philosophy we live by, whether we think we do or not," he says. "He's so amazing, he's ordinary. He's commonsensical. He discovered things that are in this world rather than inventing things beyond this world."

Some Shakespeare experts believe Peters' findings are rubbish, but the discoverer is adamant he is right.

"It's like saying Darwin is bullshit."

While he is quietly pleased to have his box-set published, Peters is careful not to get too elated, believing the downside could be depression. So, like a gold medal-winning athlete who asks, "what now?", the scholar has mapped his future. He has already outlined Volume 5 — a handbook to go with the first four — and is now working on a play commentary and plans to dissect all of them.

His dream though, is this: "What would excite me more than anything would be for somebody to say, 'I know all this, but did you know this . . .'" □

NOTEBOOK 24 Sun 28th June 98

Mallarme at the Chateau· 'Le Chateau la Esperance'·
This morning a trip from under the Ohakune Cloud into
the clear light of Rangipo exposing the snow of Ruapehu
and Tongariro onto the rising sun·
Now from the Ngauruhoe window of the Lounge of the
Grand Chateau, I dream of nothing but imagine all that
has been consummated since I first saw this over humble
castle as a child· The birth of an Idea has an exceptional
tremolo that transfigures all the expectations of even an
impressionable mind· Now as that original conception finds
its endless mirroring in the pages of anticipated clarity it
seems it is only time before the circle finds its resolution in
the intimate expression of its durable thought·

NOTEBOOK 24 Thurs 31st Dec '98

One of these years is going to open up and swallow my
peace and quiet· Why should I care who exploits everything
I've discovered when nothing that has been revealed matters
to one as much as this living eternity· River trees and
mind, birds sheep and butterflies between whom there is no
distance· I am one of you day in and day out, day by day I
share your secret muscles and succulent spots· These ritual
places cannot be replaced by any amount of distribution of
ideas, by any amount of false doctorates·
Maybe I will be unfaithful to you· I will be asked to
journey to the hospital of minds to say the words that
remove the pain· But I know in advance the sense of
exhaustion at being disembowelled so that the ants can
examine the forest floor for the secrets that are free in
the canopy·
There are flashes in my mind of those beautiful
moments of encountering a like mind that joyment carries
with the assurance that nothing I can say has been
responsible for that person discovering the true message
of themselves· That Adventure is inviolate and takes the
courage not of emulation but of a bathing in the dynamic
of original life·
Next year is full of surprises because, knowing what I
know in the way that I know, it is a surprise·

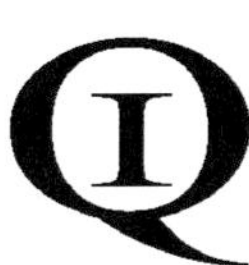